ALARIC
the
GOTH

BOOKS BY DOUGLAS BOIN

A Social and Cultural History of Late Antiquity

Coming Out Christian in the Roman World

Ostia in Late Antiquity

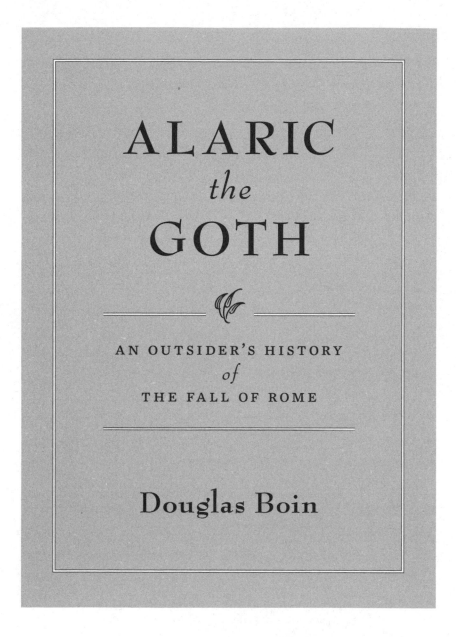

ALARIC
the
GOTH

AN OUTSIDER'S HISTORY
of
THE FALL OF ROME

Douglas Boin

W. W. NORTON & COMPANY
Independent Publishers Since 1923

For information about permission to reproduce selections from this book, write to
Permissions, W. W. Norton & Company, Inc., 500 Fifth Avenue, New York, NY 10110

For information about special discounts for bulk purchases, please contact
W. W. Norton Special Sales at specialsales@wwnorton.com or 800-233-4830

Manufacturing by LSC Communications, Harrisonburg
Book design by Chris Welch
Production manager: Lauren Abbate

Library of Congress Cataloging-in-Publication Data

Names: Boin, Douglas, author.
Title: Alaric the Goth : an outsider's history of the fall of Rome / Douglas Boin.
Other titles: Outsider's history of the fall of Rome
Description: First edition. | New York : W. W. Norton & Company, [2020] |
Includes bibliographical references and index.
Identifiers: LCCN 2019050501 |
ISBN 9780393635690 (hardcover) | ISBN 9780393635706 (epub)
Subjects: LCSH: Alaric I, King of the Visigoths, –410. | Visigoths—Kings and rulers—
Biography. | Rome—History—Germanic Invasions, 3rd–6th centuries.
Classification: LCC DG322.5.A53 B65 2020 | DDC 937/.09092 [B]—dc23
LC record available at https://lccn.loc.gov/2019050501

W. W. Norton & Company, Inc., 500 Fifth Avenue, New York, N.Y. 10110
www.wwnorton.com

W. W. Norton & Company Ltd., 15 Carlisle Street, London W1D 3BS

1 2 3 4 5 6 7 8 9 0

CONTENTS

PREFACE

A talented immigrant is denied citizenship by an unjust empire and, in retaliation, unleashes a surprise attack on one of its beloved cultural capitals, Rome. His journey from ambitious boy to disillusioned adult takes four decades. But by the time he dies, in the fifth century A.D., he will be remembered as the foreigner who forced the most powerful politicians of his day to think twice about who they called a "barbarian." He changed history, and yet his version of it has never been told. His name was Alaric, and this is his story.

Born at the river that divided two lands, he survived a border policy that separated immigrant children from their families, saw lightning success as a soldier, and became the widely respected leader of his people, the Goths. He also watched as his dream of achieving the basic dignity of citizenship slipped away during a time of political paralysis—a frustration that turned him into a champion for his people and an enemy of the Roman Empire.

Time has not looked kindly on what he and the Goths wrought. From the medieval period to today, each new trend that departed in some way from society's norms has been stigmatized with the Gothic name. Haunting architecture, disturbing horror stories, and an intimidating blackletter typeface acquired the adjective from hostile critics. A reclusive post-punk sound celebrates its moodiness, as does a modern subculture that embraces the dark, gloomy, and macabre. If being called "Roman" has always been considered traditional or classic, to be "Gothic" is different and usually a bit barbaric.

As a historian, I've always been fascinated by the origins of stereo-types and gross generalizations. The use of derogatory words and insen-sitive imagery excludes many people from the full life of a community, relegating their stories to the margins of their time and erasing them from later generations. There's something deeply unsettling in watch-ing how the reputation of an entire group can be so effortlessly, insid-iously caricatured, and I've long suspected that the Goths' name was distorted in similar ways.

Contrary to what the Romans believed, the Goths did succeed in making lasting contributions to world history. They established legal customs that shaped the histories of modern Spain, Portugal, France, and Italy. In their fight for human decency, they torched the bigotry that lay at the heart of antiquated notions of citizenship. And in an eerily prescient way, they championed the values of religious tolerance when many Christians at the time pursued heretics, imposed draconian moral laws on society, and outlawed the freedom of religious expression.

The public record of Alaric's life is frustratingly thin. Whole decades of his existence have simply vanished, and what little we do know about him comes to us secondhand. But for the past four years, I gath-ered every scrap of evidence that could tell me about him or his family, every artifact that could bring me closer to his time: from manuscripts brushed with sparkling ink to butchered rabbit bones, the leftovers from a Gothic dinner.

Much of what survives comes from the lives of people who likely never expected to find themselves in the pages of a history book: an elderly widow who lived alone in her mansion, a little girl sold into slav-ery, a farmer's son who rose briefly to emperor. Sometimes these indi-viduals are known only by a single name: Marcella, Passia, Maximinus. They may not seem like natural or helpful starting points for investigat-ing Alaric's life. But we can learn a lot from their experiences.

We can reconstruct the story of how Alaric's family settled at the frontier and, with the aid of archaeology, see how a Gothic boy spent his days at the border. We can say when young Alaric enlisted in the army and why. We can even recount in remarkable detail the political intrigue of fourth-century Rome. From this collection of odds and ends, we steal a glimpse of a real person. From the rich context of the time emerges an impression of Alaric and, with it, a world we thought we knew but never imagined from his perspective.

Alaric and his people were not the only ones living on the Roman Empire's margins during the fourth and fifth centuries. Some of these other foreigners are infamous and still frightening. The Vandals, on their march from northern Europe to their new home in North Africa, left a trail of destruction synonymous with their name. Other groups sound familiar because of their leaders. Attila, from the steppes of central Asia, is probably the most recognizable of the people known as the Huns. But it was the Goths, led by Alaric, who masterminded the most devastating assault against the city of Rome in its more than thousand-year existence. Their story intrigued me the most.

For centuries, the Goths in the Danube valley reaped the benefit of close contact with their neighbors. Yet Rome's border had always been a contested place, one where open hostility flared and xenophobia festered. Alaric himself hailed from beyond the Danube River in what constituted one of the northeastern frontiers of the Roman Empire. Although the people from this area are often called "Visigoths" as a way to distinguish them from the Ostrogoths, who came to rule Italy, no such division existed in Alaric's time. That distinction was invented later. Even the backstory to Alaric's title, "king," is more complicated. The word was the cry of his adoring fans, not a formal proclamation that came with scepter and throne.

Alaric himself chose at a young age to enlist in the army, perhaps to further his career. He succeeded marvelously. Becoming a trusted soldier who served on the battlefield with a revolutionary emperor, he bridged two worlds and spoke two languages—that of his fellow soldiers and the language of power, Rome's. These tools and talents helped him move up the ranks, tantalizing him with the hope of a lucrative government salary in the growing center of politics and diplomacy, the eastern capital of Constantinople. Alaric's view of his adopted land soured at the end of the fourth century as rampant bigotry in Roman cities, combined with a lackluster commitment on the emperor's part to reward the Goths for their service, radicalized him. By the turn of the fifth century, he had convinced his followers to exact revenge.

The anatomy of his plot to attack Rome unfolds against the backdrop of some of the most significant events in world history: the rise of Christianity, the growth of the Persian Empire, and the crumbling of a once-united Mediterranean. There's a darker history here, too, as fanatical Christians stoked the flames of civil war and turned the Roman Empire into one of history's first Christian states. In the wake of their triumph, they interpreted Alaric's three-day siege as a sign of the end of days and, with the help of Scripture, transformed seventy-two hours in Rome into a narrative of a disaster of biblical proportions. Within decades, they had weaponized fear—of another catastrophe, of foreigners—to resist their rapidly changing world, while the only political order they ever knew tilted away from Rome and toward new global horizons.

This period was no savage "dark age" of urban collapse. Nor was it a comforting "age of spirituality," a time of fevered conversion when people flocked to the church. Pervasive bigotry, state-supported Christian violence, and irrational xenophobia were the coin of the realm during Rome's later years. Those, in fact, were the shocking values awaiting Alaric and the Goths when they made first contact with the empire. This was an age of extremism, a time when moderates everywhere lost political ground and radical beliefs about religious identity, state borders, and cultural exchange polluted the air, spreading unchecked across three continents. The political, cultural, and social disintegration of the Roman Empire might have been shocking but not wholly surprising to those of Alaric's age. Their generation had witnessed dysfunction and disunity their entire lives, and one of the most divisive issues was the question of citizenship and whether foreigners would have a fair shot at becoming Romans.

It's time to think deeply and differently about the lives of marginalized people too often invisible in our history books. That's why the marquee name in this history of the later Roman Empire is not a Roman but an immigrant, a man the Romans would have understood as a "refugee," a *profugus*. Alaric ultimately did find his voice in a spectacular act of violence. But when told from his point of view, Rome's fall appears less scary than it usually sounds. This Gothic tale is a hard lesson in the realities of growing up.

ALARIC
the
GOTH

CHAPTER ONE

Seventy-Two Hours

Whoever attacks one city attacks them all.

—LIBANIUS OF ANTIOCH

August 24 began as an ordinary day in the Eternal City. As the month-long summer holiday of races and festivals neared its end, market stalls reopened. Proprietors disassembled their storefront slats, and there was a welcome return to routine. Long ago, the Romans had honored this month with the eternal name of their first emperor, Augustus. This current August 24 fell in the fifteenth year of the reign of Emperor Honorius, the forty-second man to hold the title. Much later, a Christian monk would propose a less pagan way of counting time, inspired by Jesus's birth, and the year would be called A.D. 410.

Marcella was at home on the night of the attack. While other Romans were enjoying their luxurious dinners, she had chosen to be surrounded by her books. A marvelously rich life was rolled up in the scrolls and sewn between the hardback covers of the volumes stacked on the shelves of Marcella's library. Now nearly eighty, she had dared to think differently from an early age.

While other Romans her age displayed their books as marks of status, she surrounded herself with old thinkers like Plato to satisfy her hunger for big questions, like what was good and what was just and what happened to the soul after death. Most of the authors she favored were long dead, but curiosity drove her passion to explore. The arresting tales of a hermit who warred with demons in the Egyptian desert had inspired her to tend to her own spiritual health. Cushioned by generations of her family's wealth, married, then widowed after only seven months,

Marcella had come to see the uselessness of riches, just like Saint Antony had. She turned away suitors and never remarried. A community of Christian women came to revere her as a mentor. One of those young girls was with her the night she was abducted.

The neighborhood of the Aventine Hill, where Marcella had her home, overlooked Rome's greatest stadium, the Circus Maximus. Several times a month, roars from the crowd barreled through the district's streets lined with cypresses and umbrella pines. Businessmen and politicians came in their togas and tunics to steam and soak in the local baths. Wealthy men dined at the hill's exclusive clubs, meeting in underground banquet halls, where they were initiated into the mysteries of Mithras, a pagan star god whose life story promoted an appreciation for esoteric astrology. Converts to Christianity, still a relatively young religion, gathered at houses of worship nearby.

But on the night of August 24, 410, whatever security had been stationed at the city's perimeter failed. The wooden doors and portcullises at the city's larger gates were supposed to be shut and locked, nightly. Soldiers were under orders to secure them, with night watchmen patrolling in shifts. A resident of Rome would have been reassured by the sight of flickering torches in the alleyways, carried by the fire brigade on lookout throughout the night. But none of the systems meant to protect the city functioned that night, which Roman historians calculated as "one thousand one hundred and sixty-four years since the city's foundation," when intruders stormed the city through the Salt Gate, a route that had once been popular among foreigners.

A thousand years earlier, a tribe of Italians called the Sabines had followed this same road into Rome when they came to trade their cereals and crafts for salt. By Marcella's day, the Sabines counted among the many indigenous people whose names the Romans had memorized, then quickly forgotten. But everyone still knew and used the Salt Gate. The basalt paving stones of its road followed the tawny hills of Umbria into northeastern Italy, toward the Adriatic coast and beyond, where it met the craggy landscape of the Balkans—connecting the Roman Empire to the frontier.

This time, the Salt Road brought a far different group of foreigners into Rome: men who intended to rob and kidnap its comfortable citizens and set homes and public buildings on fire. They had timed their attack on the city with meticulous precision, their chief goal to sow as much fear and terror as they could.

The quiet of Marcella's villa was a luxury very few could afford in this cosmopolitan city of perhaps a million people. She must have heard the commotion below the hill, loud and more brutal than the stadium games, before the assailants broke into her house, grabbed her from her bedroom, and marched her to a cold marble church outside the city walls. What happened next across the city and the empire has been described in countless books as three days of panic, widespread uncertainty, and high-level negotiation. Marcella died within days. The news of her tragic passing elicited a letter of condolence from the great biblical scholar Jerome of Bethlehem, who wrote to a younger friend of Marcella's to express his remorse at the sudden loss of one of "the most celebrated figures in her native city of Rome."

The fires sent many other Romans scrambling, which may have been the attackers' aim: to smoke out the residents of the city, shock the citizens out of their apathy, and punish them for their government's injustices. The city's fire brigade sprang into action, a force of men eight thousand strong carrying their buckets, ladders, poles, and blankets, yet unaccustomed to disasters on this scale. As the fires spread and smoldered, family members went missing from burning homes. Fortunes were lost.

By dawn of the next morning, August 25, residents were waking up to the extent of the destruction. The invaders had not limited themselves to Marcella's tony neighborhood, the Aventine Hill. Many quarters of the city had suffered a punishing, coordinated attack. More disturbing still, the assailants were at large. For the next tense two days, those ruthless gate-crashers—how many of them remains unclear—held the proud city and its people hostage.

Sixteen hundred years later, Marcella's final moments seem to bring an entire era of world history to an end. One bishop at the time used the tragedy to preach about the dangers of being surrounded by the world's "savage barbarians." Jerome, in his epistolary eulogy for Marcella, lamented the stunning reversal that had knocked the Romans' soaring ambitions from the city's towering heights: *Capitur urbs quae totem cepit orbem.* "The city that once captured the hearts and minds of the world has been captured!" Just six short words in Latin, even in translation, his exclamation reads like a sobering newspaper headline. For some churchmen of the fifth century, this one event, the sack of Rome, pushed half of their mighty empire into its grave. For others in the safety of the east, including nervous but vocal Christian preachers like Timothy Aelurus, the attack confirmed their suspicions about the coming of the Antichrist and the imminent end of the world.

Roman citizens throughout the empire felt the shock. As wealthier Italians fled to their second homes in Africa and cargo boats sailed from the Roman harbor, the news slowly spread across Europe, Africa, and Asia, where Rome had its many territorial holdings. In the coming days and weeks, people "in the farthest parts of the earth" were setting aside "days of public grief and mourning," said Bishop Augustine of Hippo, writing from a small city west of the great African port of Carthage. Some of Marcella's friends are known to have joined the African congregations.

Few Romans would have expected such a spectacular assault. The last documented incident of foreigners invading the city had occurred nearly eight hundred years before, in 390 B.C., when a "gaggle" of patriots had unexpectedly saved Rome.

"Choosing a night when there was a faint glimmer of light," as the Roman writer Livy narrated the history of the event, a pack of hairy, bedraggled soldiers from Gaul had stormed the capital's most sacred citadel, the Capitoline Hill. Cloaked in darkness, stealthily navigating the dimly lit streets, "they did not even wake the dogs, an animal pecu-liarly sensitive to nocturnal sounds." As the Gauls approached the hill, it seemed that nothing could stop the annihilation of the city—nothing, that is, except the birds.

At the sound of the approaching footsteps, honking geese, kept on the temple grounds and sacred to the goddess Juno, raised the alarm. Their noisy cries roused the Roman army, sending soldiers to their battle posi-tions. The Capitoline birds would forever after be honored as the heroes of that first and, for centuries, only foreign attack on the city.

A lot had changed in those eight centuries. The quaint Roman Repub-lic ballooned into an empire of sixty million people. Where one impe-rious Caesar had previously been too many, offending the cooperative sensibilities of Rome's republican government, two Caesars eventually became the norm, an important source of political stability for a govern-ment that ruled on three continents. Rome, the city the ancient writer Plutarch said had been founded as an *asylum*—the Latin word translates to a "sanctuary for refugees"—grew into a bastion of unrivaled wealth and power. By the third century A.D., the Roman people were espousing the virtues of being a "cosmopolitan," the idea stitched together from the Greek words for "global" (*cosmos*) and "citizen" (*polites*).

As the borders of the Roman Empire expanded and incorporated many different communities, however, there remained a nagging fear of people who looked or sounded different. Foreigners were called "bar-barians," an epithet the Romans borrowed from the Greeks. Stereotyp-ing was common and bias rarely questioned. People who hailed from colder climates, like the Goths, were said to be "bearish" because they had been born under the constellations of the bears, Ursa Major and Ursa Minor. Northerners were generally considered unfriendly because their climate was assumed to be far too cold to nurture warm personalities.

Superstitious beliefs about geography warped the Romans' minds, concepts they learned from colorful poets and prose writers. Although navigational charts and maps existed to guide ancient explorers, it was the imagination of artists, not the precision of experts, that taught

Greeks and Romans the contours of their world. The land of "scorched" earth, from which Greek authors like Homer derived the name for Ethiopia, was the farthest south many could imagine. To the distant north, a mythical population who dwelled "beyond the cold wind," the Hyperboreans, were believed through the age of Alexander the Great to hem in the known world. Rome's early emperors dispatched their scouts to the east and the northwest, bringing back news of Mesopotamia and the British Isles, along with luxury goods—from pears to pearls. But two centuries after Caesar crossed the Rubicon, rivers largely remained the empire's most striking territorial borders: the legendary Euphrates in the east; the north-south Rhine, which buffered Gaul; and the Danube across eastern Europe. Only in the sixth century A.D. would an explorer from the Roman world pen the first surviving account of having spied the land of China.

The center of their supposedly civilized world, as it were, was the temperate land of the Mediterranean olive trees, where sophisticated citizens lived in dense metropolises. A network of roads connected these hot spots of common culture and values. People from thousands of miles away recognized one another in a city's open forums. For the people of the fourth century, the city of Rome had long been the cultural center of their world, nearly as fixed and immovable as Earth, which lay at the center of the Greeks' and Romans' concepts of the universe.

One didn't have to leave this city to experience the riches of what lay beyond. "Here merchant vessels arrive carrying these many commodities from every region in every season and even at every time of the year, so that the city takes on the appearance of a sort of common market for the world," one ancient writer observed in the second century. "What one does not see here, does not exist." Even in the early fifth century, visitors to Rome's markets could catch a whiff of the luxurious oils and expensive spices brought in a constant stream of cargo from Yemen, Ethiopia, and India—among them, the pine-anise scent of frankincense oil and the woody resin of myrrh. And the majesty of Rome's monuments still exercised a strong gravitational pull on people. Romans of every rank came to watch the sand on the floor of the Colosseum darken with the spattered blood of the exotic prey hunted in the arena for the amusement of the crowd. Many heard rumors of the emperor's dazzling, domed audience hall, the colorful Pantheon.

The Latin language has a small way to denote big concepts. To evoke hard-to-define, intangible qualities, Romans invented a linguistic shorthand, and many of the words they composed with it are easy to recognize. The quality of freedom they called *libertas*; the quality of seriousness, *gravitas*. To name the most abstract thing of all—the quality of what it meant to live under the rule of the emperors, to call one of the hundred-plus provinces your home, and to know that the borders of your world were protected day and night by soldiers at the frontier—they coined the word *Romanitas*.

Romans who used this word knew they belonged to a community larger than one city, bigger than themselves. But as a concept, it was nearly impossible to define. Even before the attack in 410, a buffet of customs, languages, religions, and values had been set under the umbrella of "being a Roman." It included Latin speakers and Greek speakers, urbanites and rural folks, Jews, Christians, believers in the Greek and Roman gods, and atheists. Generations of Romans did the mental work of figuring out the meaning of *Romanitas* for themselves, and it was not uncommon to see a range of expressions, as varied as the residents of Athens and Zeugma.

But Romans to whom this notion appealed at least shared a vision for their society. Everyone could aspire to its united ideals, both inside the empire and beyond its borders. In reality, whether they had ever laid eyes on the rest of the globe didn't matter in order for Romans to sustain this lofty, ethnocentric self-image. The pledge of one's *Romanitas* came in the goods one purchased, in the principles of toleration one professed, and in one's personal ambitions. Visitors to Mediterranean cities could easily recognize these Roman values.

Rome was their fullest expression. In their richly decorated bedrooms, Roman wives put on airs of wealth and "gowns of lustrous, imported silk" to impress their friends, while in public, senators frittered away their fortunes on games for their sons—grisly hunts and cutthroat horse races—to ensure that junior entered the public light with a recognizable name. One politico spent two thousand pounds of gold, almost half the annual income for Rome's wealthiest households, to celebrate his son's election. Women smelled of subtle Persian musk; their husbands, of not-too-subtle wine. Elite families everywhere watched their investments grow in olives, grapes, and ceramics. Each of their villas looked like a medium-sized city, replete with its own temples, fountains, and baths. "No other city," it was said of Rome, "could ever truly call itself the home of the world's rulers." The claim was hyperbolic, but its self-centeredness was revealing.

Yet try as they might, even rabid xenophobes could not isolate themselves from the reach of foreign cultures. Every day in the kitchen, at the vegetable market, and on the dining couch brought another introduction to the customs and lands of distant people. In the first and second centuries, Romans feasted on Syrian dates and Egyptian olives as their empire expanded to the eastern Mediterranean. By the fourth century, the recipe for a popular herbed cheese spread called for Persian pears, first spotted by Alexander the Great on the frontier of the Hellenistic world in central Asia but now picked from trees grown on Roman soil. In Marcella's time, Indian parrot—the escargot or shark's-fin soup of its day—was a coveted delicacy. Busy lawyers and their demanding clients ordered it in the empire's rapidly growing eastern capital, Constantinople. Wine was imported to Italy from Gaza starting in the early days of the empire and continuing well into the fifth century.

The epicures who ordered these exotic dishes (and who possessed a modicum of self-awareness) knew that foreigners had built the Roman Empire. But by the fourth century, mockery and derision regularly greeted immigrants, as Rome's once boundless sense of freedom hardened into a rigid, two-tiered society. Citizens and non-citizens still lived side by side, sometimes in the same Roman village, but they had widely different legal rights. The language of the bureaucracy variously categorized these immigrants as "allies" (*foederati*), "transfers" (*dediticii*), or "fortunate ones" (*laeti*). But they stayed confined to these categories of Latin legalism, with no mechanism for attaining full citizenship status. As a result, foreigners could regularly expect ridicule, through no fault of their own, for their ethnic dress, their language, or the cultural practices they brought with them. "Everyone insults the immigrant," the fourth-century Latin poet Claudian sneered.

Rome had changed. The Romans entertained by poets like Claudian were highly literate elites, confident of their own standing, who preferred to remain aloof to the problems of real people. One writer told the story of two Roman dinner companions who sparred over the proper grammatical uses of the Latin word for "borders," *limites*, but skipped harder conversations about border politics. Other Romans pledged their allegiance not to the longstanding ideal of *Romanitas* but to the individual cities in which they resided. "I am a citizen of Bordeaux," one fiercely insisted—conveniently ignoring the Roman roads he traveled, the Roman money he used to buy his writing equipment, and the Roman courts that protected his property. Bordeaux's local government provided none of those protections or amenities. It was the treasury of Rome that made them possible. But for a resident of Roman Gaul, waving the flag of hometown pride had likely become an effective strategy for keeping unwanted strangers out.

As Roman poets worked populism and imperialism into their applause lines, commoners also followed suit, stoking this new combustible mix of xenophobia and cultural supremacy. The latter group did so in highly disruptive fashion at the circus or the hippodrome, where queues for the popular sporting events started days in advance. Adrenaline kept people awake in the long lines, itching to experience the potent mix of drinking and gambling; by the time the horses reached the starting gates, the spectators had often turned into a mob. They leered at drivers, bemoaned their losses, and, despairing over a lost race, howled for the expulsion of immigrants from the city. What the impassioned men in the stands seemed to have forgotten, one observer calmly remarked, was that the Roman people had "always been dependent on the help of these same foreigners for their livelihood."

Where the ancients displayed a truly impressive creativity was in demeaning these different ethnic groups. Some Romans celebrated their humiliation with war monuments or had their defeats carved on coffins, a popular decorative motif for Roman citizens who wanted to project an image of their own worldliness, even after death. A city dweller might buy colorful statues to spruce up the garden: a dying Gaul over here, a "heroic savage" from Galatia committing suicide over there. The Romans' ingrained sense of cultural superiority outlived even their own empire. By the Middle Ages, centuries after Rome fell, monks were exchanging short, sometimes alliterative lists cataloging the worst of foreigners' behavior with tropes adapted from classical authors. Persians were perfidious, Egyptians evasive, Gauls gluttons, Saxons stupid, and Jews jealous. Africans were inconsistent, Lombards bragged, and Greeks—they would never outrun the legacy of that wooden horse— were always deceitful. Some of the Latin wordplay must have provoked a few laughs around the medieval dinner table, as the Christian brothers sharpened their tongues with live targets. These monasteries kept alive the best of ancient learning and the worst of Roman behavior, for later Europeans to indulge in.

〜

Among those whose lives were remade by Alaric's attack on the cultural capital of the Roman Empire was a twenty-six-year-old boy, a late-blooming young man named Honorius. Pushed into politics from a young age, he had only ever known the "golden spoons" of palace life, as one Latin poet famously noted, and had stumbled into power after his father's early death. For fifteen years, he had held the powerful title *Augustus,* or "Emperor"; to his subjects he was master of the empire predicted by the Latin poet Virgil to have "no end in space or time."

In the years before that night of August 24, 410, whatever youthful inexperience might have hindered the emperor's judgment hadn't bothered many Romans. Family guardians and bureaucrats had always inter-vened with helpful policy suggestions. But at this time of crisis, he would have to provide Rome with leadership even though he wasn't even there. Honorius's co-ruler, his nine-year-old nephew, Theodosius the Second, was ensconced in Constantinople. Honorius preferred a palace on the northern Adriatic Sea, near the military harbor at Ravenna—safe enough that he would rule for another thirteen years after Alaric's assault.

No one blamed the two young emperors for choosing to live outside Rome. For the past century, almost every one of Caesar's successors had done so for administrative, diplomatic, and strategic reasons. To man-age its more than one hundred overseas holdings—many of which faced grave external threats—emperors had begun to reside in different cities.

Soon cities formerly on the periphery of the Roman world saw their economies and their cultural profiles boosted as the emperor, his family, and their staff settled into their new residences. Cities like Trier on the Moselle River, a tributary of the Rhine; Nicomedia in western Turkey; and Antioch near the Syrian coast became fashionable centers of busi-ness and politics. By Honorius's father's day, the emperor's duties were customarily divided between two locations—one planted in the west, one in the east—so that Rome's massive government could better collect local taxes, manage its extensive network of law courts, and deploy its troops, if needed.

Modern historians looking for a shortcut to the Middle Ages sometimes refer to these halves of the empire as the "Byzantine East" and the "Latin West," to prepare readers for the geopolitical realities that took root after Rome's collapse. But Rome hadn't split in two. Every Roman, citizen or slave, understood the unity of their empire to be unquestionable.

When Alaric's men breached the Salt Gate, Rome's local politicians, chief among them the distinguished senators, were suddenly thrust into a leadership role they had not held in hundreds of years. Because the emperors usually handled delicate negotiations, many of these obscenely wealthy men lacked any practice in the art of diplomacy and would have to wait until guidance could come from the palaces. On the cobblestoned streets, there was a lot the Roman people did not know. Why had their city just been attacked? Would there be a second strike in Rome, or in another city? And just who were these people who had dared to carry out this unspeakable, unforgivable, unjustifiable act against SPQR, the "Senate and People of Rome" and their seemingly indomitable empire?

As residents began to search for answers, the hallowed rostrum at the center of the city's forum, where Rome's citizens historically gathered in times of crisis, remained silent. No speaker rose to ascend the orator's platform with any reassuring Latin speech; the traditionally long-winded senators were choosing to keep silent about what they knew and when they had learned it. During the past decade, many had been privy to intelligence briefings and high-level deliberations about threats facing the empire, one of which mentioned the prospect of "terror." Our picture of the security threat facing Rome in the early fifth century is incomplete, but the Latin writer Claudian composed two poems during these years, *The Gothic Attack* and *Poem for Emperor Honorius on Celebrating His Sixth Consulship*, both of which suggest an outline of closed-door discussions leading up to the 410 attack. The name of one foreigner—a Goth known only as Alaric—had repeatedly come to the government's attention during this time. Claudian's poems are the most convincing piece of evidence—the smoking gun—that proves how deeply concerned Rome had grown about this one man. Advisers had assured the emperors that the danger this Alaric represented was surely contained, but many senators had already begun to doubt the wisdom of that assumption.

CHAPTER TWO

The Trailblazer

Be bold, so that someone of future generations
might praise you.

—EUNAPIUS OF SARDIS

Let's imagine for a moment a curious eight-year-old going to play with his friends in the woods at dusk one summer day. They roam away from the safety of his parents' home, and that's when he discovers for the first time in his life the wide majestic line of water—a veritable natural wonder—running right through the landscape. It's like a special language only he can read as it courses across the horizon from right to left. From that moment on, he can't erase the river from his mind. It's now part of who he is and an almost genetic component of who he will become. And yet, as a child unaware of serious things, he cannot yet guess its meaning.

Eventually, his parents tell him. They take him back to its shore and, speaking in clenched, perhaps embarrassed tones, they reveal its secret. The river is a fence, they say, and you've been born on the wrong side. How does the boy react? His first emotion might be confusion. How could the central feature in his life be a defect, a problem? Later, the boy's confusion might turn to anger—anger at finding out that he lives on the wrong side, through no fault of his own.

The water is still there. It cascades from the distant Alps and winds through Europe, the longest river on that capacious continent that flows from west to east, before discharging into the Black Sea. This fence is the Danube River, and it may have once represented everything that stood in the way of Alaric's childhood ambitions in the later fourth century.

The Romans did not look favorably on their northern neighbors. The Goths represented the opposite of a Roman patriot. Goths were scruffy, whereas Romans were clean-shaven. Goths used animal-fat pomades in their hair, whereas Romans preferred a day at the baths. And Goths made unspeakably poor fashion choices, wearing crudely sewn animal skins. A stiff white toga or a colorful tunic was the mark of civilization south of the border. When it came to culture, Goths seemed outlandish.

Alaric was a member of one of two Gothic tribes, the Tervings, who had settled in the northern territories, the other being the Greuthungs. The earliest explorers from the Mediterranean referred to their land as one of "uncivilized barbarians," but this corner of eastern Europe— where Romania meets Bulgaria, Moldova, and southern Ukraine—has a surprisingly complex history. Two centuries before Alaric was born, the local populations had watched, terrified and amazed, as foreigners from the south had crossed the Danube, invaded their land, and claimed it as a province for the Roman Empire. That landmark event, in A.D. 106, would shape Alaric's world.

The tribes who had seen the worst of that invasion, the Dacians, may eventually have heard from captured friends how a boastful general named Trajan had set up a gigantic column in Rome to gloat about his conquests. In the coming months, these Dacians joined the ranks of the empire's most notorious enemies, like Cleopatra and the Jewish rebels of Jerusalem, each of whom suffered the dishonor of being marched through Rome in a military parade. The rolling hills of the Danube lands would forever bear the traces of this invasion, its people carrying with them the memories of conquest, resistance, and abrupt change. Some nursed a distrust of Rome; others, a desire for the opportunities it offered. Even after Rome abandoned the Dacian frontier, a decision that stunned the empire in the 270s, the strong local culture manifested elements of Roman influence.

A century later, in the 370s—somewhere a stone's throw from that river—a Gothic mother would be cradling her newborn son in a quaint seaside corner of the land called Pine Tree Island, situated off the Black Sea coast. The family named the boy Alaric.

Alaric and other Goths who grew up living on the Roman frontier learned to develop an identity for themselves rooted outside of Rome, yet within its shadow. This delicate balancing act shaped Alaric's upbringing, even leading him, as a young man, to cross the river border. Roman sophisticates would always call his birthplace a "backwater," but if there's one thing we can state confidently about Alaric's childhood, it's that Pine Tree Island was no sleepy boondocks, regardless of what the Romans wished to believe.

The Romans never enjoyed living on this frontier. The first people to go to the northeast, in the early first century A.D., had hated it. The dreariness of everyday life, absent the luxurious baths and elevated dinner conversations he was accustomed to, made Ovid feel "metamorphosed." Or so he wrote in a letter back to Rome from his exile in northern Thrace, along the eastern Danube on the Black Sea. A prolific poet, Ovid knew that nothing was better for the writing process than peace and quiet. But he struggled to write in this "barbarian land, the most remote in the vast world."

Ovid penned a collection of poetic "lamentations," the *Tristia*, while living in exile, and in it he was unrelenting in his contempt for the people and the unfamiliar environment. "Privacy and ease" were in short supply. "The pine planks resound from the battering, the ropes from the shrieking wind, and the very keel" of more than one Black Sea freight ship "groans," he wrote. Every day brought a different "state of mourning." The *Tristia* is full of wallowing self-pity, interrupted only by a prayer to Dionysus, the god of alcohol.

What bothered Romans like Ovid the most was not the fact of being marginalized, at the border of their empire. The problems arose from the people one encountered: ethnic Sarmatians, Getae, Dacians, and Thracians, along with their different languages, their indigenous dress, and the unfathomable way their cultures seemed to fetishize violence.

Ovid himself never singled out one group as more frightful than the others. With a little poetic license, he and other Roman observers simply lumped these natives together in a picture that must have sounded dreadful to Romans back home.

Locals strode through villages with knives "fastened to their sides," and rarely did you pass someone on horseback who wasn't carrying a bow, a quiver, and "darts yellow with viper's gall." Even their "twang," as Ovid called it, made him wince. "If I look upon the men, they are scarce men worthy of the name," he said. "They have more of cruel savagery than wolves."

Tall tales and blunt judgments were not the only part of the Roman argot. Ovid may have been disgruntled at being sent to the frontier, banished there under mysterious circumstances involving a female member of Emperor Augustus's family. But other Romans went willingly, or at least accepted the peril and kept an open mind about the adventure. Many were soldiers, men whose families and descendants would become a common sight along the river in Alaric's day.

Romans who lived on the Danube had always noticed that the situation at the frontier could be tense, as Ovid himself remarked: "Peace there is at times, confidence in peace never." Less than a century after Ovid, Rome led its war machine to the river in a series of merciless military campaigns that would become known as the Dacian Wars. They devastated the region. Untold numbers of Dacians who lived in the area's mountains, marshes, and grasslands were captured, the people enslaved and displaced.

Carved scenes on Emperor Trajan's war memorial in Rome, a hundred-foot-tall marble column at the height of a small Roman hill, illustrated the ingenuities and the pieties of the Roman military, as well as the brutal realities of that war, for the people of the homefront. On it the Roman army chops down the local willows and uses the timber to construct a bridge to cross the Danube. Emperor Trajan solemnly presides at a pagan religious gathering, and Roman soldiers engage in a hunt for the native Dacian chief, Decebalus, who evades capture by tak-

Romans enthusiastically decorated their tombs with scenes showing the brutality of war, including images of defeated foreigners like this husband and wife, who lament their sudden captivity.

ing his own life. In all, the nearly eighty sculpted panels celebrated the story of the Roman Empire's first expansion to the northeast. The result of Trajan's conquest was a new Roman province, called Dacia, named after the people whose lands the Romans had just stolen. Its geographical center was the Transylvanian mountains.

When the Roman soldiers who had fought in the Dacian Wars retired, many of them did so in that rugged area, and their presence gradually fulfilled Ovid's hope that a "confidence in peace" might one day take root. As it did, the cities beyond the Danube River grew. Soon civilian settlers from Italy and elsewhere through the empire were arriving, many hoping to extract gold from the Transylvanian mountains, where mines had been operating unofficially since the Stone Age and had come under Roman control during the invasions of the second century.

For the next two hundred years, thrill seekers rushed to Rome's newest territories. They brought with them expectations for a different future, including hope for a better quality of life or at least one similar to what they had known in the Mediterranean. Over time, with the arrival of Roman customs—like new technology, an established industry of borrowing and lending, and the use of bronze and silver coins for everyday transactions, pressed with the official mint marks of the Roman Empire—they changed the look and feel of old Dacia. Many settlers and locals became wealthy.

A sense of the prosperity of the times is best revealed through archaeological evidence. Starting near the end of the eighteenth century, in 1786, workers in the city of Roşia Montană, Romania—near the ancient Roman metropolis of Alburnus Maior—unearthed twenty-five ancient wax tablets in an abandoned Transylvanian mine. All of them were about the size of a paperback book. They were what later writers termed triptychs, hinged planks of wood with wax panels on the inside, which the Romans designed to guarantee the security of contracts.

These wooden artifacts worked according to an early iteration of two-factor authentication. Interested parties drew up the terms of their contract and wrote them on two of the panels' faces. Each party signed the document, and then the two tablets were folded together and covered with a third. Holes were bored through all three pieces and a string threaded through them, tying them shut. Once the Roman contract was sealed, a second, identical version of the legal agreement was written on the cover, preventing either party from falsifying the original, locked inside. The process was designed to stop financial fraud.

This technology became such an effective way of preventing forgeries that in the first century the Roman emperor Nero signed a law mandating the use of it for all business transactions in the city of Rome. By the second century, locals were employing it in distant Dacia.

The Dacian contracts bring us face-to-face with everyday life in the Roman territories throughout the empire. Notwithstanding the Roman concern for law and order, it was a society of brazen behavior and calculated risk. And as the Roman gold miners moved in and soldiers of the empire retired on land given to them as a pension by the state, the worst practices of ancient Rome came with them. Men, women, even children were bought and sold as slaves. One contract, among many like it, recorded such slave sales:

> Maximus son of Bato bought and acquired, for the price of 205 *denarii,* a girl, a foundling, who goes by the name Passia (or whatever other name she goes by) through a sale with Dasius son of Verzo, a Pirustian from Kavieretium. She is around six years old. It is agreed the girl is in good health, free of crime or injury to another person, and is not known to be a runaway.

Since there was always the chance that a slave's former owner might try to reclaim his lost "property," contracts like this were the legal way for traders in Roman territory to indemnify themselves. The parties would agree that the buyer would be owed a full refund, plus fees, if ever forced to forfeit his "purchase." Many of the contracts invoked Fides, the Roman goddess of "reliability," to ensure that each signatory understood that the other was acting in good faith. Many Dacian boys and girls had their childhoods ripped away in this "lawful" system of human trafficking.

The Dacian conquests established a long history of slave trading on the river, a despicable practice that knew no ethnic distinction. Two hundred years after the little girl Passia was sold to a trader—after the Dacians mysteriously vanished and the Goths settled this same territory—many Gothic people would be forced into slavery, too. "There was hardly a region [of the empire] that lacked Gothic slaves," one Roman writer boasted in Alaric's day. Gothic labor, like Dacian slave labor before it, was considered cheap because of the overwhelming "supply." There were slaves to be found everywhere at the border, one Roman senator explained to his brother. At the river, "the price [for slaves] is right." Galatian hunters had the worst reputation and were known to snatch up any Goth "for sale in all parts, without distinction of status." As a result, Gothic children spent their youth grinding millstones like pack animals, sweeping farmhouses, or plowing fields. Every Roman home in Alaric's day was said to have at least a Gothic slave or two.

The first-generation settlers of the Danube frontier were callous, ruthless, and greedy. They were also enterprising: they purchased homes, signed leases on workshops, and made business partnerships. They had stomachs to feed and their own dreams to fulfill. Not all were as finely educated as Ovid. If we can make a safe deduction from the Latin tombstones and contracts they left behind, their spelling was frequently poor—a provincial *uxcor,* "my wive," for a dear *uxor,* "wife." Frontiersmen died and left their widows to wonder what would happen to them. Parents lived long lives: sixty years in one mother's case, seventy years for her husband. Their children, who never had known a life in another province, mourned them, honored them, and stayed.

As the hum of these colonial outposts enticed more visitors, it was increasingly hard to tell, throughout the second century, who was a Roman citizen and who was not, based on dress, language, or appearance alone. A rising tide of opportunity, which lifted both the Roman colonists and the indigenous people, was coming to three continents. As Rome established its provinces around the Mediterranean Sea, Roman culture came with it. Roman gods, writing, law, business, fashion, styles of art and architecture, tastes in wine, even kitchenware spread. The seeds of being Roman, *Romanitas,* took root in many of these local environments, cropping up in places as varied as the desert oases of modern Jordan and the damp fortified camps of modern Britain.

By the early third century, the Mediterranean world, not just Dacia, had blossomed into a multicultural, multiracial, multiethnic society. And the idea that every free person living in Roman territory might be or become a Roman citizen no longer seemed an impossible dream. In the year 212, in fact, a rebel, renegade emperor finally made it a reality.

～

Emperor Caracalla, like all political anomalies, confounded his Roman constituents. Whereas the Romans of his day expected competency, honesty, and stability from their leaders, he became best known for murdering his brother, shunning most state protocols, and refusing to outgrow his childish preference for a hooded cloak, the *caracallis,* which became the source of his nickname. His family hailed from the coast of North Africa. His father, also an emperor, had been a well-regarded administrator and talented general.

Many Romans were critical of Caracalla's judgment largely because he lacked his father's studied statesmanship. But the Antonine Declaration, which he published in 212 under his given Latin name, Antoninus, changed ancient Mediterranean life irrevocably. Every free-born resident of a Roman province was immediately given citizenship. At Caracalla's prompting, tens of millions of people across three continents began to pledge allegiance to that powerful ideal—being a Roman—which no one had yet defined. Some saw the emperor's move toward radical political equality as financially driven, an attempt to fill Rome's coffers with a new revenue stream, since citizens paid an inheritance tax but provincials did not. These cynical voices may have been correct, but the effect of the new law was undeniable. What it meant to be a Roman had changed. Anyone could be a Roman in Caracalla's new world.

By coincidence, a gruff young Gothic farmer's son named Maximinus, born and raised in the mountains of Thrace, due south of Alaric's later home, would stand among the first to benefit.

Caracalla's legal innovation revolutionized Roman society. For centuries, during the most economically robust and most stable years of its thousand-year existence, many people living inside the borders of the Roman Empire had been forced to earn their citizenship. Residents of earlier periods of Roman history did not uniformly hold the same legal status. In the time of the Roman Republic, before the rise of men like Julius Caesar, citizenship had originally been limited to free men and women who dwelled in the capital city. To vote meant physically being present in Rome, and to be a citizen, a highly prized legal status, meant living within the city walls. If they did, Roman citizens could be assured that, when they lent money, made wills, or sold real estate or human beings, their transactions—and any grievances caused by them—could be adjudicated in a Roman court.

As Rome expanded, however, and colonized the Italian peninsula, residents of small Italian towns demanded the same rights but without having to change residences and move to Rome. In the first century B.C., the Senate granted those rights, an occasion that marked the first expansion of citizenship in Rome's history. Eventually, as Roman settlements overran Italy's borders and spread throughout the Mediterranean, the process of extending these legal privileges, called "Italian rights," repeated itself, albeit at a slower pace and on a smaller scale. Only select individuals or, in some cases, entire cities were awarded Roman citizenship.

The application for Roman citizenship varied, depending on one's trade or area of residency. For example, after twenty-five years of service in the military, a veteran earned it automatically, and the citizenship status passed to his family and descendants in perpetuity. One's residence could also play a determining factor, as settlers in the larger metropolises of the frontier could, and frequently did, petition the emperors for "Italian rights," since they had taken up a life of hardship away from the Mediterranean. It was the emperor's prerogative to award it to them, and many rulers did so gladly, a thank-you to these first-generation entrepreneurs and self-made diplomats. Even before Caracalla announced his sweeping new law, settlers in the five largest towns of Dacia and their families had already been given the same legal rights as if they lived in Italy.

Citizenship ignited new hopes and dreams and turned many peripheral cities, thousands of miles from Rome, into beacons of opportunity for people on the frontier. As Roman towns boomed and main streets filled with ambitious tradesmen, vendors, and government workers, a nearby farmer might be tempted to leave behind the drudgery of his fields or the chores of animal wrangling. It was not unheard of for local residents to trade their farmsteads for an urban way of life and a modest city apartment, perhaps expecting to benefit from the next announcement of "Italian rights." Foreign-born soldiers, after their deployments, retired on land on the fringes of the empire, too. New experiments in

This bronze document belonged to a foreign soldier named Reburrus who served with Emperor Trajan's cavalry during the Dacian Wars; Reburrus later retired to Britain, where the object was found. The Latin text explains that Reburrus's unit was granted "citizenship for themselves, for their children and all their descendants."

Romanitas emerged from these intermingled communities. "Recently, we have been settled by veteran soldiers and become a most glorious colony," one Roman lawyer boasted. The sight of yet more new faces arriving in his quiet hamlet in the province of Numidia, already inhabited by members of a local ethnic group known as the Gaetulians, made him proud.

Young Maximinus witnessed this dynamic interplay every day—between Roman and local culture on the Dacian border—and it likely inspired him to aspire to escape his own small-town provincialism. Tireless ambition had always been the purest ethos of the Roman frontier. The borderlands offered its residents a freedom to experiment and a chance for reinvention. "Let someone see whether he can follow in my footsteps," one Roman frontier soldier bragged on his tombstone. He had been honored for his military valor, had performed the impressive feat of swimming the Danube "in full armor," and had strung and shot a bow like no other. "By my example," he boasted, "I am the first who accomplished such things." Generations of provincial young men were raised on this image of heroic swagger. That included young Maximinus.

Max's parents had cultivated a respect for Rome from the moment of his birth. Although they hailed from different ethnic backgrounds, they had given their son a recognizably Latin name. His father, Micca, was a Goth, his mother an Alan, one of the many native people who lived in the region of the Danube. Both of them may have harbored the common parental hope that their boy, with his stalwart Roman-sounding name, would nudge his way into opportunities they'd never had. Countless foreigners around the empire had done the same.

The journey of a provincial farm boy into the most influential corridors of the Roman state spoke to values that, according to one of the emperor's later biographers, included ruggedness, tough-mindedness, and a love of competition. The basics of a classical education, like reading and writing in Greek and Latin, never seemed to have been a priority. In other respects, Max's youth had been fairly ordinary. He herded cattle, tended his father's fields, and secretly itched for excitement, which eventually arrived in the form of a Roman military convoy. The army was on the march through Thrace. The emperor, it was announced, was accompanying them. There would be a circus of charioteers, wrestlers, and gladiators.

Young Maximinus was so captivated by the thought of seeing real soldiers and professional athletes that he raced into town. There, he stumbled into the emperor, Septimius Severus, Caracalla's father. Coming from a home where Latin had been at best a second or third language, the young provincial struggled to converse with the ruler of Rome and was ultimately forced to rely on "his native tongue." After a few false starts, Maximinus managed to express his desire to participate in one of that day's wrestling contests.

The African emperor, a native of the rich city of Leptis Magna, was impressed by this gutsy *adulescens*. Far worse reputations trailed behind Roman "young adults." Rich Roman boys were frequently lazy and unmotivated, waiting out their inheritances instead of working. Sexual assault was a regular problem, and many boys from well-to-do families wasted hours of their young lives responding to their accusers in court. By contrast, the Thracian farm boy's apparent honesty, earnestness, and deeply felt ambition persuaded the Roman emperor to take a chance on this "wild fellow," as Septimius was overheard to call him.

The ancient biographers always made a great deal of Maximinus's hulking size; one writer put him at nearly eight feet, which, even accounting for the disparity between an ancient foot and a modern one, is hard to believe. More reliable are the descriptions of Maximinus's strength and endurance, two qualities that fit a farmer's boy. On the day of the contests, the Thracian won sixteen wrestling matches "without taking any rest." The emperor applauded by drafting him into the army on the spot.

Eventually, Maximinus earned an appointment to the imperial bodyguard, was entrusted with greater leadership roles, and, after the death of his patron in 211, continued in the service of his elder son, Caracalla. The following year, in 212, Caracalla issued his decree, and Maximinus, about to turn forty, instantly became a Roman citizen. All of Rome's foreign soldiers did.

Two decades later, in 235, during a period of political turbulence following the murder of Caracalla's last surviving heir, the military acclaimed Maximinus as Rome's emperor: "the very highest station in the Roman Empire," as a later Gothic writer, Jordanes, said in his brief biography of Maximinus, written in the sixth century. Roman and Gothic readers of his day would have detected the pride in the historian's voice. It would have sounded like the pride of a Gothic father who never dreamed of seeing such successes for his son.

Maximinus was the first man who, having been born a foreigner, then made a citizen by Caracalla's law, was promoted to emperor. Three generations before him, Rome had come to the frontier. In the year 235, the frontier came to Rome in the person of Maximinus.

Fearful traditionalists immediately latched onto Maximinus's provincial origins to undermine his rule. A cadre of senators could not abide serving under this new "foreign" emperor. "Cyclops!" they shouted at him, frightening the populace with images of a fictional monster from Homeric poetry. It is clear that those already part of the wealthy establishment never thought a provincial should stand on equal footing with them, and many of their political supporters echoed their outrage. They grumbled how Maximinus had gotten his job "by luck" rather than talent. Roman conservatives, brought up to revere the *mos maiorum,* or "traditional ways," spent days grousing about the new emperor's "lowly origin" and rarely stopped to acknowledge "the honor he had won," according to a contemporary report.

Boys who grew up around the Danube, though, suddenly had a role model. Maximinus's male friends and family would no longer be, as they were in the popular Roman imagination, only the hulking, helmeted warriors who crashed into each other on game days. (Fans had long ago adopted the ethnic name "Thracian" as a shorthand for "gladiator.") Maximinus had softened that image and had turned Thracians into real people. Thanks to the citizenship decree of 212, the leadership of Rome began to look radically different, as Roman politicians could now potentially mirror the diversity of the empire's people. Any freeborn man could be the ruler of this new society, even one from the Danube.

In the years that followed, Gothic parents of a certain cultural persuasion—maybe even Alaric's—cherished Maximinus's success story because it spoke to their own aspirations for their children. The Gothic historian Jordanes composed one version of this story in the sixth century, but Alaric's parents could easily have told some version of Maximinus's biography to their son. Well before Jordanes, the tale of Rome's first half-Gothic emperor was published in a miscellany of lives, the *Augustan History,* authored during the fourth century. Latin readers devoured it, and the popularity of Maximinus's biography undoubtedly attests to what the Romans admired in the life of their first emperor who had won his citizenship, not inherited it. There were many reasons why Maximinus's biography would have remained popular on both sides of the border.

Reading biographies of the Caesars had always piqued the interest of Rome's chattering classes, and nothing titillated them more than political gossip and scandal. They enjoyed hearing about the drinking habits of their emperors; even an emperor's choice of pets could be the source of amusement or a reason for scandal. One muckraker circulated a rumor that when, in 410, Emperor Honorius learned that Rome had been attacked, he ran to his chicken pen and heaved a sigh of relief at finding his favorite bird, named Rome, thankfully still clucking.

Palace drama held Romans enrapt, and so did the rise and sudden fall of Emperor Maximinus. As he began the third year of his rule—just enough time to see a few marble portraits cut and a series of coins issued with images of his "formidable chin and jaw"—there was the assassination. In 238, unable to tolerate the radical changes his administration represented, a group of disaffected praetorian guards lured the emperor and his son out of their military tent. Herodian, the only contemporary who narrates the emperor's murder, rushes through the events only to say that the two bloody corpses "were exposed to the birds and dogs." Maximinus's head was sent to Rome, where the senators were already busy filling the constitutional vacancy. With suspiciously quick deliberation, they announced their own choice for the throne, a well-loved scion of a landowning family named Gordian, who was nearing eighty at the time. The selection marked an abrupt return to Rome's "traditional ways" and must have seemed, to many senators, the surest means of undoing Caracalla's innovation, which had upended their comfortable lives and complicated their own ideas about *Romanitas*.

The decades that followed tested the resolve of the Roman people as the very nature of what it meant to be Roman grew still more difficult to define. A succession of political highs and lows whiplashed the citizenry. As the city of Rome celebrated its thousandth birthday party, political murders both preceded it and followed by the dozens. Shortly afterward, when the government proclaimed a public religious holiday to unite the citizenry, factions of Christian citizens, believing that their Scriptures expressly forbade them to engage in such behavior, not only refused to attend; some bishops exploited the moment for their own public gain. They speciously claimed religious "persecution" and used the opportunity to unite the most ardent members of their congregations against the government. Whether motivated by expedience or idealism, Caracalla's quest for unity had widened the Roman people's deep divisions.

In these difficult years, Rome's government eventually gave up on Dacia for many reasons. The region's gold fever broke. Transportation to and from the mountain towns became too dangerous, and the logistics of security beyond the river proved too challenging. The safety of the Roman people counted among a Roman emperor's deepest concerns, and by the later third century, the need to leave Dacia clearly outweighed the benefits of staying. Towns north of the river had seen a spike in violence between Romans and the native tribes who lived on the periphery of Roman territory. One Roman emperor who had organized an expedition there, Decius, fell to a lethal arrow and died in Dacia in the 250s. Even as the Roman emperors won more and more military titles—Alammanicus ("Victor over the Alemanni"), Germanicus ("Victor over the Germani"), Gothicus ("Victor over the Goths")—with each honor lined up after their names the way athletes lined up their trophies, the general instability had convinced politicians that Dacia was too difficult to keep.

In 275, forty years after Maximinus was named emperor, the state gave up hope "that the province could be retained" and ordered the army to evacuate all Roman citizens from Dacia. There would be no more local councils, no judges, no legal protections—wills, deeds, or otherwise—for anyone living on land north of the river. The lines that careful mapmakers had once drawn were now erased. Rome's border would be reconfigured as the Danube River.

Emperor Aurelian, who ruled in the 270s, took upon himself the hard task of informing the Roman people about the change in policy. Romans fled. Developers moved south and built gated communities within walking distance of the river. Many had charmingly antiseptic Latin names, like the town of Ad Salices, which meant "At the Willows." Romans felt safer in these places.

Meanwhile, on the river's north shores, as the Roman government withdrew its workers and its tax base of wealthy citizens fled, once-thriving main streets fell into disrepair. No collection of local villagers, however organized, could match the level of Rome's financial investment in urban infrastructure. Years of neglect pushed Dacian cities into ruins. As the fourth century arrived, grasses, weeds, and flowers overtook the plots of abandoned houses and shops. By the century's end, rolling stretches of land—from the Carpathian Mountains to the Transylvanian hills to the Black Sea shore—were blossoming in a different way, as the native populations, joined by new settlers, called Goths, moved into the villages and made them their home.

What would Alaric's life have looked like if the Romans had sustained this momentum by welcoming foreigners from the Danube border? Would the Roman Empire have fractured as swiftly as it did, breaking apart into an assortment of independent territories in A.D. 476? If Alaric had been born two hundred years earlier, without any change of address, he likely would have been a Roman citizen. With that one small credential to his name, his whole life might have taken a different path. He might have followed in Maximinus's footsteps, worked his way into the emperor's attention, and been promoted to emperor himself. Gothic history would then have been woven into the tapestry of what defined *Romanitas*. But that is not what happened.

CHAPTER THREE

Stolen Childhoods

It is slow speech that brings the greatest wisdom.

—EURIPIDES

Alaric's grandparents likely remembered when the Roman government had declared their river a militarized zone. Our understanding of their experience comes through Jordanes's account of how the Goths settled the land they called Gothia. The only Gothic history book that survives from antiquity, Jordanes's *The Origins and Deeds of the Goths,* reads like a wondrous fairy tale, replete with shrieking witches and wise princes who magically conjure up fabled kingdoms. By presenting an absorbing Gothic experience of the world, it leaves a lasting impression. The story it tells captivated curious readers throughout the Middle Ages.

According to Jordanes, a long time ago, in a land far from the Mediterranean Sea, the Gothic king Berig assembled a scrappy lot of followers, packed them onto three ships, and led them from an obscure northern island, named Scandza, into the great unknown. Many miles later, Berig settled them in a strange new place. The way the Gothic legends tell it, they called this temporary home Gothiscandza and dwelled there "for about five kings" before moving again, or so the story went.

Eventually, these men and women traveled to Oium, where the tired Goths were comforted by the soothing sounds of mooing cows and delighted at the untouched fields. The sure sign that they had reached the end of their wanderings came when the bridge to Oium collapsed as they finished crossing it. When the dust cloud lifted, the Goths had found their homes, many of them near the great Danube River. Jordanes never says what befell the many Dacian people who evaded capture and remained on their land after the Roman conquests of the early second century. Even scholars are unsure why they vanished from the historical records, but the Dacians apparently recognized some benefit to keeping a low profile.

Jordanes likely knew these Gothic yarns because Goths had told them for generations and for hundreds of years. Alaric probably heard some version of the adventures of King Berig in his youth. The tales must have worked their magic on children and parents alike, connecting the mundane realities of Gothic life—hunting, fishing, cooking, trading—to a more idyllic past. Even in the fourth century, the power of storytelling would have made King Berig feel near enough to be real but far enough to remain a mystery. The unproven, yet oft-repeated claim that the Goths originated in Scandinavia largely comes from an uncritical reading of these fairy tales. No one knows the location of ancient Scandza.

The Gothic origin stories teased listeners with phantom facts but served an important cultural function. They filled in the gaps of Gothic history with intriguing, if unsubstantiated, factoids—like the idea that young Alaric was born into a family called the Balthi, or the "Bolds." According to Jordanes, the Bolds were one of Gothia's well-heeled patrician families. There's no way to verify Jordanes's ancestral account, but there are good reasons to be suspicious. Jordanes, despite his extensive research and interviews with Goths he knew, sprinkled many fanciful traditions into his books, like claiming that the Goths were related to the mythical Amazons or that the Goths had fought in the Trojan War or that they had been allies with the illustrious Macedonian warrior Alexander. None of these claims was remotely true.

Jordanes did, however, know Gothia's marshes, forests, and rivers, which he characterized as a land of "quaking bogs." Archaeologists, geologists, and botanists have, in the years since then, colored in a bit more of Jordanes's picture. Time, as it has with many majestic landscapes— the Dover cliffs, for example, or the Grand Canyon—has weathered the Danube delta. Rugged outcroppings at the river's mouth—of red, gray,

Due to the changing course of the Danube River and to centuries of deforestation, Pine Tree Island, where Alaric spent his childhood, no longer exists. But the delta's flora, fauna, and marshes still evoke its natural wonder.

and white limestone—tell a history that dates back to the Triassic and Jurassic periods. Cliffs rise six to seven hundred feet on the river's right bank, and to the north, where they level off, stretch large tracks of wetlands and fields that once teemed with wildflowers. Once upon a time, Alaric had been nothing but a boy from the grasslands.

"Communities" of plants (to use the biologists' endearing metaphor) were to be found at every roadside and hilltop of the land. Willow trees lined the rivers and provided shade for the area's thick patches of reeds and cattails. Water lilies floated atop freshwater ponds. There was wormwood in the salty marshes, and around it forests of white oaks and pines. In the ancient world, pine was a versatile commodity: in addition to the many regular uses to which a handyman might put it, the wood could be used as a writing surface. The ancients are known to have exchanged letters on pine tablets, and many of the contracts from the Transylvanian gold mines had been drafted on them, as well.

Jordanes was no botanist, but his writing still animates the landscape. Gothia, he wrote, was a land of "suitable homes and pleasant places," including its wistful-sounding nook called Pine Tree Island, where the Bolds supposedly had their home. Over the years, voracious loggers, traders, and soldiers have deforested Alaric's old neighborhood, transforming its once-plentiful timber into fuel, construction material for new buildings, and the planks of rafts and boats. As a result, the original location of Pine Tree Island has all but vanished. The Danube's own shape-shifting ways, the result of hundreds of years of flooding and other environmental changes at the delta—what scientists call the river's changing geomorphology—has also conspired to hide its exact location. But in the early 2010s, an enterprising team of scientists from Romania had a clever idea to bore holes across the wetlands and marshes and look for concentrated traces of pine pollen as a way to locate the old settlement. They discovered large deposits of pollen in an unexpected place: on a thin peninsula that extends south from the river's lip and creates a broad bay behind it. Because this sliver of forested land is almost entirely enveloped by the water on its front and back sides, scientists suspect that the Greek mariners who first laid eyes on it mistook it for an island and that their erroneous designation became fixed in all subsequent local traditions.

Every day at Pine Tree Island's ports and harbors would have brought in a different weather-beaten face. Archaeology takes us back to those modest fishing villages. In Gothia, men dug houses out of the ground to protect their families from the elements, while more enterprising Goths quarried limestone near the sea or chopped down pines to build sturdy huts. Archaeologists have found traces of these walls, spotted these holes in the ground, and carefully identified these cuts. Alaric's parents' home would have been an unpretentious abode, a place where a family could retire at night or seek protection from the rain and wind. It would have by no means been a mansion, even if, as tradition insists, the Bolds were rich.

Family life was largely lived outdoors among the members of the tribe. Many women labored at the hearth throughout the day to prepare traditional meals, but freewheeling, tattooed adventuresses roamed Gothia's villages, too. By Alaric's youth, generations of warrior men and women who lived nearby and shared the land, like the local tribe of the Agathyrsi, had long raised horses and hunted the open steppes, ranging as far away as central Asia. They inked their skin with blue-black dye, the sting of the iron needle a point of native pride and one that caused credulous Greeks and Romans to wonder, as Pliny did, why anyone would choose to write "on their own bodies."

Men in Gothia hunted, fished, explored the rivers, felled trees, and scavenged in the "swamps and forests," which, as Jordanes reminded his audience, were an important center of communal activity, the equivalent of Gothia's cities. Being surrounded by nature, in fact, was likely what taught Gothic children, both boys and girls, to be inquisitive about themselves and about others.

Goths of Alaric's day passed down the memory of many of these pioneering but now-nameless ancestors. Some of the Goths were astrologists. Others were herbalists who experimented with the natural properties of Gothia's native herbs, grasses, and trees, like the willows near Alaric's home. Romans called the willow *salix,* in Latin. Alaric's word for it, like much of his people's literature, was never written down. But fifteen hundred years later, a synthetic compound that enhanced what the willow's leaves and bark do best—alleviate headaches, aches, and pains—was finally developed by a German scientist. He won the Nobel Prize. (Salicylic acid, which is naturally derived from the willow, is the key ingredient in aspirin.)

Within the largely unstructured hours of the young Gothic children's life, adults taught them, during excursions to the forest, which stream was "sweet and fit to drink as far as half-way down its course" and which other bodies of water to avoid, Jordanes explains. On fishing trips, a child might study the nets, making mental notes about which kinds of fish were full of "fine flavor, without bones." No doubt these were the cartilaginous fish of the region, such as lampreys, eels, and sharks. For adults, days were marked by the time it took to journey from one river to the next. A child's classroom, it's safe to say, was outdoors; his parents and local villagers were akin to teachers. Throughout the year, those adults might have taught their sons and daughters how to distinguish a dainty roe deer from a majestic red one or how to creep around a lurking fox. On hikes inland to the mountains, Gothic children's eyes might have grown wide with fear as they spotted the terrifying wingspan of a vulture, learning how to tell that bird apart from an eagle, with its white tail. (Thanks to the work of zooarchaeologists, bones from these raptors have been identified in excavations at the Danube site of Dichin, near Gothia's ancient borders.)

Back home, where the landscape could appear deceptively uninteresting, even a casual stroll could offer pleasing encounters with nature. Chickens and geese ranged freely. Ducks dwelled in Gothia's bogs, and in the river, there were water voles, beavers, and screeching weasels, whose squeals may have sent children doing the same. All of these species' bones have been dug up around the delta. Sometimes they survive in fragments—a jaw bone or a claw—but as evidence, they fill out Jordanes's accounts of everyday life.

Right around the time Alaric was born, in the 370s, a series of grisly homicides disturbed one of the tribal areas far upstream. The territory was quite distant from Gothia, at the source of the Danube, a place Jordanes described as having "a great rushing sound." The tribe of people affected were called Alemanni, not Goths, but word of the violence that struck at the safety of their community likely came to Gothia.

Night after night, some of the best young Alemanni were murdered in their sleep and decapitated, their corpses left outside their huts and tents to rot. Each day, members of the tribe awoke to more news: another body had been found. The situation worsened: one day, the chief's son went missing, and suspicion fell on the Romans, who dwelled in the vicinity. A short time later, the mystery was cleared up when, in a stunning revelation, the culprit was revealed to be a disgruntled tribesman named Charietto. He "towered over everyone," it was said, with nerves that "matched his size." According to the Roman writers who documented the killings, Charietto murdered his people to punish them for their unwillingness to compromise with the Roman government. In desperation, he even kidnapped the chief's son to use as a pawn during negotiations.

It's difficult to hear about this rash of killings and not imagine the fear Gothic parents may have felt for their children at the hands of strangers, outsiders, and madmen. Beyond the Roman border, these were tight-knit villages. People recognized one another's faces and routines during the daylight hours. And after the Gothic wagons quieted down at night, the villagers met one another again around the fire for a meal. The strumming of a cithara enlivened the woods as bards sang about King Berig and people shared the evening's food.

Centuries later, Jordanes's account of those fireside meals has proved to be rather important. The same cups and plates—drab-looking gray beakers and matte-orange dishware—show up in excavated tombs across central and eastern Romania, Moldova, and southern and central Ukraine.* The shapes of these containers differ just enough from Roman wares to make them distinctive and readily identifiable, and although some occasionally mimic the appearance of well-known Roman forms, the chemical composition of the clay used to make them is unlike anything produced in Roman workshops. Their presence in the archaeological record rapidly diminishes with proximity to southern Russia and eastern Poland, and they generally look different from the dishes Roman

---

* The first archaeological sites to be connected were in Romania, at Sântana de Mureş, and in the former Soviet Union at Černjachov (today, Černjachiv in Ukraine). As specialists started to identify similarities across these artifacts, they began to refer to the people who had produced them as the Sântana-de-Mureş/Černjachov culture. Today, there is consensus that this evidence marks an important moment in Gothic history, although there is spirited disagreement about how it originated.

settlers had brought to Dacia. Most of these ceramics have been dated to the fourth century—the third century A.D., at the earliest.

From the pattern of the ceramics' distribution and the date of their manufacture, archaeologists have been able to deduce the definition of Gothia's territorial boundaries during Alaric's lifetime. No boundary is impermeable, of course, even when separated by walls and fences. And the artistic expression of a people's culture, like their ceramics, rarely fits snugly within a line, however neatly drawn. Some of those humble Gothic dishes, archaeologists know, did cross the Danube border and are occasionally found in excavated Roman settlements south of the river, a point of archaeological curiosity that suggests that the Goths' sphere of influence reached beyond their own political territory. In fact, the presence of Gothic-style ceramics on Roman land can be explained as the sign of a robust trade between Goths and Romans, as testimony to their shared taste in styles of kitchenware, or as the everyday house-hold cups and plates of Gothic individuals and communities who had crossed the river. Not all of these Goths would have been slaves or refu-gees. Throughout the fourth century, many Goths went south by choice.

In the end, what's astonishing about Alaric's rather hidden child-hood is not that nearly all information about it was lost but that young Alaric survived at all. Like Charietto, numerous headhunters stalked the woods near his home. And just as in old Dacia, slave traders lurked near the water he played in. In his youth, civil war ravaged the Terv-ing tribe, to which Alaric's family belonged, and terrifying nomads from the central Asian steppes, Huns, invaded Gothia's northern bor-ders, even disturbing towns and communities as far east as China. Dur-ing one intense period of conflict, the despondent Gothic chief of the Greuthung tribe, who had been unable to protect his people from the marauding Huns, killed himself out of shame.

Many Gothic families, in both the north and the south, eventually made the decision to leave their homes. By 376, thousands of them had fled Gothia for Rome. Like generations of immigrants before them, each would become a refugee, a *profugus*. That simple Latin word, which generally referred to a "wanderer," resonated deeply with Romans, who remembered it from their school days. The unmatched storyteller of the first century B.C., the poet Virgil, had made it an inseparable part of Rome's national identity when he enlisted it to describe the hero Aeneas in his epic poem *The Aeneid*. Generations of schoolchildren memorized the opening lines of Virgil's poem and, in doing so, taught themselves that Rome's founders had been immigrants.

Yet a widespread affinity for Virgil never guaranteed that the Roman people would formulate a sympathetic response to the Gothic crisis. As one fourth-century commentator pointed out, Virgil specifically said that Aeneas had immigrated "by fate," *fato*. Without that important caveat, Servius explained, readers might have misjudged the poem's protagonist and transformed him into a dangerous criminal or a murderous invader—the implication being that, in fourth-century Rome, immigrants were frequently disparaged as both.

This generalized hostility probably explains why, as Goths crossed the border in 376, lacking much money with which to purchase food or water—what the Romans recognized as "life's necessities"—many fell victim to the border guards, who preyed on the immigrants' vulnerabilities. Goths in the camps were sold second-rate dog meat as food and promised better meals if they handed over their sons. For twenty-four months, these indignities went unaddressed by the government. The new immigrants were acting like wild animals who had escaped from their cages, Romans said. Goths made decent cooks and butlers, but why were they camped in their wagons on Roman land?

Demoralized Gothic men, the heads of families, learned to be wary. Dinner invitations were extended by enthusiastic Roman soldiers, with a pretense of camaraderie, only the Goths never came home after the purported meal. Violence against foreigners, even state-sponsored acts of murder, had become an ugly part of Roman life. Even foreign dignitaries could be eliminated, if the circumstances so demanded.

Unbeknownst to the Goths during these years, Emperor Valens, fearing the defection of Armenia as a key ally against Persia, ordered one

such assassination, targeting Armenia's young king, Pap. Two years
before Goths boarded boats to cross the Danube, the rising star of Armenia had to use a makeshift raft to save his own life. The emperor invited
Pap to the Roman city of Tarsus, purportedly to persuade him to adopt
a more aggressive stance toward their mutual Persian neighbor. In fact,
the emperor planned to murder him. As soon as Pap suspected Valens's
treachery, the young Armenian and his entourage fled home through the
Syrian desert. Trapped by the Euphrates River, they raided farmhouses,
stole mattresses, and rigged the beds together with inflated wineskins
to improvise a float. Pap crossed the river and thought himself safe. He
was not. Roman spies used forged documents to lure the king to a "banquet" that would feature wine and "drummers, flutists, lyre-players,
and trumpeters." During the middle of the meal, Rome's representa-
tives walked out, mercenaries were sent in, and Pap was felled with one
stroke of an axe, as "the wine of the [king's] cup mingled with the blood
from his throat."

At the Danube border, nervous Roman cities increasingly often
locked their gates when they saw ragged Gothic mothers with children
coming to the markets. Jordanes says that some Gothic parents relin-
quished their children to slavery during these hard years because they
concluded it was "better to lose liberty than life." One Roman called the
human trafficking morally unjustifiable. "Even if they were the judges
of their own case," he opined, the actions of the soldiers "could not be
acquitted by any excuse." But solutions were slow to come.

Valens's government finally intervened. Rome agreed to offer the refugees handouts of food and arranged for some of the hundreds of thousands to settle on open fields. Christian writers praised the emperor, after
his death, for his "compassion." But his measures proved insufficient to
address the ongoing horrors of famine, slavery, and immigrant deaths.

More trauma followed when, sometime that year or early in 377, the
border patrol began indiscriminately separating Gothic boys from their
parents. The government had decided upon this policy of forced relocation to ensure that the young Goths grew up pledging "faithfulness" to

the values of their new home. The plan, instituted by Emperor Valens, was to distribute the Gothic children "into various towns to prevent them, when grown to manhood," of plotting what many Romans feared would be an "insurrection." According to the Roman writers who lived to witness this episode, the government's policy applied to Gothic boys eight to ten years old—"those persons," it was said, "who were too young for war." Following the usual Roman military practice, many of the older boys were likely enrolled as cadets.

The young Gothic boys were identified, processed, and sorted, the impersonal nature of the border guards' tasks little different from the inhumanity of the colonial-era Dacian slave trade. In fact, many Roman soldiers capitalized on the general confusion to acquire their own slaves. They separated Gothic wives from their captured husbands and took possession of unmarried Gothic girls. One Roman soldier, it was reported, "was smitten by a fair and pretty boy," who endured a different fate from his peers, all of whom the Roman government classified as "hostages."

State resources were soon allocated to implement the border separation policy in full. An office of the Roman government was set up to oversee the relocation program, and a military appointee received a government salary to manage it. The rugged plateaus and cities beyond the Taurus Mountains, in Roman Asia, were identified as suitable holding pens for the children. Gothic children were forced to say good-bye not only to a familiar landscape of childhood memories but to their actual parents, grandparents, and siblings. No documentation was ever kept, as far as historians know, that would have identified the children or helped reunite them with their families. An obvious paper trail, in fact, is quite likely what the Roman government wanted to avoid. Cruelty was the intention. Many Gothic parents never saw their sons again.

In the late summer of 378, the distracted fifty-year-old emperor Valens, tabling his military plans to lead an attack against Armenia and Persia, decided to visit the Danube frontier to address the growing crisis. Gothic spokesmen asked for permission to farm on more Roman land, as they felt it would give their families hope for a better future. But Valens was in no mood to bargain. The land they wanted belonged to the Roman people, and he could no longer help them. When it became clear that the two sides would not reach a settlement, the aggrieved Goths circled their wagons. Rome readied its legions. On a field at Adrianopolis in early August, some distance beyond the eastern capital's outer territory, tens of thousands of Roman and Gothic soldiers died in a pitched battle.

On the night of August 9, 378, Valens, pestered and weary, was likely asleep when Gothic arsonists torched the Roman farmhouse where he was lodging, close to the battlefield. The roof of the property fell under the weight of the flames. One version of the incident says he was killed in the fire. Jordanes contradicts that account, saying Valens actually died the day before on the battlefield. But as a Gothic historian, he might have scrubbed the murder scene to exonerate his people. The real tragedy of Adrianopolis was that the story of a murder by arson under the cloak of night appeared to confirm the Romans' ugliest fears about the Goths. These people, the Romans told themselves, were savages.

Within the year, the young Gothic boys separated from their parents were dead. In the wake of the farmhouse massacre, lingering doubts about the benefits of the program had convinced the Roman official in charge, Julius, to end it on his own initiative—with Gothic blood. He ordered officials in Asia Minor to call a public assembly. A false promise was made to assist the Gothic boys financially. Town councils were instructed to gather the refugee children. Julius ordered archers to be "mounted upon the roofs of the houses in the respective marketplaces." When the boys were led forth, they were murdered, one by one.

The lone Gothic source that survives, written by Jordanes, omits this episode, but the Roman people who learned of it never forgot about the stolen childhoods of the Gothic youths. The ancient writer who gives the most complete surviving historical account of the tragedy, the radically revisionist historian Zosimus, wrote well after Alaric's life. An outspoken champion of the older empire, Zosimus lived in the early sixth century during an age of political instability and Christian overreach, and he romanticized the Roman Empire's earlier history: a time of competent rulers, stable government, and religious toleration. Frustrated by the realities of his own day, he published a work called *A New History*, which offered a blistering critique of the empire's ills. In it, he lamented the loss of Roman territory and savaged the empire's Christian leaders for their intolerant zealotry.

Skeptics protest that no writer working two centuries after the fact could definitively have documented what happened during the border separation crisis of the 370s. And Zosimus, it is true, was not an eyewitness to those events. Moreover, news of the atrocities was barely mentioned in contemporary reports at the time, which means that Zosimus might have fabricated some details. Even the magisterial Roman historian of Alaric's youth, Ammianus Marcellinus—heir to the noble tradition of Latin history writing begun by Livy and Tacitus and author of a weighty tome on the fourth century—buried this episode in a brief aside. He praised Julius's "wise plan" to hold the young foreigners in detention but was vague about the moment when Roman public squares were turned into a killing field.

The reticence of the Roman sources prior to Zosimus is also unsurprising. Given Rome's usual reluctance to understand the predicaments of foreigners and the relentless mockery immigrants endured at the hands of poets and writers, it makes good sense that Romans in Alaric's day never really wanted to confront the tragedy. Roman writers frequently did claim to prize objectivity—but usually only if it suited their own personal agendas and glorified the empire.

Zosimus, on the other hand, was an avowed troublemaker. As a historian, he chose to expose some of his culture's dark memories when most of his audience would have preferred such scandalous details to remain hidden. Provocation was his goal. From the pages of his *A New History*, he gave his sixth-century Roman audience a different way of remembering the life of the Roman Empire: not just as a series of military victories and cultural triumphs but also as a sequence of political setbacks, missed opportunities, and disappointing leaders.

Zosimus wrote so that history would not be forgotten. And like other historians, he had his biases and his own perspectives. Yet he also seems to have recognized something modern practitioners of his discipline have come to appreciate. Writing history is more than a routine chore of hanging events one after the next, like laundry on a clothesline. Questions of how people remember their past and why they choose to forget parts of it are just as important to shake out.

For that reason, even accounting for Zosimus's distance from events that occurred during Alaric's childhood, it's probably unfair to dismiss his findings. He might have uncovered evidence deliberately ignored or simply unavailable to earlier writers like Ammianus—private letters, military journals, or official memoranda that survived into his time but are not, like the majority of those written artifacts, available to our own. If so, then far from being guilty of embellishment, Zosimus might represent the historical profession's most dogged commitment to the truth. By describing how the children's extermination was coldly, methodically planned—with secret communiqués sent to Constantinople and an "oath of secrecy" sworn by the collaborators—he might well have documented an atrocity that earlier generations of Romans had judged too painful to record. Zosimus also preserved many details of Alaric's adult life that are otherwise unconfirmed; it doesn't follow that he was misinformed.

Alaric came of age at a time when high-placed politicians wanted Gothic boys like him dead, when few ordinary Romans cared to acknowledge the cruelties that had occurred at their own borders, and when even the casual comments of educated Romans dehumanized his people. Still, almost inexplicably, the Gothic boy from Pine Tree Island imagined there might be some better future awaiting him on the other side of the river.

CHAPTER FOUR

Opportunity

All of us, beginning with himself, are sojourners here and
strangers and exiles.

—PLUTARCH

There were many reasons why citizens and immigrants from the borderlands decided to join the Roman army. Some did so for the basest reasons, out of necessity, as was the case for many economically hard-pressed communities who lived at the Danube. In good times, a provincial citizen or a Goth could earn a lucrative career by buying or selling amber, furs, and hides at the many Roman trading towns stationed above the riverbanks, like the imposing fortress at Noviodunum, whose tall stone walls loomed over the hills. Soldiers surveilled the river border from its high watchtowers. A naval base was nestled beneath its escarpment. Wealthier provincials often avoided military service by opting to work in one of the town's essential trades.

The fort lay a short distance from Alaric's home, and many Gothic hunters throughout his childhood earned a modest income bringing their skins to market, where they would have haggled with the Roman buyers. The regular comings and goings of ships kept Noviodunum thriving throughout much of the fourth century. On any given day, at the Danube delta's cliffs, one could hear the sound of oars and the grunts of the enslaved men who rowed the long-distance ships on the choppy sea. Shiploads of crates and jugs arrived daily and were "transferred to river barges and transported to towns along the bank so that the soldiers have their supplies." By the late fourth century, a chain of forts like the one at Noviodunum extended along the Danube—at places like Capidava, Sucidava, Cii, Bireo, all of them located in modern Romania.

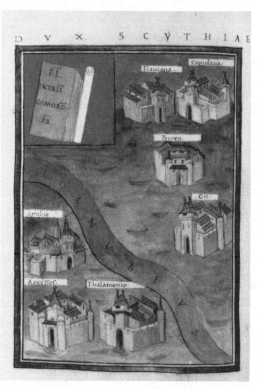

Rome's river border with Gothia hosted naval bases and forts, as seen in this provocative Renaissance illustration. To emphasize Rome's mastery of the landscape, the artist has depicted Roman camps on both sides of the river, although all of these Roman settlements were historically located on the right bank.

The cargo provisioned Rome's soldiers on the frontier with their needed bread, oil, and wine and fed the engine of the local economy.

But the situation did not last. As a heightened anxiety about Gothic criminality settled over the area following Emperor Valens's murder, many harbor towns closed their ports and markets to Gothia's traders, as the Roman government itself had encouraged during the worst years of recent fighting. Goths suffered even after Valens's war concluded. So did the Romans who lived in villages near the border. The latest archaeological research has revealed the extent of the economic downturn. In 2014, as a team of Romanian workmen near Noviodunum began building a new station for the border police, the workers discovered a series of collapsed brick walls. (The site sits on the southern riverbank, across from the southern appendage of Ukraine.) Work stopped as wheelbarrows full of ancient ceramics were hauled from the ground. The construction team had stumbled upon a Roman pottery factory. Its industrial-strength kilns had fired hundreds, if not thousands, of lamps and dishes for people to use in local villages near Alaric's home. The modest group of potters had provided a service as vital to its region as a small-town general store.

By the end of the fourth century, however, its kilns had gone cold. The factory had been shuttered and workers forced to abandon their jobs.

Rome was still an empire of immigrants in those years. From Greek speakers who had come to the city of Rome to work as tutors and teachers in the early first century, to the architects from Damascus who engineered some of the Roman world's most iconic monuments in the second century, to the often overlooked female politician, Zenobia of Palmyra, from the Middle East who claimed the title Augusta in the third century, Rome had long pulled foreigners into its orbit. Not all of them were treated warmly. As her sphere of influence grew beyond local Syria, into Egypt, the shocked establishment captured "Queen" Zenobia, as they derided her, and marched her through the streets of Rome to punish her for her audacity. Yet it was far more common that foreigners who wanted to make a name for themselves were applauded, recognized, and earned lucrative rewards.

Many immigrants advanced their families' reputations and their own careers by settling inside the Roman Empire's borders: Franks, Armenians, Vandals, Moors, Ethiopians, and more. Unless conquered and enslaved in war, every man and woman who lived inside the empire's territorial border held the status of a free person. A kaleidoscope of options for where to live, what to enjoy, and how to earn a living kept society colorfully in motion. Latin may have famously been the common language, but all around the ancient world, multilingualism was the norm. A basic definition of *Romanitas* emerged from this array of diversity. Privilege, education, wealth, and one's own dreams filled in the rest.

Nevertheless, an unavoidable level of precariousness had always defined the immigrant experience in Rome. Both before and after Caracalla's citizenship law, immigrants, refugees, and exiles faced an uncertain reception wherever they went. Plutarch, a widely traveled Greek speaker who had a sympathetic ability to see both the fascinating and the frightening in people's lives, captured some of their challenges in his biographies and essays. He is best known for his *Lives,* a series of biographical portraits of ancient statesmen that paired Greek figures with Roman ones to draw out parallel lessons. But at the end of the first century A.D., he also wrote an essay, "On Exile," that explored the predicament of finding oneself in new surroundings.

Being forced to leave one's home is an ordeal no one should be forced to endure, Plutarch began. Geographical dislocation causes undeniable suffering. Everyone admires how the ancient bards channeled that emotion into their soulful poetry and music, he acknowledged. But, he went on, fortunately, hardships are never immutable, and one's circumstances can often improve. In the same way a good cook can recognize when a dash of "sweet and pleasant" spice might help mask the "disagreeable" flavor of a "bitter and pungent" dish, a readiness to experiment and a willingness to be creative constitutes one's basic recipe for survival in a strange land. The culinary comparison was especially apt for Plutarch's audience, since it was food, after all, that taught many isolated Romans about cultures beyond their borders.

Plutarch's essay preached a civic gospel—of hard work and optimism— that nudged many Roman readers to sympathize with the *alieni* (to use the Latin term for "strangers") they encountered. The examples Plutarch chose to illustrate the pain of displacement told a powerful story about the need for perseverance and acceptance. Hadn't the city of Athens at one time banished the mythical hero Theseus from its community? Now the Athenians worshipped him as a founding father. And hadn't a migrant from Thrace started the Eleusinian Mysteries, which expanded to become one of the ancient world's longest-running religious festivals, at Eleusis? The lesson was that human beings were eminently adaptable—"No place can take away happiness"—but only if citizens and "aliens" worked together.

"Do you see the boundless aether overhead? / That holds the earth within its soft embrace?" Plutarch asked, quoting for his readers a now-lost Greek play. "This is the boundary of our native land, and here no one is either exile or foreigner or alien." Any small-minded provincial foolish enough to claim that the moon looked better at Athens than at Corinth, he asserted, deserved to be ridiculed. In Plutarch's mind, the wonders of the world knew no geographical boundary—a message that was undoubtedly easy for him to preach as a native Greek speaker, a friend of the emperors, and a Roman citizen.

Two hundred years later, even with its flaws—a legacy of colonialism, an aggressive foreign policy, unchecked rancor toward foreigners in its own cities—an immigrant could settle down in the Roman Empire, learn a trade, raise a family, and make a decent living. A simple plot of land might be sufficient. Opportunity plus patience equaled happiness. By the Middle Ages, that formula became proverbial. "Rome wasn't built in a day," people quipped.

Ambitious foreigners, both men and women, sensed the possibilities. Despite the limitations of not being a citizen, an immigrant to the fourth-century empire could legally go anywhere, work any craft, and be anything. Each of Rome's territories had its own unique allure, from its climate to its food to the careers its people pursued. Simple, ordinary friction—between a region's local customs and the broader trends whirling around the Mediterranean Sea—propelled the Roman Empire in interesting directions. Intellectuals went east to the distinguished centers of learning at Athens, Antioch, and Alexandria, where they conducted their highbrow conversations in the taverns run by sons of local farmers. By the fourth century, businessmen had struck it rich on the North African coast by investing in kilns, digging and processing local clays, and manufacturing heavy-duty ceramic containers for wine and olive oil to be shipped throughout the Mediterranean. Gradually expanding their production into a popular line of home goods that included cups, cookware, and plates—a style archaeologists call African red slip ware because of its glossy orange color—these entrepreneurs soon dominated the Roman market.

Given the empire's enormous size, an immigrant's search for a home was constricted only by the dreams he aspired to and by where he could afford to live. Spanning three continents, the Roman Empire of the 380s was an atomized world of about 120 small provinces, clustered into twelve dioceses and grouped into four prefectures. Each level of the government required political appointees and an extensive staff, who oversaw their small section of it. The Roman Republic, at its inception in 509 B.C., had never employed such a large federal system; nor did the empire until Emperor Diocletian brought it about in the late third century A.D. to stabilize the state after the half century of rancorous, often violent political divisions. With the new government structure, peaceful transitions of power returned, the horrors of civil wars faded, and the self-confidence of the Roman people took root again.

The people of the Roman Empire would have seemed as diverse as their tastes. Syrian merchants ventured to the northern frontiers. A Roman of Jewish faith had been the director of the customs station at Intercisa, on the Danube. With this constant mix, stereotypes were, perhaps, unavoidable. The father of Emperor Valens, whose family hailed from the middle Danube frontier, had often boasted of winning a strongman rope competition, an ancient variant of tug-of-war, in his hometown province of Pannonia as a young man; boorish and unrefined was how the Romans thought of that northern neck of their empire—on good days.

The culture of the Roman provinces themselves varied widely from high to low, in terms of everything from deeply held religious beliefs to the food served on their tables. Some communities were famous for their gods, like the Gazans, who worshipped an eccentric deity named Marnas, protector of crops; other places were renowned for their dishes, like the much-beloved salty mackerel of the Iberian provinces. In some Roman kitchens, olive oil reigned; in others, a pat of butter was the first ingredient a *coquus* plopped into the pan. Even the tiniest dregs at the base of a cup presented fascinating portraits of the Roman people. The Romans in Gaul, Egypt, Liguria, and Lusitania were said to enjoy a good *cervesia,* or beer; the Romans of Italy and Greece, a glass of *vinum,* or wine. Animals lived at the whim of their human neighbors. One modern historian famously quipped that in the lead-up to Rome's Jewish Wars, pigs in Judaea "could look forward to a tranquil old age" because so few people ate them. With the Roman conquest of Jerusalem in A.D. 70 and the burning of Jerusalem's Second Temple, however, menus changed to include plenty of pork.

⤝⤞

As the Danube trading centers went quiet and local pottery production shut down, the Roman military became the most prominent industry at the northern border by the end of the fourth century. Both Goths and Romans enlisted.

The empire's border patrol worked as a wall and a mirror, with the faces of the watchful soldiers reflecting the faces of those living on the other side. The Romans had long drawn upon a network of "loyal confederates," or *foederati,* as they were known in Latin legal terminology, to police the empire's frontiers. The benefit of this arrangement to Rome was financial: foreigners could be paid less than citizens. The enlistees received payment in coin but also accrued more intangible forms of capital. Years of service facilitated their introduction to the cut-throat world of politics since the emperor, even when he did not take the battlefield, served as commander in chief of the army. Wealthy, connected civilians on the emperor's staff provided these soldiers with the real-world training in values and ideals essential for advancement, as Emperor Maximinus had so deftly proved.

Children who grew up on either side of the Danube border understood these basic facts of life. Standards of living were lower here than they were in the bigger cities. For those born at the river, the horizons were limited. Young men from rural areas were known to make enthusiastic soldiers, however. Roman recruiters identified them as rugged self-starters who came to the military ready to work. They were undaunted by digging a ditch or shouldering a load, and unlike fussy aristocrats from the Mediterranean coasts, no one in these remote regions was afraid to dirty his hands. Because of their experience in family trades, many of them already knew how to forge iron, and if they didn't have metalworking skills, they had at least grown up "enduring the sun, careless of shade, unacquainted with bathhouses, ignorant of luxury," as Vegetius, a fourth-century Roman military writer, said.

In one of his less judicious moments, Vegetius calls these recruits "simple-souled, content with a little." Even if he bungled it, he was trying to pay an honest compliment. City dwellers made fine soldiers, too, but they usually needed more attention. It took time for them to adapt to the simple food and the discomforts of living in a tent—a housing arrangement that generally made them shudder when they were introduced to it.

A soldier's life brought tangible benefits not exclusively reserved for Roman citizens. A soldier's pay—what Romans called a *stipendium*—was on the whole a good living wage, with ample spending money. Enlistees received provisions and a small bonus every five years, through the emperor's generosity. It cost the government twenty-five or thirty *solidi* a year to fully fund a soldier, including housing, food, weapons, and uniform. It is impossible to determine a modern equivalent in today's currency, but even if a recruit never saw most of those gold coins (which chiefly covered his overhead), that amount of money could, in theory, go far.

At the open market, four coins bought a camel, and three purchased a book—a luxury indeed, in a society where only 10 percent of the population could read. The annual salary of an infantryman, as Alaric likely was when he started, was probably five gold coins, roughly equaling 7,045 *nummi,* the handier form of currency used for everyday transactions. That added up to a good meal off the base every once in a while and an excuse to leave the barracks. The bill might run to six to fourteen *nummi* per person, depending on the extravagance of their taste. Twenty-four *nummi* bought soldiers a full spread of some bread, a pound of meat, and a jug of wine. A moderately indulgent night out cost about 1 percent of a starting soldier's monthly take-home pay.

The men who were drawn to this highly disciplined way of life came, like Alaric, from many backgrounds. The army was open to anyone, and Rome's citizens were not compelled to enlist. By the fourth century, many foreigners from the Danube, not just Goths, filled the ranks, including members of local tribes like the Quadi, Marcomanni, Taifali, Alans, and Sueves. Across the empire, the dynamics were similar. African Moors joined at the Saharan border, Isaurians in southern Asia Minor, Arab soldiers on the Arabian frontier. Even in the fourth century, foreign service members earned significant rewards that surpassed the occasional promotion.

Roman law explicitly granted these men many legal protections when they retired, including farm equipment, arable land, tax exemptions, and health benefits. An imperial law signed in the early fourth century extended to members of the Danube River patrol "the same privilege [as the cavalry and infantry] without distinction if they should prove that they have been discharged because of wounds received in action." Both foreign and citizen soldiers were given valuable start-up grants of oxen and assorted grains, which sensible legislators apportioned so that veterans could start their own farms. The farmland itself was awarded to them tax-free, and laws permitted an additional personal exemption for service members' fathers and mothers "if they should have these kinsmen surviving." For the soldiers, many of them the heads of Gothic families, a lighter financial burden brought more economic security to their household at the end of the year. All retired military personnel received these same government benefits, whether they had been born outside the borders or were Roman citizens, *cives*.

Unlike other immigrant men his age, however, when Alaric crossed the border, he did not immediately seek out a Roman military recruiter. The Roman sources, usually hostile to Alaric, in this case help us reconstruct what happened in the early 390s with some clarity. In a poem extolling the dubious accomplishments of Emperor Honorius, Claudian—the most partisan writer of his day and an unofficial spokesman for the emperor—tells us that in 391, Alaric was a little-known menace who had made a dubious reputation for himself terrorizing the swamplands of southern Thrace: "Hailing from beyond the Thracian frontier, he kept your father, Emperor Theodosius, from crossing the waters of the Maritza River."

Traffic had clogged the roads in northern Macedonia ever since Valens's successor, Emperor Theodosius, started working in Constantinople. The new emperor had enticed long-standing associates from Roman Spain to join him in the eastern capital, and the sons of wealthy friends went, too, in pursuit of government jobs. Even the Roman postal service, the armed couriers who delivered an emperor's correspondence, likely contributed to a steady increase in the number of horses and carriages on the roads across the Balkans. With them, most likely, had come a corresponding rise in one of a traveler's worst nightmares, highway robbery.

While it is clear why opportunity seekers would follow the emperor, it is less clear why men followed Alaric, a rebellious twenty-year-old Gothic agitator. Yet men were already trailing after Alaric, a phenomenon that must have looked not unlike, as the ancients observed, the way "a magnet attracts iron." He must have been a good strategist and communicator. In 391, his band of guerrillas had crossed into Roman land to cause trouble more than once, concealing themselves in the muck of the marshes. If Claudian's sketch is reliable, Alaric's men, daggers at their sides, were waiting to ambush a passing military convoy, perhaps to loot it, when they confronted the cavalcade of the emperor himself.

The episode at the Maritza River is the earliest known about Alaric's life, but his confidence and attitude at that moment made him infamous as an insurgent. By 392, he had become a Roman soldier during the start of a period of easing Gothic-Roman hostilities.

Recently appointed to share power with the western ruler, Valens's nephew Gratian, Theodosius had, from the moment of his installation as the co-emperor in 379, demonstrated a commitment to distancing himself from his predecessor's heartless border policies. As one of his first acts, Theodosius opened diplomatic channels with the Gothic Terving chief, extended him the offer of a state visit, and eventually welcomed him to Constantinople. Roman citizens and foreigners jammed the young city's usually open plazas to participate in the pageantry. Boats filled the Bosporus. The Terving chief, whom the Goths referred to with the honorary title "Judge," marveled at "the coming and going of the ships" and at the city's "splendid walls." The aged Judge Athanaric was old enough to remember the conflicts of an earlier day, which had nearly decimated his people. Emperor Valens's administration had strained Gothic-Roman relations, and as a result, the proud judge had promised on his father's deathbed never to set foot on Roman land. When the time had come to sign a treaty with Rome, the judge stipulated that he would do so only if the parties agreed to meet on rafts and logs in the middle of the Danube. Now, at Theodosius's invitation, the judge was strolling through Constantinople on an official state visit.

According to Jordanes, who reports on the ceremonious occasion, Emperor Theodosius's generosity overwhelmed the judge, as did the myriad faces of the Roman people. The throngs of so many citizens from such different backgrounds looked, the judge said, "like a flood of waters streaming from different regions, into one basin." What affected the judge the most, Jordanes continued, was that Roman society could be so ethnically, racially, and religiously diverse, yet so united at the same time, an esteemed ethos that had only ever seemed like a myth to many Goths. "I see now what I have often heard of with unbelieving ears," the judge said, in wonder. Within months, Goths were joining the army.

By one count, upwards of twenty thousand young Gothic men, including Alaric, were known to have signed up to serve by the end of Theodosius's administration. Like all new soldiers, their names were written on their shields, with their cohort number and their unit. They were fitted for helmets; if the one they were issued was too loose, they were told that a Pannonian cap could be purchased to keep it from rattling. Then they were sent to camp.

The months of basic training that followed, especially for a young man of growing self-confidence like Alaric, would have come as easily as playing in the Gothic woods. Some of the more platitudinous lectures he and the other Goths would have been forced to endure from their officers—"Bad water is a kind of poison and the cause of epidemic distempers"—were among the lessons Gothic parents and grandparents regularly taught their sons and daughters. Alaric likely already knew how to do everything his drill sergeants demanded, which included running, jumping, throwing, vaulting over horses, and, an exercise not to be omitted, swimming. Soldiers had to practice it "in melting snow or washed out in the rains."

For recruits, drills were run twice a day, morning and afternoon. They lugged sixty-pound sacks on marches. They practiced with weighted swords to add power to their swings and hurled weighted javelins, which, a trainer knew, "strengthens the arm and makes the soldier a good marksman." If the twenty-year-old Alaric was anything like the Latin literary sketches of an ideal recruit, he would have been good at all this, too. A hypothetical Roman soldier, it was said, was supposed to have "alert eyes, a straight neck, broad chest, muscular shoulders, strong arms, and long fingers." Unlike the plump gourmands of Rome's leisured class, he also "needed to be small in the stomach, slender in the buttocks, and have calves and feet that are not swollen by surplus fat but firm with hard muscle." Height and weight could always be fudged. "When you see these points in a recruit," Vegetius said, "you need not greatly regret the absence of tall stature. It is more useful that soldiers be strong than big."

Birthplace didn't really matter to the Roman commanders of the fourth century; nor did raw talent. Even if Alaric wasn't a natural-born soldier, he would have had the next best thing when it came to learning a new sport or teaching the body a new physical activity. He had youth, which military men prized. It meant that a soldier's training would be "more quickly imbibed and more lastingly imprinted on the mind." No scout liked to take a risk on bones and muscles "stiffened by age." For Alaric, the physical exertion he endured during these months was likely surpassed only by the terrible weight of history—chiefly, the murder of Emperor Valens by his own countryman—that he and his fellow Gothic soldiers had been forced to carry. Yet the opportunities to be more than an expendable foreign infantryman were real.

In a Roman army barracks from the early 390s, a new recruit would have spied a dizzying variety of trades being practiced. There were roles for blacksmiths, butchers, and hunters. Doctors and their staffs cared for the sick and injured. Crews of carpenters were tasked with the challenge of bringing the military's ingenious weapons to life, like the platforms on casters camouflaged with branches and painted to look like trees that could be rolled up to a city wall to attack it. The cooks and pastry chefs were some of the most beloved people on the base because of their culinary creations, particularly their desserts—a skill that occasionally earned them scorn from curmudgeonly generals, who believed their men should "be content with crackers." Accounts had to be balanced, larders to be logged, inventories kept. If Alaric had never used a stylus before, the army may have taught him how.

Among the many benefits Rome's army bestowed on its recruits, however, a well-rounded, almost humanistic education was among the most valuable. Commanders gave their soldiers both formal and informal lessons in geography, math, engineering, collaboration, problem solving, and new languages—a suite of essential skills for anyone wishing to make a future in the rapidly changing world. Years of living with officers and drinking in highway inns also gave the more economically disenfranchised something they had likely never dreamed of gaining: a passable knowledge of Latin.

The need for Latin, if not Greek, was obvious to many discerning foreigners, who could see that a lack of either language might be used to keep them out of Roman society. The Roman people had long been raised to see the two classical languages as hallmarks of culture, an expression of one's credentials, and keys to advancement. Parents believed that their sons' and daughters' futures depended on acquiring a proficiency in one tongue and at least working knowledge of the other language.

They imparted this value to their children starting at an early age, and the precocious ones excelled at both, like the eleven-year-old Roman boy named Quintus Sulpicius Maximus, who won a language contest for his ability to speak in Greek. Pretending to be Zeus, he extemporized a poem in which he took on the persona of the king of Olympus reacting to the news that the Sun had foolishly lent his chariot to a mortal, who'd crashed it. With its astute, mature reflections on the nature of responsibility, Quintus's performance astonished his mother and father, no less so because their boy delivered it in a second language. When he died—at eleven years, five months, and twelve days—his parents paid to have the entire text of the prize-winning composition chiseled on their son's tombstone. They erected it at a highly visible place in Rome on the old Salt Road, outside the Salt Gate.

Three centuries later, when Alaric galloped by young Quintus's tomb, wealthy parents still expected their children to learn the schoolhouse languages of Latin and Greek as a pathway to success. But as a matter of practical survival, a Roman coming of age in the fourth century would have also needed a basic familiarity with other languages in order to engage with his or her neighbors. With the expansion of Roman citizenship, Punic was regularly heard in the Roman bathhouses of the major metropolises in North Africa, like El Djem. Many new citizens of Roman Egypt preferred to communicate in Coptic, whose alphabet combined Greek and Egyptian letters to create a colloquial Egyptian language. Hebrew and Aramaic came to fashionable cities, as Roman Jews built prominent synagogues in Sardis and Ostia. Gothic was overheard at the northeastern border, and early forms of Arabic on the southeastern frontier with Arabia, in the territory of the Nabateans. With so many pronunciations and dialects, the Roman Empire of the fourth century would have resembled the kind of boisterous menagerie the poets described—places of "yowling wolves, roaring lions, grunting boars, lowing cattle, hissing serpents, [and] yapping leopards," as the contemporary poet Nonnus once wrote. Most Romans connected with one another in Greek and Latin on formal occasions, but beyond the classrooms and courtrooms, the streets would have been, to borrow Nonnus's phrase, "a babel of screaming sounds."

The lesson of the Roman educational system was not how to engage these other voices but how to keep them out. By Alaric's time, gatekeeping had a storied history. It was the role of schoolteachers, as one official aptly put it in an earlier day, to guard the sanctity of Latin just as the Roman emperor was responsible for bestowing citizenship. In the minds of Rome's elite, proper language skills were a prerequisite for admission to the high-society clubs of politics and letters.

In the fourth century, the elite's claims of cultural superiority were difficult to defend. Still, parents, Roman and immigrant alike, pushed their children to study the classical languages. "Letters are the greatest beginning in understanding," one teacher instructed, writing the sentence in Greek at the top of a wax tablet, so that a student could practice copying it. Families from Gaza sent their sons to bookish Alexandria to learn from highly qualified science instructors. Boys from the Numidian town of Thagaste trekked to fashionable Carthage, provided they had the money for their tuition and could afford to travel. One student bounced "from Greece to Rome, from Rome to Constantinople, from one city to another, going about practically the entire earth," to chase down his education. Without it, the chances of a career were nil.

"All arts and trades are brought to perfection by continual practice," it was said in Alaric's time, and that maxim would certainly have applied to the study of Latin and Greek's many confusing declensions and conjugations. Yet not every immigrant had the time to pursue an education or practice a second language. Learning filled the spare hours of an already compressed day. Two Gothic churchmen in the late fourth century grew so frustrated with teaching themselves Latin that they compiled a list of questions, addressed them to the most talented living linguist they knew, and handed the papyrus scroll to a messenger, with Bethlehem as the destination. They prayed that the great language instructor Jerome would give them a response.

The simple monk, absorbed in the enterprise of making a new Bible translation, the Latin Vulgate, received their letter and paused his scholarly work just long enough to answer them. The Goths had been puzzled by certain biblical passages they did not understand among the Psalms, and Jerome admired their efforts at wrestling with their meaning. "Who should believe that the barbarous language of the Goths would try to compete with the Hebrew in establishing the true text of the Scriptures?" he told them in return reply.

His poor opinion of their Latin was as unrestrained as his condescension for Gothic. "The word 'water' should be plural in Latin, written 'aquae,' instead of the singular 'aqua,'" Jerome wrote, in one of several grammar corrections he made to their original letter. He gave the Goths copious notes, ticking off answers to their queries, including an *asteriskos* (star) here, an *obelus* (dagger) there—the marks of a careful editor's hand. And how was it that they didn't yet know the difference between the nominative and the accusative? The critique would likely have stung, but the diligence with which Jerome had read the churchmen's letter was rare to find in a Roman teacher. Most immigrants, especially those who worked trades, never received such a detailed assessment and stumbled through their foreign language acquisition with whatever improvements they could glean from casual encounters in the market or at their place of worship.

Nonetheless, no language ever did acquire official status in Rome, probably because no Roman, not even the most culturally conservative Latin-speaking politician, advocated it. But for centuries Latin did retain its place as the Roman Empire's first language, largely because it fulfilled a useful function. It provided sixty million Romans a tool for communicating with one another—in the halls of justice, in the town councils, and in the military camps—until the government in Constantinople replaced it with ancient Greek in the sixth century A.D. In western Europe, Latin would remain entrenched in the courts, the corridors of government, and the schools throughout the medieval period.

Yet rewards and recognition came to immigrants with the time, money, or ambition to practice their classical languages, and by the

380s, that group of overachievers included prominent Goths. "Would that many of our people could imitate your upright conduct," one eastern bishop wrote to an upstanding immigrant Gothic soldier named Modares. Modares's character and work ethic impressed this stalwart Roman churchman, who went on to confess that he had experienced a change of heart about these new Gothic immigrants. Modares, the bishop said, had shown him that "the difference between being a Roman citizen and a barbarian is a matter of the body, not of the soul." The compliment was entirely backhanded and not unique for the time. What the bishop really admired was the way Modares had developed language skills and Roman cultural practices that concealed his Gothic identity to make himself seem less "a barbarian."

The choices immigrants made during these years were personal and tortured, and scholars will never really be sure why men like Modares put so much effort into the study of language and culture. Some probably saw their actions as a down payment toward citizenship, which, they believed, would come with the next administration. Yet that dream never materialized. Throughout Alaric's lifetime, to be a Roman citizen meant one's family had been born within the physical borders of the empire as they had been set in the time of Caracalla, and to be accepted as a Roman immigrant came with tacit requirements about proper language, behavior, and dress. That blunt reality weighed on citizen and immigrant alike because, in the formulation of one modern historian, "There was no process by which a foreigner became a Roman citizen except by functioning as one."

For immigrants, this unwritten rule of cultural assimilation would prove an especially cruel trap. While it was true that immigrants could always settle down wherever they wished, and that the Roman government never closed its borders—not even after the spike in immigrants during the Danube crisis of the 370s—one's physical characteristics ("a matter of the body," as the bishop said) dictated whether one was perceived as a Roman. After Caracalla's law, to be treated with dignity in the later empire always depended on how one dressed, how one spoke, and how one behaved. The acceptance of immigrants in Alaric's time was not, as it were, based on tolerance or on open-mindedness or even on protected legal principles. It was based on a self-righteous sense of Roman cultural superiority. Basic rights were never guaranteed, for apart from its volumes of laws and the emperor's occasional declarations, the ancient Romans lacked any formal, drafted constitution. If the lowliest Roman citizen disapproved of how a foreigner looked, sounded, or acted, there was no recourse from discrimination.

Foreigners were at the mercy of these racial and ethnic structural biases and suffered disproportionately for them; even soldiers felt slighted in their day-to-day routines. Toward the end of the 380s, as Alaric was approaching adulthood, a xenophobic incident rocked the world of Roman sports and led to one of the most notorious public scandals. At the majestic imperial city of Thessaloniki, whose pleasant seaside location had made it a favorite residence for fourth-century emperors, an immigrant police officer named Butheric arrested a local star athlete—a popular chariot driver, never named in any of the accounts—and jailed him for making improper advances "on a barman's honor."

The streets of the usually reserved imperial city, where diplomats strolled with their entourages and government workers congratulated one another on the signing of foreign treaties, erupted in violence as the fans expressed their fury at what they deemed to be the unjust arrest of their favorite athlete. Games and races were postponed while the accused immigrant officer, Butheric, was held, awaiting trial. The legal justification for making the arrest was never clearly established, and Butheric was eventually killed by a mob before his case could proceed before a judge. In an iron-fisted demonstration of his authority, the Roman emperor Theodosius rounded up the mob—seven thousand unruly citizens, one ancient writer claims—and executed them for contravening Roman justice. Yet many foreigners continued to immigrate to Rome to start their new lives, undeterred by the horror of Butheric's public murder.

"Great enterprises are always left to the free choice of those who hear of them," it was said in Rome at the time. But why Alaric ultimately chose a soldier's life was never clear to anyone. The thawing of Gothic-Roman relations in the 390s helps explain, at least in part, Alaric's decision to enlist. His recruiters had probably been impressed by his brawn. Theodosius had, we can assume, been taken with his brains. It required a great deal of guile to execute a highway ambush. Alaric's strategy sounded, truth be told, like the textbook planning Rome's military prescribed. "Let [the soldier] set up ambushes in complete secrecy at river-crossings, mountain passes, wooded defiles, marshes and other difficult passages," Vegetius explained in his military manual. Alaric, the cocky twenty-year-old Goth, had passed that test already, working on instinct. The boy showed promise.

❦

CHAPTER FIVE

The Mystery of Conversion

Nature leaves us free and untrammeled; it is we who bind
ourselves, confine ourselves, wall ourselves off, herd ourselves
into cramped and sordid quarters.

—PLUTARCH

As Alaric began basic training, Rome teetered on the cusp of civil war, with Emperor Theodosius's eccentric religious convictions and his authoritarian demeanor pushing society to a precipice. But the radicalism of the day would have easily escaped the notice of a young Gothic soldier. The economically comfortable, culturally permissive, and largely independent world that constituted the Roman Empire of the 390s A.D. showed few outward signs of stress.

In Rome, the Colosseum, with the musty odor of a three-hundred-year-old sports arena, hosted blood sports multiple times a week. Athens's Parthenon stood firm after a glorious eight hundred years, its technology virtually Stone Age to the many Roman tourists who flocked to Greece to admire it. The pharaoh's pyramids were now the Caesars' trophies. And where there was noticeable rubble, such as at Jerusalem's Temple Mount, a site that had been left in a state of disrepair since the punishing Jewish Wars of the first century, the scattered rocks and ancient boulders drew odd looks from the hordes of Christian pilgrims, who preferred to reflect on sites they associated with Jesus's execution, burial, and resurrection.

The gossip circulating about the Roman people—which Alaric probably overheard—would only have reinforced the impression that the empire was still a hedonist's paradise. In the world of the grand public baths, fearless predatory men pushed the boundaries of lewd behavior, leering at every passing female. Sweet "Cleopatra," they clucked at

Egyptian girls. Dear "Zenobia," they called out to the ones from Palmyra, each clichéd expression no different from a wolf whistle in its disregard for female dignity.

Respectable Roman men and women alike were shameless attention
seekers. Parents had become so nervous about their children's future
career prospects that they falsified their ancient pedigrees to boost
their family's reputations. Cities became stages for intensely personal,
pathetic dramas. Aging female darlings of high society, mourning their
lost youth, would wrap themselves in gowns and slink slowly through
the streets, with legions of fawning admirers paid to trail after them.
Everyone in these sad troupes looked as if they were "bringing up the
rear of an army," said Rome's sharpest social critic of the fourth century,
Ammianus Marcellinus.

Ammianus sermonized against Romans who seemed catty or overly
posh and lacked any hint of modesty. *Where is the night's fashionable
party?* they twittered. *How much is it costing the neighbors to renovate
their house?* Intolerable self-absorption filled each hour of the Roman day.
The Roman society of the late fourth century was infatuated with itself.

Scales were brought out at fine dining establishments because hosts
thought it would be fun to showcase the price of the fish, birds, and dor-
mice they had purchased. Notebooks and pens became the new utensils
of the Roman table, used to record the weights and measures of the food
before the meal was served; guests salivated while their hosts scribbled
away. Vanities like this had been known to ruin a pleasant evening on
more than one occasion, Ammianus complained. Everyone had that one
friend who could turn a nice dinner into an intolerable lecture.

The Romans of the late fourth century did not lack a sense of humor.
The satires of the Latin poet Juvenal, with their bawdy rants about
ethnic minorities, still elicited rounds of laughter, even though he was
more distant to the Romans than Mark Twain is to us. A fondness for
these old classics reveals how much of Roman society was stuck in its
ways, though. New learning, new languages, and a different range of
experiences remained by and large anathema. "They ought to be read-

ing a variety of books," Ammianus grumbled. But few Romans cared to indulge his vision for a more literate, more educated society.

Glib conversation was more the Roman style. Romans joked about the hardship of walking short distances in fashionable clothing in unbearable heat. Taking the yacht out around the bay was expressed, in the mythical language of an epic hero's journey, as "going after the Golden Fleece." They were relentless about mocking people with lower living standards. Urbanites decried the possibility of having to endure life in the remote wilderness of the Cimmerians, envisioning the horror of having even a critter as small as a fly ever land on their skin. Bathers didn't just bring extra clothes with them for after a swim; they brought whole wardrobes, several closets' worth of colorful tunics and robes. Living was performance art.

But amid the oblivion and indifference, fissures were widening across Roman society. Unbridgeable disagreements manifested in debates between senators on the floor of the Roman Curia, in nervous gossip traded between peers at parties, and in tense exchanges between strangers on the street. There was more talk in these years of a pagan Rome and a Christian Rome, a glaring divide between rich Rome and poor Rome, one Rome for citizens and another for immigrants. The public conversation was more polarized in the late fourth century than it had been in generations, notwithstanding the comfortable position of the Roman Empire's class of privileged elite.

On some days, it must have felt as if each of the empire's 120-some provinces fell into one of two camps, Blue Rome or Green Rome. The fraying of the empire's social fabric might have been illustrated by the jackets of its two most popular chariot-racing teams, the Blues and the Greens, whose supporters disrupted otherwise peaceful city centers with their notorious rioting and instigation. "Burn here, burn there. Not a Green anywhere," went their chants. "Set alight, set alight, not a Blue in sight."

The moralist, lover of classical history, and member of British Parliament Edward Gibbon found a lot to love and much to condemn in Ammianus's unflattering stories. By Gibbon's era, the eighteenth century, it was quite common for commentators to condemn the Roman Empire for its depravity and decadence using these same examples. A child of the Enlightenment, Gibbon pointed to the irrational forces of religion and barbarism as two key factors that caused Rome's eventual collapse, and he argued his case against them with a prosecutorial vigor and a smooth prose style that still wins over sympathetic jurors. In the centuries since Gibbon published the first volume of his extended manifesto, *The History of the Decline and Fall of the Roman Empire,* which appeared in 1776, critics of every world empire have found some excuse to quote his analysis.

Gibbon, like the voluminous ancient writer he drew upon, Ammianus, was a sharp cultural critic, and Gibbon's sketches of Roman life in Alaric's day were, in many cases, brutally accurate. But on closer inspection, there's a noticeable deception in the way Gibbon so casually relied on Ammianus's testimony to create a negative impression of the fourth-century Roman Empire. In *Decline and Fall,* Gibbon summarizes Ammianus's episodes immediately prior to his own account of Alaric's attack in August of 410, as if the eminent Latin historian had profiled the Roman people in June or July of that year. But Gibbon's presentation is misleading and distorts how we understand the military career Alaric embarked on.

Ammianus composed these amusing profiles in the 370s or 380s. If they are representative, one can argue that they represent the Roman Empire of Alaric's late adolescence and early army years, the early 390s. Ammianus was not describing a society of moral profligates, womanizers, and self-absorbed adults that Alaric wanted to tear down, as Gibbon would like us to believe and as modern critics of the Roman Empire would insist. This world was the very empire Alaric had just signed up to defend. It's worth puzzling over the mystery of his decision.

Although difficult to see from thousands of years away, the Roman Empire did have its redeeming qualities. The position of "Augustus," regardless of an individual emperor's family lineage, his geographic origins, or whether he identified as a pagan or a Christian, demanded a cohort of associates and assistants, who helped the emperors govern. The master of the imperial letters, the count of the sacred treasury, the jurist of the sacred palace, and all sorts of other official postings had to be kept filled for Rome's government to run efficiently. There was no shortage of candidates for these jobs.

The positions were essential, and for the most part, the Romans who staffed them in rapidly growing cities like Milan, Gaulic Vienne, Trier, and Ravenna were at least minimally qualified, sometimes expertly so. They had the language skills to handle correspondence from the empire's citizenry and from Armenian and Persian diplomats, the communication skills to articulate the emperor's policies, and a knowledge of accounting and law. Some excelled at managing an emperor's schedule, a particularly desirable trait for well-regarded politicians who were flooded with requests for public appearances.

The limited number of jobs created a fierce competition for them but also promoted a broad respect for the offices. There was a value in maintaining one's connections with a rising colleague, a well-placed friend, or a former interviewer. Even if a candidate was passed over, another option might arise. A Roman didn't need to hold Rome's religious office of *pontifex*, or "priest," to understand the importance of building bridges. ("Bridge builder," an important public office in early Rome, a city built on a river, is what the Latin *pontifex* literally means.) In short, although the empire was autocratic, Rome never ran on autopilot, and that tension generated opportunity at every level of the government for civilian and military men. It also established an almost sacred bond between the Roman people and their leaders. Excellent emperors were elevated to gods. A *divus*, he was called posthumously, if the man was deserving of such an immortal claim. It would place him in the hall of divine honor alongside Julius Caesar, the first Roman to earn the title for, among other audacious opinions, having championed the economic fortunes of the lower class.

During the sixteen years Theodosius wore the imperial diadem, from 379 to 395, he used every tool available to an emperor—the laws, imperial decrees, a soft touch, veiled threats, and actual physical force—to implement his vision for a single-party Christian state. And he changed Roman society irrevocably.

Dreams of becoming a god were not, for this soldier's son, the future he likely envisioned for himself; nor were they ones Theodosius's Christian family would have encouraged. In Roman Hispania, where the emperor's family had its home, wealth was abundant and politics usually a distant concern. Fortunes were made in olives, grapes, and horses. Spanish horses were some of the fastest in the empire, prized as far away as the racetrack in Constantinople. Theodosius's father had had a promising career in the army, seeing action in Europe, Britain, and northern Africa, and young Theodosius had traveled with him.

The soldiers had respected Theodosius's father. He distinguished himself as a rugged warrior, a leader who wore his helmet even in the scorching heat of a Libyan summer. But palace insiders looked suspiciously on the elder Theodosius's accomplishments, and in 375, at an uncertain directive, Theodosius's father was arrested while in Carthage and beheaded by the state. The charge of treason, although alleged at the time, is unlikely to have been true; it's more probable that a nervous but ruthless adversary arranged to have his fast-ascending rival from the provinces not so quietly removed. The son entered politics soon after. Although no historian can be sure, he probably did so with the intent to avenge his father's death.

The Roman people generally knew what qualities they admired in an emperor. The hallmark of political professionalism was someone who traveled relentlessly, inquired sincerely about the many provinces, and promoted stability, what Romans called *securitas*. A good emperor was capable of being firm when needed and thoughtful about deploying the army if necessary. The best kind of leader, in the estimation of the well-regarded fourth-century historian Ammianus, was a man of committed principles with a devotion to the common good in public services, in the distribution of food, and in the cultivation of the well-being of his people. These were the qualities ordinary Romans also hoped to find in their emperors and were pleased when they did.

After Mount Vesuvius's eruption in A.D. 79, for example, Emperor Titus had impressed many with his empathy and been heralded for acting as a surrogate father to the people of Pompeii, one of the cities destroyed by the volcano. He had listened to the displaced families and promised to use the state's resources to assist them. Pagan Rome had not ignored the basic needs of its people.

Likewise, in Christian Rome, the emperor's moral compass continued to remain important. An unconditional generosity toward those less fortunate ranked among the most admired traits an emperor could show and influenced how members of the emperor's family were expected to act in public, as well. When a famine struck the city of Rome in the winter of 408, both Emperor Gratian's widow and Gratian's aging mother-in-law hastened to help. Their dispersal of emergency food to needy Romans earned them the public's deepest respect. Both women were Christian, but citizens of all faiths expected these norms of civic behavior from their leaders. (That unexpected food shortage, incidentally, would be Alaric's malevolent doing.)

After accepting the position of emperor in 379, Theodosius agreed to move to Constantinople, a rapidly rising city located on the Golden Horn and the meeting place of two continents, both ruled by Rome. Four decades earlier, soldiers who fought under Emperor Constantine had helped the victorious general build Rome's second capital as a living trophy to his military accomplishments, which the immodest Christian emperor named for himself and which he decorated with a bricolage of vintage Greek and Roman statuary amassed during his travels. The city's grand but largely empty streets and open plazas still showed these bric-a-brac beginnings when the thirty-two-year-old Emperor Theodosius moved into the palace and took command of the eastern army. Contemporaries said Theodosius did so "like a youth who is heir to new wealth." He would change the look and feel of Constantinople, too.

It was expected that the new emperor would demonstrate his ability to serve as a willing collaborator, a partner to his co-ruler, Emperor
Gratian, Valens's nephew and the man who had appointed him. Theodosius did, even as he also quickly displayed the two essential talents of
a successful Roman politician. He proved a natural speaker and could
express a genuine interest in the affairs of his constituents. *Alternos
cum plebe iocos* ("He traded jokes with the people"), it was said after one
of the emperor's first trips to the stadium. More removed, less affable
emperors were criticized for answering their correspondence during
the games, barely raising their heads from their stylus and tablets.

Over the next decade, Theodosius maneuvered for greater authority.
After the death of his first wife, Flacilla, he married into the western
emperor's family, then swiftly quashed a resistance movement led by
Magnus Maximus, a political opponent with an oversized ego. Battles
aside, the politically untested emperor often acted on principle in those
years, even going so far as to reprimand soldiers for their abhorrent
treatment of refugees. In the 380s, his sensitivity stopped the outbreak
of another war.

In 386, a tribe from Gothia contacted the border patrol and asked permission to immigrate, en masse, onto Roman land—a logistical night-
mare for the communities on both sides of the river. The guards made it
known that the empire would grant the Goths' request and instructed
them to come back at night, when, they said, it would be easier to cross.
The unsuspecting members of the tribe waited as told, then rowed into
the middle of the Danube in the darkness, at which point the Roman
border patrol "sailed up to them in large and strong ships with firm oars
and sunk all that they met." After filling the river with Gothic corpses,
they sent the survivors to the auction blocks for the slave trade.

The fiasco at the border outraged Theodosius. He hastened to make
amends by releasing the Gothic prisoners and drafted the most capable
Gothic men into the army. The emperor's quick intervention averted a
diplomatic disaster although news of the incident unfolded rather differently on the streets of Constantinople, where the still relatively inexpe-

rienced emperor used it to promote his young administration's prowess on the battlefield. By the end of that year, the Gothic "encounter" at the Danube had been presented to the public as if it were a military victory. The emperor imported an Egyptian obelisk, nearly sixteen hundred years old and originally quarried for Pharaoh Ramses II, to mark the occasion as a fitting trophy and ordered his staff to hoist the pink granite monument into place in the center of the city's racetrack, where he could see it from the windows of his palace. Scenes of groveling foreigners were carved at the base of the old Egyptian monument to enliven it for the Roman audiences. Its presence put a pharaoh's imprimatur on Theodosius's increasingly grandiose rule.

Much had already changed in Rome. An unrealistic desire for unity defined the emperor's approach and had led to undeniable milestones, such as the signing of a landmark treaty with Persia, which concluded decades of hostility on Rome's eastern borders. But a confidence in his own convictions also sent Theodosius in pursuit of more quixotic ideals, which others enabled. Early in his tenure, Theodosius and his like-minded co-rulers, Gratian and Gratian's half brother, Valentinian the Second, had announced a law that cut funding from the society of Vestal Virgins, likely with the intent of starving the group into nonexistence. Hundreds of women of all ages had been honored to serve in the Vestals' exclusive priesthood, whose origins went back several centuries and whose duties, including the protection of Rome's eternal flame, offered one of the few visible roles for powerful females in Roman society. The law, although it did not bar women from joining the association, made it all but impossible for it to continue its mission. In A.D. 380, the emperors declared that the only permissible religious option for citizens of the Roman Empire would henceforth be Christianity.

Eager churchmen enforced the radical decree by requiring their congregations to make a formal recitation of faith, enforcing technical language drafted fifty-five years earlier during a contentious bishop's conference at Nicaea. This Nicene Creed, which made bold proclamations about the eternal nature of Jesus's being—"light from light, God from God, begotten, not made"—offered Christians important clarifications about the identity of the Son of God. But its adoption also marked an abrupt change from three hundred years of church precedent, when no such statement of belief had been required of any Christian, let alone imposed on pagan Romans. The intrusive imperial law, requiring every Roman to acknowledge that Jesus and God were "one in being," as the Nicene Creed articulated, represented an aggressive new track in an ongoing political fight for the soul of Rome.

Within a decade, the old sights and smells of pagan Rome—of incense wafting from outdoor altars and of pagan priests dressed smartly to visit the stately temples, religious activities that men like Cicero and Virgil would have instantly recognized as an essential part of being Roman—gradually disappeared. Zealots patrolled the empire's streets. Places of worship, stunning architectural monuments, were attacked. In 388, after Christians burned a synagogue at Callinicum, in Syria, no one was held accountable; Theodosius refused to punish the guilty faction of Christians because they counted among his most loyal supporters.

Three years later, a cell of militant Christians, perhaps inspired by notions that the elimination of idolatry would hasten Jesus's return, took hatchets to the city of Alexandria's wondrous Temple of Serapis, whose tall columns overlooked Cleopatra's harbor. In 392, after Gratian's half brother, who had succeeded Gratian, was discovered hanged in the palace, Theodosius solidified his own position as the single most powerful person in the empire. Tens of thousands of Roman citizens watched as a religiously motivated hatred engulfed their towns and as state-imposed Christianity came to the empire during these years, in the form of an aggressive coup coordinated by Theodosius and enforced by fanatics. Romans of every denomination, pagan, Jewish, and Christian, felt anger and frustration as their world slipped away.

Flavius Eugenius seemed a smart choice to marshal the opposition. A well-liked Latin teacher and a professor of rhetoric whose "high reputation for eloquence" had earned him a coveted palace position as chief of correspondence, Eugenius was nearing fifty and, in principle, an ideal standard-bearer against the rising tide of Christian radicalism because he was also a moderate Christian. Although there were many Christian public figures who taught their congregations to see Rome's smoke-filled altars as the frightening home of pagan "demons," Eugenius read his Scripture with a critical mind, apparently finding little of practical value in its pugilistic stories, like the tales of righteous angels who battle demons in the book of Revelation. As a Christian, Eugenius had not been raised to demonize his neighbors.

Eugenius's Rome had always been a society where people of all faiths could worship as they pleased. Roughly three decades before he was born, the state had granted Christians a protected status, and it's almost certain that those years hardened Eugenius's commitment to the legal principle of toleration. It was one he had been taught to value and, if necessary, to defend. One tyrant, Eugenius believed, should not man-date the use of a strict formula to promote his vision for *Romanitas* and remove the freedom of religious choice from the Roman people.

In 392, as the cultural situation deteriorated and an imperial vacancy opened in the western palace, a high-placed foreign general named Arbo-gast, with the support of several distinguished senators in Rome, asked Eugenius to bring a temperate influence to Theodosius's increasingly despotic rule. The professor consented to their plan. Fine Roman men in Eugenius's profession won debates and wrote well. They knew their history, literature, and art. But whereas those qualifications might have distinguished a candidate for high office in an earlier day and ensured some measure of success, none of them mattered in the bruising arena of fourth-century politics. Mavericks ruled Theodosius's world, and Euge-nius would always be a cautious academic.

Notwithstanding his evident gifts for Latin grammar and composi-tion, Eugenius's background was largely unsuited to the task of leading an urgent movement that crossed religious lines. His upbringing almost certainly lacked anything comparable to the sidekick heroism Theodo-

sius had acquired during the years spent on military campaigns with
his father; Eugenius's own contemporaries were keen to point out that
he was "unused to the blast of war." His reputation suffered a fatal blow
when, asked by the Roman Senate to assume the role of Theodosius's co-
ruler, he made the timid decision to write to Constantinople to ask for
permission to share authority. The bull-headed emperor assented, pre-
serving a fiction of collegiality in a time of rapidly vanishing consensus
and irreparable partisanship.

Over the next several months, Eugenius and his diverse group of supporters grew more vocal in their opposition to Theodosius's policies,
confident that they would be able to turn public opinion against the run-
away emperor since, they reassured themselves, they had the force of
history on their side. Pluralism had formed the basis of the empire's legal
system for generations and had been enshrined in a famous edict. "We
gave to Christians and to all people," the Christian emperor Constantine and the pagan emperor Licinius had announced on June 13, 313, "a
free ability to follow the worship practices that each one wished, so that
whatever divinity there is in the heavenly seat above may be appeased
and made favorable to us and to everyone who had been put under our
rule." The emperors' constitutional decree, brokered at Milan and forever bearing that city's name, safeguarded the legal status of Christianity by overturning decades of state-sponsored discrimination but did so
in a way that protected everyone's religious rights, not just Christians'.

The successes Rome's Christian community won with the Edict of
Milan can lead historical interpreters to wild speculation about how Christianity proliferated in a supposedly hostile pagan environment. Christian
writers of the fourth century, like Bishop Eusebius of Caesarea, the author
of *The Church History,* which covered the period from Jesus's execution
under Emperor Tiberius to the time of Constantine, labored hard to tell a
story about Christianity's tireless evangelism and the outspoken witness
Christians gave to their faith. Although it would become commonplace
among the more pious Christians to attribute the momentous act of toleration in 313 to their uncompromising forebears, the reasons for Rome's

about-face were less dramatic. Simple acts of patriotism had, by and large, guided the conduct of the earliest church and profited the community.

In the first century A.D., as Jesus's apostles passed down the first oral traditions about his life and crucifixion, a new generation of followers emerged, drawn from a wide social and economic background. Gathering in the houses of wealthy sponsors and relying on well-heeled patrons to provide lodging during their travels—like Prisca and Aquila, Chloe, and Stephanas, known from the letters of Paul—they built a network for their movement. These small communities, usually no more than a handful of people, lived in large Roman cities like Thessaloniki, Philippi, Corinth, and Ephesus, where, to the consternation of sterner men like Paul, they often gathered with their fellow citizens to celebrate animal sacrifices and share public meals during their cities' patriotic pagan festivals. Sometimes they encouraged one another to embrace antiquity's most questionable values. In several letters attributed to Paul, Christian wives were told to obey their husbands, children were told to listen to their parents, and slaves were told to submit to their masters, in each case to conform with the widely accepted standards of patriarchy, parental authority, and slavery prevalent at the time.

By the second century, as war threatened to open an unbridgeable chasm between Jews and Rome after the burning of Jerusalem in A.D. 70, the next generations of early Christian patriots began attending a wider variety of festivals, like those celebrating Rome's dead emperors. "Honor the emperor," the biblical letter of Peter instructed its readers, and many Christians did. By the third century, at least some Christians were so confident about their unassailable social status that they renovated their houses and apartments to create bigger worship spaces and, in the process, contributed to the creation of the first recognizable church buildings. Wealth, connections, and a degree of calculated risk brought these fearless Christians, amid the noises of demolition and construction, into the main streets of their cities. Fifty years before Constantine and Licinius granted Christians a protected status, acceptance had already become a regular fact of life for many towns.

Rome witnessed many senseless acts of violence against Christians in these same years. Christians would always remember those difficult times when opinionated individuals suffered for their outspokenness and an imperious magistrate could bring criminal charges against the members of their group, leading to trials and sometimes public executions. Born of Roman ignorance and fear, these acts of discrimination made heroes out of many Christians, who were glorified by their friends and loved ones for the daring witness they had given to their faith. Much later, the stories about these *martyres,* as the "witnesses" were called in Greek, were twisted into fanciful legends about an age of widespread Roman persecution against the early church. But such was never the case in the first 250 years of Christianity; nor did every Christian in Rome endure threats of open hostility, suffer bodily harm, or seek out occasions for public confrontation. Many found their solace in Scripture, in passages that reminded them to steel themselves against the world. "No one after lighting a lamp puts it under the bushel basket, but on the lampstand, and it gives light to all in the house," Matthew's Gospel taught them. Other Christians committed themselves to enacting popular civic values, like *philanthropia,* as they would have expressed it in Greek, meaning "love of one's fellow human beings." In the visual language of the day, pagan artists personified the idea as a shepherd caring for his sheep, usually with a fluffy animal wrapped around the shepherd's shoulders. Wise, noble, and caring emperors were said to fit the model.

When Christians started appropriating the image during the third century in their catacomb paintings, tombs, and houses, their choice to do so must have flabbergasted hardheaded Roman traditionalists, especially those raised to think of Christians as dangerous religious radicals, unable to mold their beliefs to Roman culture. Yet with the birth of the "Good Shepherd" artwork and other nods toward popular culture, Christians subtly pledged their *Romanitas.* Even as Christian writers omitted this side of history from their narratives of the early church, preferring, instead, to portray the faith as relentlessly besieged by Roman culture, the stoic confidence that inspired these and other patriotic Christian displays must have blazed a path to toleration.

No one could have foreseen the difficult times ahead. The backlash came swiftly. As much as the group's robust public presence angered cultural traditionalists, the support Christians were earning from pagan society probabaly upset them more. Everywhere they looked, it must have seemed, to rearguard Romans, as if their established way of life was quickly disappearing. It's understandable, then, that discrimination was soon written into the Roman law code. During these darkest years of persecution, from 303 to 311, almost a century after Caracalla expanded the definition of a Roman citizen, a faction of politicians used the legal system to punish Christians for their growing but, to the officials' minds, unjustified self-confidence. Emperor Diocletian threatened Rome's Christian citizens with the loss of civil liberties and, in some cases, their lives, if they did not hand over their Bibles and empty their church coffers. Attending civic events, like pagan sacrifices, was no longer a matter of individual conscience. It was mandatory, the emperor said, and the government would strip all Christians of "their freedom" if they chose not to comply with the directive.

Diocletian's invasive, oppressive edicts were crafted by a simple-minded politician at a time when civil war was common and Rome's experiment with empire faced grave threats. The emperor, an efficient problem solver whose surviving portraiture shows the face of a tireless but perhaps beleaguered administrator, had already implemented a radical constitutional reform, in A.D. 284, by announcing the creation of two emperors, each of whom would reside away from the capital and be served by two close assistants. The push for greater collaboration and renewed government oversight saved the empire from political ruin.

Convinced that Christians were a threat to the state by virtue of their religion and scrambling to preserve the unity of his empire, Diocletian enacted his edicts during this tense time. The edicts were also published at a time when pagan Romans and Christian Romans had been amicable neighbors for nearly three hundred years, and by a politician whose own wife and daughter, Prisca and Valeria, publicly identified as Christians. Countless Roman Christians suffered needlessly during Diocletian's hardheaded campaign, and the laws were later repealed by Valeria's husband, Diocletian's pagan son-in-law, Galerius. In 311, he reversed his father-in-law's edicts and announced that Christians could "be Christian again" without fear of reprisal. Yet just as the new law was set to take effect, Galerius died. His sudden passing stranded the Roman people in a social crisis.

Two years later, in 313, tolerance would finally, and irreversibly, be enshrined in the Edict of Milan. Eugenius and his supporters aspired to uphold the noble spirit of the centuries-long fight that had led to the formulation of Constantine and Licinius's law.

Not every Christian shared their vision. In Theodosius's day, radical Christians claimed that their faith was still under attack by Rome's predominately pagan culture. They expressed hysterical claims that the dreaded emperor Nero would rise again from his grave to persecute Christians, just as he had supposedly done in the first century A.D. In Milan, Bishop Ambrose preached about the contentious debates in the Roman senate and reminded Christians that they were locked in a spiritual war against the forces of evil. Fed a regular dose of his vivid, apocalyptic language, many Christians came to believe that angels were fighting demons for control of their empire and that only the emperor Theodosius deserved their unqualified support.

The question of how, when, and why Rome's predominantly pagan society converted to a Christian one is a topic many scholars have pondered with unnecessary bewilderment and undue credulity. In ancient Rome, the decisions of a single emperor could have far-reaching systemic effects. The emperor could marshal an army to enforce his will, had the power of the magistrates and courts to prosecute his enemies, and could ask his spokesmen to stand at the rostrum to communicate his wishes to the public. The clearest path to implementing a Christian takeover of society was for the emperor to mandate it, which is exactly what Theodosius did.

Christian conversations about culture, politics, and values—traces of which survive in the sermons, letters, and theological treatises produced at the time—turned the public arena into a frightening place. Christians demanded that the Roman government prevent Jews from rebuilding their temple in Jerusalem, based on interpretations of biblical passages that set forth the requirements for the Second Coming of the Messiah. Churchmen preached a gospel of fear, whipping their congregations into a moral frenzy about the need to eliminate the evils of pagan society. Their favorite fixation was protesting the horror of pagan animal sacrifice, a practice whose abolition they had been demanding since the time of Saint Paul, even though it had never interfered with the practice of their own beliefs. Their obsessive complaints about this single issue consumed the attention of Roman politicians for nearly three hundred years. Other Christians composed misleading prophecies, modeled after a collection of widely regarded pagan writings called *The Sibylline Oracles,* and shared them with other Christians to stoke anxiety about another coming age of persecution.

These people puzzled other Christians. According to Lactantius, the Christian tutor of Emperor Constantine's children, who had witnessed these and many other spirited conversations in his lifetime, the best word he could find to describe the character of these fanatics was a simple Latin adjective he drafted into service as a noun. *Deliri,* Lactantius wrote. They were "crazies."

Yet by the time Eugenius and Theodosius were sharing power, the rhetoric of Rome's Christian "crazies" was threatening to destabilize any attempt at consensus. Christian senators who negotiated small acts of compromise with their pagan colleagues were branded as "apostates," deniers of their faith, by members of the church who'd appointed themselves to police the behavior of other politicians. According to a fifth-century church historian named Sozomen, Eugenius himself was told during these partisan attacks that even he was not a "real Christian," because he supported a broad open right to pagan worship.

The spreading wildfire of Christian intolerance marked a stunning reversal for Rome, considering that, four centuries earlier, it was the pagan government that had executed Jesus for sedition. Gibbon blamed the rising narrow-mindedness on the very soul of Christianity, an opinion that, though surely wrong, was quite understandable, given the general intellectual distaste for the irrationality of religion that characterized the Enlightenment. Throughout *Decline and Fall,* he underscored Christianity's flaws, overlooked its upright believers, and pilloried the faith as a hypocritical sham of a belief system, a superficial religion of peace masking an ugly zealotry at its core. But one religion cannot bear all of a society's woes, and the Christians of the Roman Empire are known to have resisted easy labels, as did the Christians of Gothia.

The Christianity Alaric and his Gothic followers professed differed in one tiny but profound way from what many Christians in Theodosius's Roman Empire believed, an *iota*'s difference. The smallest of the Greek letters had set off an explosion of theological disagreement at the Council of Nicaea, one of the headier church conferences. Constantine had convened it to determine whether Jesus and God were made of the "same" substance (*homos*) or of a "similar" substance (*homoios*). But the council's attendees, including Arius of Alexandria, who proposed the latter view, never reached a unanimous agreement on the issue. When they adjourned, the presence of a single letter of the Greek alphabet in one technical term had created two lasting fissures between the Christian attendees. By the middle of the fourth century, there would be two Christian creeds, a Catholic one formulated at Nicaea and a second at Rimini, affirmed by Arius's men, and countless ways of conceptualizing the mysteries of the faith. The fallout affected centuries of church dialogue.

The divisions spread across the Roman-Gothic border, arriving with the first Christian missionaries, who came in the years following the Council of Nicaea—famous among them a much-admired Roman figure whose adopted Gothic name was Wulfila, or "Little Wolf." After teaching himself to communicate with Goths by living in their villages and adapting to Gothic customs, he carefully selected a set of Greek and Latin letterforms, combined with a handful of runes, and devised

A combination of Greek and Latin letters and tribal runes, the Gothic script was the invention of a Roman missionary named Little Wolf. This sixth-century Bible, the Codex Argenteus, which takes its name from the expensive "silver ink" brushed across its luxurious purple parchment, is one of the only texts in Alaric's language to survive.

the Gothic alphabet. With it he taught Goths how to write, made the first translation of the Christian Bible into Gothic, and, through these efforts, gained a reputation as the Gothic Moses. One of his most radical acts was to omit the Jewish books of Kings from his Gothic Bible translation because their belligerent tales, he feared, would do lasting harm to the already bellicose Gothic mind, which "needed its aggressiveness curbed rather than kindled."

Faint resonances of the language Little Wolf captured in print echo in modern English. The Gothic tongue belongs to the Germanic language family tree, and many words with Gothic roots have been handed down to Nordic and Germanic languages, the latter of which include English. The Gothic word for an entryway, like a gate, was *daur* (pronounced "door"); the person assigned to protect it was a *daurawarda* (a "door warden"). Provincial Roman children, despite generally low expectations for their intelligence—implied from the many unflattering stories of brawlers, bruisers, and brutes that proliferate in Latin and Greek literature about the frontier—probably acquired a handful of similar Gothic words and a familiarity with Gothic script as a result of living near the border. It probably helped them and their parents navigate daily interactions with foreign friends and immigrants.

Christianity's arrival in Gothia did not immediately tear many small villages and communities apart. Most Goths converted to Arian Christianity, based on Little Wolf's teachings, but religious demographics likely remained mixed. Catholics found their place in this society— pious men and women like Godda, Inna, Rema, and Pinna, whose names are known, even if the details of their lives are hidden. Where trouble did manifest in Gothic cities during these years, it stemmed from the many early converts who were vocal proponents of their faith and uncompromising about their new beliefs, like the Goth Saba. A little-known man from an undistinguished Gothic family whose pious way of life was recorded soon after his early death, Saba was the kind of radical Christian Alaric might have become under different influences. Saba's problems began when a group of Gothia's political leaders visited his pagan village for Gothic fellowship and a meal. As the time approached for the usual plates of meat to be shared around the tent, the villagers grew anxious. For some time, they knew, their acquaintance had obstinately refused to eat any meat from a butchered sacrificial animal. If Saba's peculiar eating habits were exposed during such an important visit, the elders feared, it might be interpreted as an affront to the distinguished dignitaries. No one wanted to make a scene at such an important tribal occasion.

To avoid embarrassment, the pagan Goths devised a ruse. With the help of a sympathetic chef, they prepared a second, identical plate of meat from a beast that had not been sacrificed, and they asked Saba to eat it while pretending it was the original dish. Their elaborate plan, motivated by genuine concern, was designed to ensure that no Goth should

be made to feel like an outcast at a tribal gathering simply because he
held different religious convictions.

Saba, who with the aid of Scripture saw the world around him in
dualistic terms, a place where good and evil fought daily spiritual battles, had developed a different set of Christian values. He didn't overturn the tables at the banquet, as Jesus did with the money changers
in the Temple. But he upset the villagers' plans. "If anyone eats of that
meat, this man cannot be a Christian," Saba declared, crushing any hope
for compromise. The elders chased him out of their village. In their language, they might have said Saba had acted like a *dwala*, a "fool."

According to the story, Gothic vigilantes then rode from village to village, torching the grass outside towns and terrifying the villagers with
the sounds of their approaching wagons, until they hunted Saba down.
The inquisitors found him hiding in a priest's house, shackled him, and
tortured him—at one point, by slamming a heavy club into his chest like
men crudely storming a city gate. When they had nearly finished bloody-
ing him, the men led him to the Buzău River, where Saba had one last
vision. "Over there, on the other side of the river, I can see what you cannot," he said, as his captors prepared him for death. "Standing in glory
are all the holy ones who have come to receive me." The Goths muscled
their fellow tribesman into the muddy water and held his neck down
until the gurgling stopped. Saba's body was left to rot near the bog.

In the coming decades, as Christians in Rome argued about the mal-
leability of their own faith, the story of Saba's death worked as a litmus
test among Christian and pagan Goths. Around meals of boiled game,
with the scent of a broth wafting through the air, Goths chewed on the
choices that had led to Saba's tragic end. Christian apologists revered
him and heaped on him a litany of praise. He had been "temperate, self-
controlled in all things, uninitiated in woman, abstinent, observed all
fasts, steadfast in prayers without vainglory and someone who sub-
jected all men to his good example," they insisted. Other Goths, Christians included, would have seen him as a menace, and Alaric himself, as
it is known, never modeled his own faith on Saba's example.

Goths who converted during these years grafted Christianity's teachings onto practices that were largely familiar to them and, in the process, made the faith uniquely their own. As more and more Goths settled in the Roman Empire, their penchant for adapting to their new surroundings elicited comment from critics who interpreted it as a form of studied deceit. One Roman, Eunapius of Sardis, took a jaundiced view of the immigrants' faith:

> Each tribe had brought along from home its ancestral objects of worship together with their priests and priestesses, but they kept a deep and impenetrable silence upon these things and spoke not a word about their mysteries. . . . [Furthermore,] they all claimed to be Christians, and some of their number they disguised as their bishops. And having dressed them up in that respected garb and having provided for them, as it were, a large fox-skin, [they] brought them forward. . . .
>
> The barbarians used these devices to deceive the Romans since they shrewdly observed that these things were respected amongst them while the rest of the time, under cover of the deepest secrecy, they worshipped the holy objects of their native rites with noble and guileless intent. Although the situation was such, the Romans had fallen into such folly that even those who appeared to be sensible persons were clearly and readily persuaded that they were Christians and bound by all Christian rites.

How widely Eunapius's suspicions were shared by other Romans is unknown, but the fear that Goths were using their religion as "fiction and sham designed to fool their enemies," like a menacing Trojan Horse, was largely a product of Roman hysteria.

Christian "crazies" in Rome frequently preached about the supposed purity of the early church during these years, claiming that their faith had shot forth from its pagan surroundings miraculously unsullied.

Their pronouncements were high on faith and light on facts, told by pious churchmen who espoused a one-sided view of Christian history, separatist and militant to its core. Instances of Christian compromise or of tough decision making by Christians in the public sphere, either before or after Constantine, never fit their strict definitions of Christian behavior. Unsurprisingly, a more complicated understanding of Christian history was usually ignored by the medieval church. But by the fourth century, there was no disentangling early Christianity from the messiness of its Roman environment—no pure original church for Christians to dig up.

The Christianity practiced by Goths and Romans alike intertwined Jesus's teachings, the Bible's stories, a preacher's unique set of interpretations, and the idiosyncratic practices and beliefs of the environments where it was lived. Even as the Roman community recited the "Our Father" and the Gothic community the "Atta Unsar," preserved in Little Wolf's translated version of the prayer, these strong ties of faith lay just beneath the rocky surface of Rome in the fourth century.

⚓

In November 393, Theodosius put moderates everywhere officially on alert by criminalizing nearly every aspect of pagan worship. No candle could be lit at a pagan shrine, no honey cake left for the spirits of the dead, neither in public nor in the privacy of one's home, without risking arrest, the emperor announced. As early as the fifth century, Christians would herald these radical moves as their long-prayed-for religious triumph. Many deeply devout men—Socrates of Constantinople, Sozomen, Rufinus, and Theodoret among them—wrote popular partisan histories of the church that taught other Christians to see their faith's success in these years as a divinely ordained turning point in world history. By the Middle Ages, churchmen regularly reminisced about the Theodosian age as a time when the deepest truths of Christianity were written into the charter of Europe as a civilizing force designed to protect the world from the dangers of the barbarians beyond.

Each cultural victory made militant Christians more ecstatic. Pagan animal sacrifice, which Christians had opposed for hundreds of years, citing biblical passages to justify their political crusade, was outlawed in most Roman cities. The emperor's men locked the doors of the empire's once-stately marble temples. The thick streaks of incense, usually seen at shrines, attenuated, as the devout and the superstitious alike feared being associated with any public act that could be interpreted as a demonstration of political resistance. Marble and bronze artwork that depicted pagan gods and beloved heroes was removed from display in sacred precincts, packed into crates, and taken to wealthy people's homes or melted down. The many richly decorated spaces where the ancients had exuberantly worshipped their gods now looked barren and empty.

The ultimate tragedy of ancient history is that tens of millions of Romans—Christians, Jews, and pagans—were in no position to resist Theodosius's changes unless they dared to form their own rebellion. If they lost, they would be called usurpers and killed, an ignominious fate many noble men had suffered throughout Rome's long history. But if they did not act, if they chose not to organize, they would move toward a future they could already see without any prophetic help. The freedom of expression and of religious belief that had been a defining feature of Rome was at risk, replaced by a selected set of biblical values that would be imposed on everyone.

Such was the tense situation facing the Roman Empire on the eve of 394, the year Alaric and the other soldiers in Theodosius's army received notice that they were called up to war.

CHAPTER SIX

Love, War, and an Awakening

But this is slavery, not to speak one's thought.

—EURIPIDES

W ar in antiquity was raw, ugly, and regrettably unavoidable. When armies lined up and generals squared off, the prospect of a sudden death match brought dread to the air for everyone involved. A soldier's armor could do only so much. A rudimentary helmet and shield protected the skull, but they were hardly foolproof. Whizzing arrows could pierce an eye socket the way a silver toothpick stabbed an olive. In one ancient battle, a flying projectile hit a soldier in the head and he "kept on pursuing with the javelin still embedded." As the fighting ebbed and the sun set, he rode back into the city, the javelin in his head still bobbing.

Soldiers sometimes slipped "in the blood of their comrades on the muddy, treacherous ground." Some struggled for their last breath at the bottom of scrums, suffocating under the weight of the other soldiers' armor. It was a terrible fate to lose one's life in war "without being wounded," Romans said. Broken bones meant a warrior had been lucky to survive. The pageantry of a pitched battle, two uniformed legions fighting on an open plain as in the age of valiant Scipio and Hannibal, was an old-fashioned gentlemen's game by Theodosius's time. Understandably, Rome's generals did everything they could to mitigate against fighting these savage contests. Sneak attacks were smarter, raids even better. The element of surprise was known to shock an enemy and kept your own casualties low.

A culture of toughness fostered pride. The men of the Roman army were the "bravest, greatest, most dedicated" fighters the ancient world had ever seen. The superlatives spilled from Latin writers' pens: *fortissimi, nobilissimi, devotissimi*. A field army, such as the battalions ordered to take their positions in the late summer of 394, when war looked all but inevitable, would have comprised between fifteen and thirty thousand men, ranging in age from their twenties to their forties and varied in both experience and physique from cavalier to strong to battle-tested.

The combat theater where Alaric likely expected to see action exercised a large hold on every Roman soldier's imagination. The safe bet that summer would have been that he and his fellow soldiers were going to the Tigris and the Euphrates, the two powerful arteries of the Middle East, which drained into the Persian Gulf, just beyond the Roman Empire's sphere of influence. Mesopotamia was the military hot spot of the fourth century. Emperor Julian, Constantine's nephew, had commanded troops in Persia in the middle of the fourth century, many of them drawn from Gothic recruits. The men had sacked cities, designed machines for desert war, and returned with stories of having dodged lions in the marshes. The dry carpets of sand and the many oasis towns had been known to disorient and humble generations of Roman soldiers, including Gothic soldiers from the bogs.

Persia stood at the epicenter of a growing network of trade, linking Asia, the Middle East, the Arabian Peninsula, and the eastern African kingdom of ancient Ethiopia. The local kings from the powerful Sasanid family—the shah of shahs, the subjects called their ruler—held an unshakable reign on their kingdom for four centuries, until they fell to an invading Islamic army that brought the Sasanids' dreams of empire to a crushing end.

During that time, the shahs emerged on the world stage as true impresarios. Patrons of the arts, literature, and music, they modeled their kingdom after the great Persian Empire of the fifth century B.C., when Darius and Xerxes had reigned unopposed. The shahs cultivated a love of philosophy, scientific inquiry, and theological debate and commissioned scholars of Zoroastrianism, Persia's official religion, to inves-

The Persian palace at Taq Kasra, whose catenary arches soared over the capital Ctesiphon, functioned as a center of art, culture, and intellectual exchange through the sixth century, impressing visitors, diplomats, and foreign soldiers alike with the grandeur of the shah's ambitions.

tigate the origins of the world. They invited foreigners to do so as well. At the shahs' request, Christians from the Roman Empire came to Persia and lived at the court as cultural ambassadors.

Persia's kings built monuments to their worldly ambitions. At the Persian capital Ctesiphon, outside Baghdad, huge catenary arches soared into the sky and formed the great hall of the palace. The size of its stone vaults awed the government's many foreign guests, and the elegant curves of its parabolas would be surpassed only in the modern age. At dinners, food was served in expensive silver dishes decorated with scenes of hunting. Horseback riding, polo, and archery were popular leisure activities.

The reach of the shah's authority extended even to those outside the Persian Empire. Archaeologists regularly discover Sasanian currency in Chinese tombs, attesting to the many Persian traders who worked the Silk Road; Roman coins are incredibly rare in these contexts. Even after the Persian Empire was conquered, a capacious curiosity about the world remained the region's hallmark. The Muslim 'Abbasid dynasty preserved that rich tradition into the thirteenth century.

Despite Persia's achievement and the shahs' extraordinary drive, Roman armies were regularly being deployed to the Persian frontier by Theodosius's day, and the Roman people themselves often viewed their eastern neighbors with suspicion and distrust. Persia had long been Rome's most bitter foe, sacking garrison towns and harassing emperors since the 250s A.D. The memory of conflicts lingered into the fourth century, with the tense standoff stymieing Rome from pursuing the riches of the Far East. Rome knew that Persia occupied "the middle of the earth" on the route to Asia and China, but the Persians' unwillingness to allow foreign merchants to cross their land without paying stiff tariffs had forced Rome into the Red Sea and the Indian Ocean, a more perilous journey. Emperor Julian's military objective had been to break through Persia's barricade. He never returned from that campaign.

The soldiers who had fought with him toiled to cross the desert. The "stiff clay and marshy ground" of the Tigris and Euphrates frustrated their otherwise determined march, and their horses fared no better, frequently getting stuck in the mud. Morale sunk. While there, Gothic men, in particular, witnessed and participated in some of the Roman army's most egregious behavior. They raided Persian warehouses. Rampant theft went unchecked and was sometimes encouraged by the soldiers' own commanders. Grain was stolen, packed onto carts, and loaded onto "ships for the maintenance of the soldiers." A Persian general's charming private zoo, "planted with all kind of trees, in which were wild beasts of every description," was turned into a Roman shooting gallery, in which his prized collection of animals—very likely "lions with long manes, bristly wild boars, [and] bears of the extraordinarily savage type peculiar to Persia"—were indiscriminately slaughtered.

Still, even with these occasional bouts of insensitivity, greed, and indecency, the soldiers received a valuable apprenticeship in teamwork, strategic planning, and creative problem solving, which supplemented their more practical knowledge of how to wield a sword or brandish a shield. They learned how to construct scaffolding to hoist troops over a city's walls, studied how to enter a fortified town by tunneling beneath it, and devised techniques to cripple a city's gates by melting its iron bolts. Goths returned home with stories as fantastic as any fairy tale, like the one about the time they dug a passage underneath a Persian woman's kitchen and startled her while she was preparing the next day's food. Many immigrant soldiers met men of unmatched valor and leadership during these years, including one of their own generals, Hormisdas.

Hormizd, as he had been known during his youth in Persia, had also crossed a river, fled his country, and immigrated to the Roman Empire. A member of a well-established Persian family, he was a generation older than most of his troops and had come of age during a Persian coup. The men who'd tried to overthrow the shah had captured and imprisoned him. Horrified by the thought of her spouse's being jailed for life, Hormizd's wife conspired to release him by concealing a thin metal file inside a fish, which she sent to the jail as a gift for her husband. Hormizd, finding the tool buried in its belly, used it to free himself from his chains and escaped, eventually securing passage to neighboring Armenia. From there, on the back of a dromedary, it was on to Constantinople, where he curried favor with Emperor Constantine's family. He changed his name, using the Greek spelling, Hormisdas, perhaps to make his foreign heritage less threatening, and eased himself into the world of baths, markets, and parties. By the 360s, General Hormisdas was back in Persia as the commander of Roman cavalry.

Many Goths saw combat under his command and were at Hormisdas's side when the charge of "Traitor!" was spat in his face by Persian locals. The ferocity with which the Persian people upbraided a Persian man in a Roman general's cloak must have been an abrupt awakening for the Goths, if they hadn't experienced that cultural shock for themselves already. An immigrant who fought successfully on the side of the Romans could never safely go home.

Alaric had not known Hormisdas personally but, by 394, had likely gleaned that same lesson. Many Goths wrestled with it during these years, asking themselves how long they could live as unequal partners in Roman society, whether their political status would ever change, and whether it would ever be possible to return to Gothia, where civil war had destabilized society, economic hardship had devasted the quality of life, and invading Huns had ravaged the northern territories. Their answers to the question of how to find a new Gothic future in Rome often exposed deep divisions among close friends, turning political disagreements into personal animosity.

Sometime before the outbreak of war, two Gothic men, Fravitta and Eriulf, had been invited to a dinner at Emperor Theodosius's palace. The elaborate nature of a Roman state dinner sent the cooks scrambling. Wine had to be selected and pastries baked. The two Goths agreed to attend because they respected the emperor and knew he would not repeat the tragic mistakes of his predecessor's day, when Goths were lucky if they escaped from a dinner invitation with their lives.

That night, the two Goths fell into a heated argument about politics. Fravitta always encouraged his fellow Goths to adopt a stance of deference and humility in their daily interactions with the Roman people. Since the Roman government had given farmland to some of the Gothic immigrants, the Goths should be gracious, he said. Eriulf, the more impatient, belligerent man, espoused the opposite view. The Goths needed to demand more action and not let complacency determine their fate. At a time when children could be sold into slavery at whim and families had no legal recourse in the towns where they settled if their property was damaged or their bodies abused, Goths were justified in owing the Romans nothing.

The conversation grew heated as alcohol inflamed the situation, and the shouting finally erupted into violence. In the middle of the dinner, Fravitta plunged his sword into Eriulf's side, murdering him in front of Rome's leading family, a bold act that impressed Theodosius. What a just, virtuous man Fravitta was, the emperor coolly remarked, as slaves

rushed in to mop up the mess. From that one thrust Fravitta would draw
a promotion, a Roman wife, and the emperor's lasting support. Goths
who advanced in society often did so by making horrendous personal
decisions like this one. It was not the last Gothic slaughter to bloody
Theodosius's feet.

✂

The Frigidus River, the sight of Alaric's deployment in the late summer of 394, would have struck any soldier as an odd battle site. If history
had offered them any guidance, the men in Alaric's regiment would have
been preparing themselves for months of an insufferable swelter in the
Persian desert, not a day or two of mild discomfort from the lower Alpine
winds. The location, to the northeast of the Italian peninsula, which had
taken them weeks, if not months, to reach from the Danube frontier, was
neither at one of the empire's borders nor the site of any checkpoint or
known invasion. On September 5, 394, it was just a pleasant, if slightly
out-of-the-way ravine that would eventually be claimed by the modern
country of Slovenia. Its grasses were a rich green in spring, summer, and
late fall. Few places throughout its lush hills warranted the status of a
real city. There were just isolated farms in the valley, which amplified
every yodel.

The identity of the soldiers' opponents might also have puzzled them.
Theodosius had ordered them to face Flavius Eugenius, who, after
nearly two years of growing frustration with his co-emperor's fanatical
religious policies, had been unable to broker any peaceful compromises
to stem the advance of Theodosius's Christian state. With the western
army behind him, an alliance of senators supporting him, and the aid of
his field general, Arbogast—widely recognized as a volatile personality—
Eugenius had gone to the Frigidus River that summer to face the now-
unavoidable prospect of civil war.

To Eugenius's army's credit, the Battle of the Frigidus River was
remembered as a bloody, protracted fight. The Roman writers who
described the outcome, none of them an eyewitness, estimated that it

lasted two days. However long it took, by September 6, 394, Theodosius had quashed his opposition, and ten thousand Gothic soldiers had fallen fighting for him—killed as a result of the emperor's cold tactical decision to overwhelm the "enemy's" front lines by sacrificing an extraordinary number of his Gothic troops, the *foederati*. Alaric was among the few to survive. As news of Eugenius's defeat reached the cities, ecstatic cultural warriors rushed to convince their Christian followers that their triumphant emperor owed his victory to a heaven-sent miracle: a sudden gale-force wind had barreled through the valley, one bishop claimed, lifting the enemy's arrows and blowing them back at the soldiers' faces—proof that God had wanted Theodosius to defeat the coalition of pagan and Christian forces that had risen in opposition to the emperor's reign.

Christians could believe the propaganda if they wanted, but the reality of what had led to the civil war was more mundane and its effects on society more sobering. Eugenius's side had been outmanned, outplanned, and outmaneuvered the moment he'd tentatively stepped into a leadership role, and Theodosius was the more successful field general. By the end of day, Eugenius's own field commander, the Frankish immigrant Arbogast, had deserted his men and committed suicide on the lam. Eugenius, the moral leader and public face of the last hope for a resistance, lay in the valley, decapitated. Theodosius impaled his head on a stick and toured Italian towns with it.

⚬

For the ancients, the morning after any death offered a fitting time "to look out a little through the mist" and reflect. And September 7, 394, was no different in this regard.

All soldiers sought fame and victory. After an ancient battle, messengers delivered victory reports, an ancient genre of writing called *epinikia,* to the major cities. The news was announced in theaters, in open forums, and in stadiums. In Theodosius's time, the details of a recent battle were sometimes delivered to the public in painted pictures set up at the racetrack. Victory became a patriotic ideal: Victoria, as she was personified in Latin, Nike as she was called in Greek. Emperors put "Victor" in their signatures. Any surface that could bear her image was covered with it: party cups, dinnerware, linen curtains, wool clothes, ivory boxes, writing tablets, mosaics, arches, columns, and equestrian monuments. The defeated, meanwhile, were customarily shown groveling for mercy, trampled under a general's bulging calf muscle.

A victorious emperor cut a stylish figure. Fashion was a triumphant Caesar's favorite form of self-expression. An emperor flush from victory became a model of excess in an age of vastly simpler tastes: decked out in red leather shoes, a golden robe, a rich purple cloak thrown around his shoulders, gilded chains, and shiny brooches. The winners thanked God for their blessings and prayed to God for more success. Even after Theodosius's day, many relied on Christianity to inspire their troops: "Be not disturbed, O brethren, by the multitude of the enemy," it was said in the seventh century A.D. "For when God wills it, one man will rout a thousand."

Theodosius's trouncing of Eugenius's coalition occurred at a unique time in Roman history when the papacy was in its infancy and the quickly growing global religion of Christendom, with its inroads into Persia, Africa, and central Asia, lacked any unifying leadership. Church and state routinely vied for power in these years, and it was Rome's politicians, not churchmen, who had the authority to define Christian creeds, conversations, and identity. Theodosius's bloody triumph ensured that his Nicene Christian party could confidently stride onto the landscape of Roman Europe, the Middle East, and Africa with a self-assuredness born of having vanquished the other side.

Hard-line Christians, feeling the political winds at their back, spent lavishly in the coming years to remake the image of the empire. The look of ancient cities started to change, in some places dramatically. Pagan artists, eager for work, sought out commissions from this powerful class of cultural arrivistes who, almost overnight, suddenly constituted the arbiters of tastes and style. In the coming decades, expertly trained architects aspired to impress and collaborated with Christian financiers to reshape the core of Mediterranean cities, building more churches and fulfilling their patrons' demands for more explicit Christian symbolism in every aspect of daily life. Artisans depicted biblical stories on ceramic lamps and dishware and used gold mosaics and other colorful tiles to animate the walls of churches dedicated to Mary, to the apostles, and to numerous martyrs. In the sixth century, the Roman engineers who designed the great domes at the church of Hagia Sophia, in Constantinople, could be confident that they had surpassed the splendor of Rome's Pantheon. Few such secular commissions existed anymore in this new, faith-driven version of classical society. Moderates adapted to the new realities.

With the emperor's victory at the Frigidus, a Christian identity was virtually required to maintain one's Roman citizenship status. The government establishment of Christianity brought with it a need for new public buildings, called baptisteries, where pagans could be welcomed into the faith through the waters of baptism, as church law required, a practice of cleansing and initiation adapted long ago from Jewish ritual. Buildings that housed these spaces had largely been unknown in the classical world of pagan temples and shrines, but they soon became ornate civic structures, usually adjacent to a city's church. The fancier ones, like those of tall brick, colored marble, and intricate mosaic work in Ravenna and Rome, would not have looked out of place in a later city like Renaissance Florence. Preening bishops loved raising money for them, each town surpassing the next in its magnificence, each structure a subtle boast about its congregation's wealth.

Alaric may not have understood the full implication of Theodosius's victory at the Frigidus in that hour, but he certainly felt loss and perhaps some tinge of regret after the battle. If it hadn't been for the chance of a passing caravan three years earlier, the thrill seeker from the marshes might never have become a Roman soldier. And if he hadn't joined Theodosius's army and worked his way up the ranks, he might never have stood in the silence of the Frigidus River valley after the battle, where he

counted and mourned his fellow warriors and might easily have num-
bered among the dead. There was quite a lot for a Goth to mull over, in
fact. Within a few years of the Battle of the Frigidus River, Romans would
say that the loss of Gothic lives that day had secretly been Rome's "gain"
and that whenever the Goths had suffered, it was Rome's "victory."

In the coming weeks, there was a duty to bury the fallen soldiers on
both sides. Funerals assisted "the morale of the living," the Romans said.
But even with the help of rituals, there would have remained for many
families and loved ones an overwhelming sense of grief. Daughters and
sons waited for their absent fathers. Wives prayed for their husbands to
return. Aging parents hoped to see their grown sons again, but many did
not come home. The news of a soldier's death always struck, it was said,
like a thunderbolt.

While it was not unheard of in Rome for a wounded soldier to survive
long enough to pass away in his loved ones' presence, that was probably
rare after the Frigidus. In an earlier Roman war, one man's wife nursed
him in his final hours and listened to him explain how to protect their
property from thieves who preyed on widows; unlike many couples,
they parted with a kiss. In 394, others found comfort in the memory of
their love. As one preacher said of the horrors of war:

> [Love] embraces and unites and fastens together not only those
> who are present and near and visible but also those who are far
> distant. And neither length of time, nor separation in space, nor
> anything else of that kind can break up and sunder in pieces the
> affection of the soul.

If there was any solace to be found, one preacher said in a touching
moment of empathy, it would come from the realization that death was
not an end. The passing of a loved one was "only a kind of emigration," a
journey from this life to a second home in heaven. Many bereaved families were reminded to take heart in the words of the Hebrew prophet

Hosea: "For He Himself," John Chrysostom said, quoting the prophet, "has smitten us, and He will heal us; He will strike, and He will dress the wound and make us whole."

Whether a wife remained faithful to her deceased husband was a different matter. Roman law required widows to wait four years before they remarried. Some did—and, after the Frigidus, are known to have wedded Gothic husbands. Traditionalists never condoned these mixed marriages. One highly exaggerated but illuminating tale, written anonymously well after the war, told of a Roman girl who fell for a Gothic soldier; it offered a powerful lesson in the dangers of associating with immigrants. According to the story, the young bride, named Euphemia, came to regret the day she met her future husband.

From Euphemia's earliest childhood, her mother had displayed a fiercely protective maternal instinct. When the girl grew older, eventually befriending a slightly older Gothic soldier billeted near their town, Euphemia's mother grew suspicious of his motives and morals. According to the tale, the Goth, also unnamed, occasionally showed a "fierce temper." Persistent in his pursuit of Euphemia, the Goth eventually persuaded Euphemia's mother to relent, and she allowed her daughter to marry. The couple announced a honeymoon in Gothia.

As soon as they crossed the border, the young bride's journey turned dark. Having escaped from the prying eyes of his overly possessive mother-in-law, the Goth revealed that he already had a Gothic wife. In a moment of terror for Euphemia, he ordered the girl to remove her wedding dress and hand over the gold she had been given as a dowry; then he forced her into slavery. Euphemia, whom the story portrays as a devout Christian, escaped the Goth's clutches by praying to God. At the conclusion of the tale, she safely returns home and is reunited with her mother. The moral of the story was never to let your Roman daughter marry a foreigner, particularly a Goth.

But love did find a way to cross borders, and weddings often created extended families of citizens and foreigners. There were no Roman laws that forbid ethnic or racial intermarriage in these years—the strictest legislation in Theodosius's day prohibited interreligious marriage and unions between people of two economic classes—and amorous partnerships between people of the same gender were not unknown, even if these relationships did strike the majority of Romans as highly unconventional.

One male Roman citizen wrote a touching letter to a foreign beau asking him to overlook what made the two of them different. There were many pairs of things that struck simple folks as incompatible, he said: the soul with the body, the nightingale with the spring, and the swallow with an indoor home. Elephants terrified many Romans. Rumors of the phoenix, the bird that rose from its own ashes, entranced the people of India, and a kingfisher rarely perched on a cliff. An uneducated mind was often taught to view these odd pairings as exotic and strange. But two men who felt a deep love for each other should embrace their strangeness, he reasoned:

> Don't be shocked if I, as a foreigner, reveal my love for you. It's not a crime to look. Beauty, like fire, kindles the eyes, and what is beautiful should shine. It should light up the eyes, right away. Don't worry about trying to distinguish a foreigner's eyes from a citizen's, or a foreigner's ears from a citizen's. The eyes and the ears are messengers of the soul.

Foreign lovers were especially beautiful, he went on. "If you want someone who will stay faithful to you, write my name down in your list of citizens. Be my Zeus and my Apollo, my protector of citizens, my guardian of native cities. And if they ask what tribe I belong to, go tell everyone my tribe is the tribe of Love." Many immigrants to the Roman Empire were shocked to find war and bigotry and fanaticism in their adopted home. But with luck, some also found the spark that led to poetry.

The end of 394 brought the triumphant but lonely Roman emperor to Milan. The northern Italian city was nestled below the central Alps and close to the battle site. Despite its winter rains and fog, which clouded its porticoed streets, it had the usual Roman amenities that offered a comfortable respite at any time of year: hot baths, warm wine, and a pleasant selection of parties. It also hosted a fully staffed palace, where a cadre of officials would be awaiting their postwar instructions.

Even surrounded by the extensive bureaucracy and Milan's opulence, the accomplished emperor must have been troubled by a feeling of isolation. His second wife, Galla, had been pregnant when she died on the eve of the Battle of the Frigidus River. Preoccupied with war, "Theodosius mourned the dead Empress for about one day," it was remarked. The child would have been Theodosius's fifth. His sons and his daughter, also named Galla, were living in the east or in Rome. The only pastime that seems to have brought the forty-eight-year-old emperor some distraction was his love of chariot racing. There were games in Milan's stadium between the Blues and the Greens on January 16, 395, and Theodosius took his seat in the stands, where, as most popular politicians did, he likely made a show of cheering on the teams as diplomatically as possible.

On January 17, 395, one day after he had been in good spirits, the emperor succumbed to a vague medical condition the ancient doctors called "dropsy." As the shocked establishment scrambled to prepare a state funeral, a degree of confusion settled over the government. The emperor's corpse remained in Milan for more than a month.

The funeral filled Milan's modest cathedral with imperial dignitaries as Bishop Ambrose, likely dressed in a solemn but elegantly embroidered robe, ascended to the pulpit and delivered a strident eulogy, extolling the Christian state the emperor had muscled into existence. An incurable partisan, Ambrose used the service to praise Theodosius for his fortitude, militancy, and resilience to heathenism. There was much for the Christian community to celebrate, the bishop said.

In this dramatic painting by the seventeenth-century artist Peter Paul Rubens, Saint Ambrosius and Emperor Theodosius, *Ambrose, the bishop of Milan, prevents the emperor from entering the church after Theodosius has ordered the massacre of thousands of residents of Thessaloniki—a confrontation Ambrose won and which he mentioned during the emperor's eulogy.*

God had given them a fearless and merciful emperor who fit the profile of the best biblical kings. Had Theodosius not been a model of humility, as well? After all, he had sought forgiveness in church after the horrible massacre at Thessaloniki during the Butheric affair—when Ambrose, upon learning of the killing of the seven thousand citizens, denied Theodosius Holy Communion unless the emperor publicly kneeled before him in church. By bowing to the pressure, the emperor had tacitly acknowledged the power of the bishops to hold politicians morally accountable for their actions and policies. Prelates rejoiced at the precedent Ambrose won for the church throughout the Middle Ages.

At the funeral, the bishop told the crowd of mourners that just as "the horse returns to the stable when it has completed the race," so the moment of their beloved emperor's eternal slumber had arrived, and soon, Ambrose predicted, Theodosius would be honored as "a citizen of paradise."

His earthly remains came to rest with rather less swiftness. In late February, the emperor's body was finally loaded onto a carriage for

Constantinople; it arrived nine months later—a sluggish pace even for an ancient delivery.*

Whatever receptacle Theodosius's body was in as it traveled to Constantinople and whatever its physical condition when it arrived that November, it was interred in one of Constantinople's most sacred sites, the Church of the Holy Apostles. Before his own death in 337, the pious emperor Constantine had sent men to scavenge the Mediterranean for Christian relics. When they returned with a collection of old bones of dubious provenance, he sorted them into twelve piles, credulously called them "the apostles," and ordered architects to build a church to house them, leaving instructions for himself to be buried among them as "the thirteenth." From that point on, this church was the preferred mausoleum for the empire's sterner Christian rulers, especially those who sought to distance themselves from the pagan collaborations and expedient partnerships of Eugenius's Rome. Theodosius, in an expensive stone coffin, joined Constantine there as the peculiarities of managing the government occupied his two sons.

---

* The Romans had rudimentary forms of refrigeration, although ancient funeral workers occasionally practiced embalming. Excavations in 1962 in Thessaloniki, Greece, uncovered the corpse of a wealthy Roman woman with parts of her eyebrows, hair, and skin tissue still preserved. Archaeologists speculated that the woman's lead coffin could have prevented decomposition after she died, sometime in the third century A.D., but so could the oils and resins applied to her corpse and shroud, including patchouli, alcohol, and the compound vanillin, perhaps derived from cloves or storax.

CHAPTER SEVEN

The Lion and the Fox

The designs of a general should always be impenetrable.

—VEGETIUS

For Alaric, the shock of seeing the ten thousand Gothic soldiers dead must have demanded a frank discussion about what kind of ruler Theodosius had been and whether the Roman Empire was truly a hospitable place for men like him to remain in its service. In the most generous assessment, Theodosius's record on immigration had been mixed: selected promotions, greater opportunity, but, tellingly for Goths and other immigrants, no announcement of citizenship. Alaric's mentor, a Gothic leader named Gainas, was transferred to Constantinople in a lateral move, at least ensuring him continued prospects. Alaric, the less experienced soldier, faced an uncertain future and a moment of reckoning.

Options were few. Centuries earlier, he might have earned a *diploma,* the bronze plaque that bestowed citizenship on veterans, from a grateful emperor in return for a soldier's military valor. But those rewards no longer existed. Alaric could continue to draw his soldier's stipend and maybe move up the military ladder in the process. But with decades of military service still expected of him before he could legally draw a pension or receive a land grant, and without any clear path to citizenship, he may have let his youthful impatience build to an intolerable frustration. Even a career as a civilian officer seemed out of question, unless he made the difficult choice, as Modares had, to soften his Gothic image or, following Fravitta's more radical approach, to stab someone at dinner. All

Alaric had on offer was to continue to fight for Rome without acknowledgment of his service, to hope for change, or to walk away.

Confrontation with the Roman government—an open protest against the unjust treatment of the Gothic people—seems, in the final calculus, to have offered Alaric the most satisfying solution. By the summer of 395, after he was told by the new government without any further explanation that he would be denied a chance to "command more soldiers"—a subtle, if ultimately belated, acknowledgment of his knack for motivating his fellow warriors—a fuming Alaric left the Alps for distant Constantinople. While the contemporary historian Socrates of Constantinople admits that some consolation prize awaited him there, remarking that "on account of his service in the war," Alaric would be "deemed worthy of Roman honor," the exact meaning of this "honor" has been endlessly debated. Was it a medal for valor? A gift? An official title, one of a list of empty Latin abbreviations the Roman upper classes loved to add after their names: "Distinguished," "Illustrious," "Admirable"? Whatever it was, Alaric soon discovered that it was not a promotion, a rejection he seems to have taken personally, inspiring visions of storming the palace and overthrowing its staff in a spectacular coup.

To little surprise, for a man with a demonstrated track record of charisma, Alaric had garnered a growing number of Gothic supporters on his march eastward: rallying behind his cause were husbands and wives, families and friends, and former soldiers, like him. Because so little about Alaric's company is known, beyond the spontaneity that brought them together, scholars often debate whether they constituted a formidable "army" or a burgeoning Gothic "nation"—either option a none-too-subtle attempt to fashion a band of menaces and marauders from a collection of people who, on any fair assessment, were mostly poor and disenfranchised.

Their march against Constantinople probably would have succeeded, too, had not an ally inside the palace presented himself to Alaric at the last moment. Rufinus, one of the key advisers to Theodosius's son Arcadius, contacted Alaric as he neared and persuaded him to change his plans. If Alaric could wait patiently outside the walls, Rufinus said, he could run interference during the chaotic palace transition and perhaps broker a deal to secure Alaric more money. Alaric waited.

The eighteen-year-old Arcadius, whom Rufinus served, was a surprisingly assertive young man—unlike his younger brother, Honorius, who had the wavering confidence appropriate to an eleven-year-old and a voice that had not yet deepened in age or wisdom. For years Honorius would migrate between the palaces in Milan, Ravenna, and Rome with his entourage, while Arcadius would always remain in Constantinople. The two boys, who had lost both their mother and their father and were said to be "in the bloom and flower of young manhood," had inherited all the bureaucratic mechanisms of the Roman government, but their political experience was as green as their age.

The leadership transition in 395 after Theodosius's death was every scheming politico's dream, which explains Rufinus's confidence that he could manipulate the new administration and find a way to funnel money to Alaric. Every week offered a new opportunity for insiders to test the boys' impressionable will. Ideologues capitalized on it immediately, inundating the palace with requests for clarifications on religious policy, foreign policy, cultural legislation, and immigration. Surely the abhorrent practice of animal sacrifice would remain outlawed, correct? Would the Caesars now end the gladiatorial games? What did the emperors wish to do with the marble and bronze statues and the painted and jeweled artworks dedicated to the closed pagan temples?

Passions spiked. Even ordinary citizens volunteered policy suggestions in creative ways. One Christian leapt down onto the *arena*, as the Romans referred to the sandy floor of their Colosseum, and interrupted a gladiatorial match to protest the savagery of the sport, which Theodosius had allowed to continue. The crowd, apoplectic at the stoppage, stoned the man to death. But Christian culture warriors hailed him as a veritable martyr and used his example to persuade Theodosius's sons to close the gladiatorial schools. In 399, Honorius bowed to their zealotry.

Everyone in Rome sensed what was at stake in all these debates. People speculated about "whether the ears would show themselves on the stalk," as a famous proverb went. During his sixteen-year rule, Theodosius had engineered the radical upheaval of society, but those accomplishments risked unraveling if the boys did not aggressively defend their father's legacy. Advice came from every direction, even from beyond the grave. "I can't warn you often enough. / You live in sight of the whole world," the poet Claudian wrote, conjuring the ghost of Emperor Theodosius to inspire the young men. "Be a citizen and be a father," he said, reminding the boys that their constituents admired even-keeled statesmen.

Other poets pleaded with the boys not to undo Theodosius's policies. The Roman Empire had always been changing, the Latin poet Prudentius wrote to Honorius, and previous Roman emperors had undoubtedly built a great society. "Earthly glory made these men famous, and mortal valor raised them to the heights of renown," he noted. But, he said, those weaker pagan emperors had fallen "under the power of a superstition adopted from the earth." The God of the Christians knew no limits; Theodosius's Christian son should not allow Rome to slip back into its heathen ways.

Prudentius's Christian argument was quite novel for conservative Rome, a society that had long run on the principle of the *mos maiorum,* or "customs of one's ancestors." The poet was propounding a theory of progressivism in which it was time for Romans to abandon their outdated ways. The ancient pagan gods, Prudentius explained, had come to Italy hundreds of years ago as "foreigners" and "outcasts." The old graybeards, like the god Saturn, had been "fugitives" and "exiles" from their home on Mount Olympus. Roman poets dutifully preserved their memory through entertaining stories, but centuries later, a blind faith in tradition, he suggested, was no reason for so many to believe silly tales of "homeless strangers." The stampede of Christian progress had eliminated the need for antiquated religious fables:

If we have to hand down all our ways,
    including customs from rough days of yore,

THE LION AND THE FOX

then roll back time to the earth's origins
and list what's different between then and now.
There was no farming long ago; plow and
mattock came much later. We should all be
eating acorns if we're history's hostages.

It was time for traditions to change, the poet pleaded, and change meant
that Romans should embrace Christianity, rid society of its foreign influences, put the goddess Victory's altar away, and end the pagan blood
sports. It also meant separating immigrants from the Roman citizens.

"What is Roman and what is barbarian are as different from each
other as the four-footed creature is distinct from the two-footed or the
dumb from the speaking," Prudentius wrote, neither the first nor the
last to compare immigrants to animals. The emperors' sons, who signed
most of their early laws jointly, largely fell in line with his opinions. Foreigners who hoped that the new administration might bring a welcome
change to their murky legal situation would have to keep waiting. No
new citizenship initiative would be taken during Arcadius and Honorius's rule.

The new young emperors repaired crumbling infrastructure, assigned
public money to patch broken pipes, and acted swiftly to prevent the
misappropriation of public goods, as when residents of Rome illegally
siphoned water from one of the city's most powerful aqueducts, the
Aqua Claudia. As soon as the government discovered the instances of
theft, the emperors authored legislation prohibiting the modification of
state infrastructure for private use, and thieves were required to pay
"as many pounds of gold as the number of inches of water [as] have been
appropriated"—one of the most creative fines in the annals of crime.

Civic-mindedness was not entirely lost in these years, but a foreigner
like Alaric would have had a hard time naming any other values shared
with former times. As Theodosius's boys, raised to share their father's
strict Christian sensibilities, doubled down on their father's radical
religious laws, the sense of disorientation among Rome's population

widened. The usual places where citizens had celebrated *Romanitas,* the plazas and streets around the pagan temples, remained closed. Weeds overran some of the oldest and greatest, like the beloved Temple of Jupiter on the Capitoline Hill, whose presence dated back to the early republic. Marble torsos, bronze limbs, and painted pots cluttered other sites of worship.

The boys, nevertheless, did at least strive to appease, in a small way, Rome's more demoralized citizens: by offering a few nods to religious temperance, punishing synagogue thieves and arsonists, and specifically warning Christians not to demolish any more pagan monuments. "Just as We forbid sacrifices, so it is Our will that the ornaments of public works shall be preserved," the emperors decreed. But the fight for preservation was an uphill battle. Christians knocked down pagan statues, then invented laws to justify their acts of vandalism—a ruse that did not fool the young rulers. If a Christian "should produce any rescript or any law as his defense," they announced, "such documents shall be torn from his hands and referred to Our Wisdom." Much of the fabric of classical pagan Rome survived because of the brothers' heritage preservation laws.

Romans of every background prattled about the direction of Arcadius and Honorius's administration. The great Latin writer of Alaric's early years, Ammianus, who had almost single-handedly recorded the deliberations, back-channel dealings, and tavern gossip of the fourth century, was dead by then. And with his passing, sometime during Theodosius's reign, there was no longer any widely acknowledged, living authority for perspective on current events. If it weren't for two emerging, enterprising writers who set themselves the ambitious task of documenting the events of these years, in fact, modern historians would largely be guessing at what ordinary Roman people talked about.

Like all insatiably curious artists, Eunapius of Sardis and Olympiodorus of Thebes knew the rewards of lingering and listening on tavern trips and of laughing with the locals. One hailed from the wealthy city of Sardis near coastal Asia Minor, the other from the rich southern

Egyptian city of Thebes. They left their family homes to pursue a life of research and writing and used their education and personal connections to interview politicians. They spent hours in city libraries, visited oily taverns, and frequented many cities, where they doubtlessly enjoyed themselves. But after the fun was over, they returned to their studies, consulted their notes, and wrote with rigor, a love of history, and their own inimitable styles. Although they probably never knew each other, they produced two of the most fascinating works on the life of the later Roman Empire.

Eunapius's flair was for exploring new frontiers in the language. Writing in Greek, he invented words that translate as "piggier" and "monkeyish," which he sprinkled into his account of Theodosius's reign and the reign of his two sons. Stodgy academics loathed his literary exuberance. "He spoils and debases the nobility of the rest of his vocabulary," they charged. But people read Eunapius's fourteen-volume *Chronicle* into the Middle Ages. Olympiodorus, a poet at heart, was often spied sitting at the local bar with his pet parrot. There was "hardly any human action it could not imitate," the people guffawed. "It could dance, sing, call out names and do other things." Oly, whose name is usually abbreviated in scholarly notes, must have cut quite a "buccaneering figure," one modern historian has surmised. A scribbler constantly writing "material for history," as Oly described it himself, he published a widely regarded twenty-two part series, probably called *Histories,* that narrated the reign of Theodosius's sons. By the time he died, in the early decades of the fifth century, he was enjoying the fruits of his literary successes on the streets of Constantinople.

Eunapius and Oly made a name for themselves as smart, well-traveled, and hardworking writers. But their books have all been lost, represented by the survival of only a few crucial fragments. In the Byzantine era, an anonymous admirer may have copied one or two chance sentences into a notebook, which was then shelved in a monastery and, later, discovered. At other times, an ancient librarian may have preserved threads of their information by transcribing key passages, as Photius of Constantinople did in the ninth century. Zosimus, the revisionist author of *A New History*, which detailed the border separation program of Alaric's years, quoted both Eunapius and Oly extensively.

Eunapius and Oly recorded the exploits of contemporary Gothic men, like Gainas, Fravitta, and Eriulf, and critiqued the cautious first steps of Honorius and Arcadius's reign with emotional depth and analytical insight. They identified and characterized other chief players on the stage, too, like General Stilicho and his influential and intriguing Roman wife, Serena. By the time Alaric himself left the Frigidus River in 394, trading the battlefield for some well-earned respite, their gaze had found the boy from Pine Tree Island, too. The Goth whose childhood slipped through ancient sources had finally merited someone else's regard. Romans knew about him, and they wanted to read about him, judging from the amount of attention Eunapius and Oly paid him in their chronicles. Alaric's movements, his conversations, even his dreams and his frustrations thicken considerably in their pages. Thanks to them and to Zosimus, who incorporated much of their reporting, historians can reconstruct key episodes from this pivotal moment in history: from the period of Theodosius's funeral right up to the fateful evening of August 24, 410.

⟩⟨⟩

What was Alaric's mood as the two children came to power, ten thousand Gothic bodies lay unmourned, and Rufinus searched for hidden funds? Zosimus, borrowing information from the two lost writers, says Alaric was "displeased"—a decent translation but perhaps too genteel. Zosimus's word also means "violently ill." In Greek medical texts, doctors used the term to describe the effect of a chill coming over the body, as when people feel sick to their stomach.

In late summer, while the wagon with Theodosius's body was still rattling through the Balkans, Alaric lingered impatiently outside Constantinople, waiting for news from Rufinus, the palace's most colorful personality. But the undeniably deft Rufinus won no affection for positioning himself as a sympathetic Roman ear in a time of widespread anti-Gothic sentiment. His political opponents accused him of Gothic collusion.

Vituperation took a healthy amount of ink in Latin, but the poet Claudian had plenty. He swiftly penned two broadsides against Rufinus to shame him for negotiating with the Goths and trying to appease them. As every political veteran knew, the best way to smear a rival was to caricature him, and Claudian's poetry rendered Rufinus almost unrecognizable to the average Roman. Working the literary magic that would earn him a bronze statue in Rome, Claudian turned the upstanding officer of Arcadius's court into a man of questionable morals who preferred animal skins to a toga, the wardrobe of a real Roman man:

> Have you seen his yellow-stained pelts?
> How he slings barbarous fur round
> his shoulders, sporting harnesses,
> quivers, and arrows—the kind that
> make an inhuman screech? Clothes make
> the man, but this man's make a beast.
> It's disgraceful that he signs our
> laws while sitting in the curule chair,
> ruining our Roman way of life
> with his poor taste in Gothic "style."

The Roman government couldn't risk having a Gothic sympathizer in the palace, Claudian huffed. The writer Eunapius, who also caught word of the hastily called meeting with Alaric, reported that Rufinus was conspiring to become emperor.

The savage lines of Claudian's lively portrait, widely shared after Rufinus's assassination, do not need to be read literally to convey the extent of anti-immigrant sentiment coursing through Rome. If Rufinus was a politician ready and willing to listen to Alaric, the furs and arrows could have been the poet's carefully crafted fiction, a warning that men garbed in animal skins could not be trusted to take positions of authority "in the curule chair." With a message that underscored the young emperors' Roman patriotism and verses that trafficked in inflammatory stereotypes, Claudian bolstered Arcadius and Honorius's tenuous position in the palace.

In November, Rufinus received an odd request from Arcadius's advisers: a meeting in a secluded neighborhood outside Constantinople's towering walls. Rufinus went at the agreed-upon time and, at the insalubrious place, found Gainas, who, on his own advisers' command, murdered Rufinus. Eunapius's fragments and Claudian's poetry leave the bigger picture of what happened obscured. Why a Goth as politically sensitive as Gainas would have agreed to take part in an assassination is never explained—and stretches belief. Even given Claudian's villainous description of Rufinus, the cautious trust that Alaric had placed in him suggests that Rufinus was the Gothic people's most well-placed government asset, an open-minded Roman ready to support the Gothic cause and, thus, someone to keep around. Gainas would hardly have agreed to kill him unless the Gothic general had been promised greater rewards by the conspirators. Maybe he had.

Roman politics had always relied upon augury, taking the flight of birds as a prediction of good beginnings, for example. But the start of this new administration would have marked one of the most inauspicious in decades. Fewer than twenty days had passed since Theodosius's burial, and there had already been one assassination, quite possibly the result of Rufinus's scheme, albeit nebulous and vague, to enlist Alaric's forces against Theodosius's sons. The assassins conveniently disposed of Rufinus's corpse on the periphery of the capital. Rufinus's wife and children fled to a church for protection. Within a year his family sought political asylum outside Constantinople.

The assassination left Alaric marooned. As the year closed, he led his followers away from Constantinople's inhospitable gates. According to the Roman sources, they spent the next two years causing disturbances in Greece, but the reality of 396 and 397 is more revealing and less melodramatic.

After the icy barracks of northern Thrace, the precarious existence of combat, and the swift reversal of fortunes in the shifting political winds of Constantinople, the city of Athens offered Alaric a respite from heavy military and political matters. For generations, even wealthy Romans had come to Greece and to Pericles's city, in particular, in search of escapism. Athens in the fifth-century Roman Empire did not disappoint. Roman generals had taken a strategic interest in Greece in the second century B.C., identifying the Isthmus of Corinth—between the Greek mainland and the Peloponnesian peninsula—as a vital sea route to and from the eastern Mediterranean. After Corinth fell to a Roman army in 146 B.C., the very same year Rome annihilated its nemesis, the Phoenician city of Carthage, several once-proudly independent cities on the Greek mainland and peninsula merged into a Roman province, called Achaea. Athens, a city that shot to life under Pericles's leadership in the fifth century B.C. and had fallen to its enemy Sparta a generation later, was eventually sacked by the Roman general Sulla in the first century B.C. It remained the shining star at the center of this network of Greek cities. Roman families with wealth prided themselves on sending their sons to study at its schools.

Inspirational figures had long taught in Athens's shaded gardens. Justice walked, personified, across its stages, within sight of the olive groves on Mouseion Hill and the pines of Mount Lykabetos. Beautiful as Athens still was in the late fourth century A.D., however, Rome had stamped a brutalist mark on the solemn monuments that the great statesman Pericles had commissioned. The Athenian market, the agora that Socrates had once strolled, was smaller in Alaric's day, befitting the city's reduced population, down to perhaps twenty thousand. Rome's military had erected unsightly new walls, which carved odd neighborhoods out of the old city. Governors lived in garish mansions built amid once modest dwellings. The city's crown jewel, Athena's sanctuary on the Acropolis, the Parthenon, looked more like a fortress, thanks to the recent addition of Roman defenses near the formerly elegant entranceway, the Propylaea.

Yet even in the Roman Empire, Athens always remained a desirable address. Compiling a top-twenty list of the best cities to live in, a fourth-century Latin poet ranked Athens as fifteen, behind delightful Capua's "fields and fruits" and the picturesque canal at the merchant city of Arles. A Roman could do worse, he said, than settle down under the "peace-bearing olive trees" of Athens. By Alaric's day, the Greek city had lured people away from the Roman Empire's crass political hubs, like Constantinople and Trier. Fine imports, like the quality wine from Rhodes and Gaza, were inexpensive there. Tourists looking for an educational experience kept Athens on their itineraries, keen to visit famous sites from the history of the Peloponnesian War, which Sparta fought to stop Athens's imperial expansion. "It is indeed a wonderful experience," one Roman remarked, "to view the fabled war of bygone days as told in the monuments standing there." Above all, the Romans came to see the "the beauty of its Acropolis."

The Parthenon's translucent marble was weathered by Alaric's day, but not very much had changed in its decor. Athenian artists and architects had carved bombastic ideas of self-importance onto its exterior, creating a jingoistic billboard, a statement about Athenian superiority over the barbaric forces of Persia. It's not hard to understand why, centuries later, the Romans loved it. Braggadocio featured on the monument's every side. Panels showed drunk centaurs, half man, half horse, harassing the guests at a mythical wedding party. The noble humans who fought back, the Lapiths, effortlessly repelled their attackers—a much-loved Greek story. The fact that the men could foil such threats without wearing any clothes spoke to the power of restraint Pericles had cultivated in his citizens. Classical nudity conveyed heroism, and Athens had always, with little hint of modesty, viewed itself as a civilized society under attack. That was how the Romans viewed their own world.

The beauty of the Acropolis affected Alaric too, if Zosimus can be believed. When Alaric arrived outside the city, in 396 or 397, he supposedly spied the goddess Athena striding atop the city walls, joined

by the ghost of the great warrior Achilles. Zosimus says that the effect
of the two apparitions on Alaric convinced him not to attack the city.
In the novel written in the 1930s by the French writer Marcel Brion,
La vie d'Alaric, released in English as *Alaric the Goth,* the "Barbarian"—
as Brion occasionally called his title character—requests a reading of
Plato's *Timaeus* at an elegant Athenian dinner and, later, delights in a
performance of Aeschylus's *The Persians.* At least in the novelist's imagination, Athens enchanted him with all the élan of fin de siècle Paris, but
there is no evidence to substantiate any of it.

⋙

Over the years many scholars have doubted Zosimus's presentation
of events, as well. Among them are religious skeptics who scoff at the
possibility of divine appearances. Others, pointing to the unmistakable signs of vandalism on the Parthenon's exterior, are convinced that
Alaric pillaged it. Who but an angry Goth could have toppled the building's elegantly fluted columns—arranged with mathematical precision to heighten the Parthenon's beauty from a distance—and bowled
through the ancient statues arranged around the precinct? "A destruction of such magnitude and terrorist overtones could only happen in the
hands of foreigners," one modern archaeologist has claimed, depicting
Alaric as a centaur for his time.

In fact, the question of who and what may have damaged the Parthenon in antiquity remains hotly debated. One square marble carving,
on display in Athens's Acropolis Museum and showing an enigmatic
encounter between two gracefully attired female figures, is the star witness in these arguments. On it, a winged but now headless woman stands
at the panel's left side, her dress cinched tightly at her waist in the aus-
tere classical style, and addresses a second faceless woman, seated at the
right, clothed in a billowing gown. Even to those who have never looked
at sculptures from the Parthenon before, the panel will seem familiar
because of its composition. Asked to identify the subject of the scene, a

For many years, this marble carving from the roofline of the Parthenon was falsely believed to be the only artwork on the famous Athenian temple not destroyed by Alaric's men, presumably because the Goths confused it for an image of the Annunciation. The angel on the left is, in fact, the goddess Hebe, and the figure assumed to be the Virgin Mary is the goddess Hera.

Renaissance master like a Giotto or a Fra Angelico, steeped in Christian storytelling, might have said it depicted the Annunciation, the moment the angel Gabriel revealed to Jesus's mother, Mary, that she was with child. The pieties of many historians would lead them to believe that this is what Alaric recognized, too. After seeing it, the mad Goth supposedly halted his attack on the Acropolis and ordered the Goths to protect this lone panel—one of a set of thirty-two metopes from the building's north roofline—because he mistook it for a scene from the Bible, although, in reality, it's a picture from the myth of the fall of Troy. The tortured explanation for its "preservation" is supposed to reassure us that even a barbarian like Alaric must have had a crumb of decency stuck somewhere in his matted fur. But that reconstruction is pure fiction.

In truth, a potent mix of ancient bigotries and modern prejudices makes it hard to tell the later history of Athena's Parthenon. Over time, the Parthenon itself would welcome visitors as a church and as a mosque, assume the role of a gunpowder warehouse, and, by the nineteenth century, would become an empty shell of Athena's former glory. But there's no real evidence to blame Alaric for the destruction of its classical glories.

Outside Athens, many Greek towns did report Gothic invasions during these years. As cities fell and towns were taken, the people of Sparta, Megara, Argos, Corinth, and Thermopylae suffered. Alaric's nearly two-year stay in Greece was a *katastrophe,* in Zosimus's Greek tongue: "an overturning of an entire way of life." Claudian labeled Alaric "destroyer of the Greek people," though for all we know, he based his accusations on reports from Greek villages where homeless, starving Goths received poor welcomes and reacted in desperation. As happens during the mass movement of any foreign people, there were probably legitimate conflicts during these years. And yet what happened at Athens was noticeably different.

Zosimus states that the Roman residents opened the city's gates to the Gothic stranger and extended him "all possible civility," which Alaric graciously returned. The Athenians invited him on a refreshing visit to the city's baths, gave him gifts, and probably ensured that he dined well. Why they chose to do so, and other towns did not, says a great deal about the political values dividing the people of the Roman Empire at the time and exposes the fault lines that were rupturing Roman society, more broadly.

Foreigners, Roman residents of Athens had been taught, deserved guest friendship, *xenia,* an ancient Greek concept to which Romans still subscribed. As adults, they internalized it in the stories they consumed. Escapist romances, such as the novel *Daphnis and Chloe,* about lovers separated by fate and stranded in strange towns who survived with the help of thoughtful locals and found their way back into each other's warm embrace, filled the hours of casual readers. More educated Romans recalled the heart-tugging scene at the end of the *Odyssey* when the swineherd fussed over a meal for his homeless guest, Odysseus in disguise. "Every beggar and stranger comes from Zeus," the swineherd says, winning Odysseus's sly approval. Romans of the fourth century still quoted that Homeric scene to make a point about wealth, privilege, and the need for small acts of kindness. In pagan antiquity, concern for the poor was never an exclusively Christian value.

The 90 percent of the empire's citizens unable to read learned this lesson at the theater, where many ancient people received an education in the liberal arts. What qualities made a good citizen, what was the right moral course of action, and what was fair and equitable provided the basis of dilemmas that had long been dramatized on the Athenian stage. A girl wrestles with the injustice of seeing her brother's body lie unburied in the street, his funeral forbidden by the king. What should she do? Sophocles asks the audience in his play *Antigone*. A despondent mother watches while her two ambitious sons kill each other in a struggle for power. Why should cities suffer senseless violence? Euripides posed that question to theatergoers in his *Phoenician Women*. For a thousand years, the Athenian stage was the place where the ancients sought challenging stories and surprising viewpoints to teach them to see the world differently.

Sometimes audiences didn't know what to expect when they sat down on the stone seats of Athens's marquee performance space, the Theater of Dionysus. Euripides's drama *The Phoenician Women*, while purportedly a family drama about two warring brothers, also concerned a chorus of traveling foreigners peripherally caught up in the outbreak of violence that brought about the collapse of a Greek city. Euripides titled the play after its protagonists, the foreign women. Telling the story through their eyes was a way of teaching his audience empathy, asking them to imagine an outsider's perspective on well-known events. Such inspired displays of originality—taking well-loved plots, rearranging the pieces, and reassembling them to achieve new results—earned Euripides a lasting renown. The Athenian audiences adored him for it.

The Romans loved him, too. Throughout the Roman Empire, Euripides remained the most read and performed Greek playwright from classical Athens through the fifth century A.D. His characters, settings, and plots offered timeless entertainment, even if, by the fourth century, full-scale productions had become rare and the way his plays were staged had changed. By the time Alaric arrived in Athens, Roman audiences preferred to watch mimes, stories performed by one or two silent actors, or pantomimes, stories retold as interpretative dance. Both had become popular forms of expression in the early Roman Empire. But Greek theaters never went dark, and Greek writers remained part of the cultural and political conversation of the time. The work of three of the biggest names in Greek literature—Homer, the humorist Menander, and Euripides—would continue to provoke discussion in literary salons throughout the medieval and Byzantine periods.

Perhaps the Athenians' long-standing appreciation for the well-being of guests, cultivated for centuries on the Athenian stage, played a part in their decision to extend Alaric their hospitality. Contemporary Romans recognized that cities had their own distinct personalities. "Just as children have different spirits allotted to them at their birth," it was said, "so to each city, when first its walls rise up, its own hour and day bring a destiny or genius under whose government it shall bear rule." Zosimus, whose discussion of Alaric's visit is terse, implies only that Athens's antiquity was its best defense.

The Goths were far from their own homes in 396 or 397, but Alaric's leadership gave them the sense that they belonged to a larger community. Oly says that during these years Goths regularly started to call Alaric their "tribal leader," or *phylarch*. Jordanes gives the announcement more of a trumpet blast. Goths began to hail Alaric as their "king," he claims. Scholars like to dismiss that news as an unreliable fiction, since the title would not have carried any real weight in the late 390s. But what it would have carried, to a migrant Gothic society whose hierarchical structure we cannot reconstruct, was ethnic pride, which might have meant something to the Gothic migrants who settled in Athens. Alaric's magnetism in these years might have given them a tangible hope for the future. Meanwhile, the tales of destruction in Greece from Roman sources suggest that fear was in the air. With the Goths' occasionally violent outbursts and rumors of their unity behind a daring young leader, many Romans would have felt justly nervous. And Alaric likely knew he could not stay in Athens forever; he was being sought by one of the most accomplished, high-profile Roman generals, Stilicho.

General Stilicho took a huge risk by coming after Alaric. Theodosius had welcomed Stilicho into the government largely because of the credentials of his female family members. Stilicho's mother had been a Roman. So was Serena, Stilicho's wife, Theodosius's niece. Her father, Theodosius's brother, had passed away young, and she had been raised by her emperor uncle, who took dearly to his niece, involving himself in her education and upbringing. It was he who had arranged for her to marry his loyal Vandal chief of staff, and in all possibility, it was Serena who made Stilicho's career. Her unimpeachable pedigree gave her Vandal husband the confidence he needed to invent a powerful position for himself. For two decades, he worked as a combination of chief of staff and general, and excelled at it, tasked by Theodosius himself to travel to Persia to negotiate the emperor's landmark treaty. By the time he was in his forties, few people could have given Stilicho orders. But he worked quietly, as a cautious Vandal might, and was commanding the western army when the emperor died.

At the funeral in Milan, there had been talk of Theodosius's last wishes; the deceased emperor, it was rumored, had appointed Stilicho, his son-in-law, as guardian over both his boys. No one in the government was able to corroborate the story at the time. But as news of Alaric's actions in the east began to spread beyond Greece and Constantinople, it became increasingly clear, to Stilicho and others, that the recent spike in

Gothic violence demanded a proper military response. And Stilicho was not a soldier who waited for permission to act. While Arcadius looked to his court for guidance and Honorius dawdled, Stilicho's impatience proved incurable, and he informed the two indecisive children that he would resolve the matter himself. Within a year of Theodosius's death, the thirty-seven-year-old Vandal general set out to track Alaric down in Greece. Stilicho knew Alaric's qualifications as a soldier. The man was battle-tested, and Theodosius had clearly admired his talents, which is likely why Stilicho went after him: with the intent to give Alaric more responsibility in the empire and to ensure that he was not alienated from it. Stilicho would have much to gain if he could corner Alaric in Greece and extend him an offer of aid. And if there really was conflict, then General Stilicho would stop it.

A predictable level of hemming and hawing arose from Arcadius's litigious staff in Constantinople at the prospect of a western official transacting business in the eastern territories, let alone a Vandal. Romans by and large scorned the Vandal people as an "effete, greedy, treasonous and sorrow-bringing race." The northern location of their tribal lands, beyond the central Danube, left them susceptible to Roman notions of their own centrality and others' cultural inferiority. During Stilicho's day, they were said to bring destruction, arson, and "madness"—*rabies,* in Latin—a word that forever tarnished their popular perception. From Stilicho's day to the moment when the Vandal Kingdom was established in North Africa in 435, Vandals endured a relentless whispering campaign about their character. It was Stilicho's people, not Alaric's, who birthed an "-ism" for cultural destruction.

Within months, if not weeks, of Rufinus's assassination, Stilicho was galloping into Greece, technically Arcadius's jurisdiction, unequivocally without Arcadius's authorization. The Roman government usually took an almost sadistic pleasure in watching ethnic groups savage one another; at the time Stilicho set out for Roman Greece, the Roman government was funding a mercenary Moorish soldier, Mascezel, with the expectation that he would kill his brother Gildo, who had begun harassing the empire's North African provinces. Policing the empire often required these complicated arrangements, persuading foreigners to betray their own tribes or to turn on their own kin. But this time it was a Vandal who pursued an upstart Goth.

It is highly likely, although not firmly established, that the two men eventually met sometime in 397. The Ionian coast of Epirus, with its scattering of pleasant fishing villages nestled below the region's rugged hills in the western Balkans, would have been an ideal, tranquil setting for a moment of diplomacy between two hardened soldiers. As each cautiously felt out the other, a decade's difference between them, the tone of their conversation must have been guarded and terse. Couldn't Alaric see himself in a position of greater authority, leading a campaign of his own? Stilicho asked. The funding was not a problem. Honorius would sign the order, and Alaric could command the troops. The mission would be to take the weapons factories of Illyricum, so that Stilicho could annex the Balkan territory for Honorius. It would be dangerous, but a good soldier never turned down a challenge, right? Government maps would have to be redrawn, of course, and Constantinople would not approve. So was Alaric in?

The reconstruction is not entirely fictitious. Zosimus, using Oly's testimony, places Alaric in Epirus after the turmoil of Greece. He describes Stilicho's intent to requisition the western provinces of Illyricum, and he documents Alaric's knowledge of and involvement in Stilicho's gutsy plot. The only questionable area of Zosimus's reporting is the date. Zosimus puts Stilicho's offer to Alaric a few years later, in the early fifth century, not in 397. But that detail might not be too important. If Stilicho had grand plans for seizing the provinces—and he did—it would have been smart to plant the seeds of an offer with Alaric during their first meeting, in Epirus.

Nothing came of Stilicho's proposal. Before any promises could be exchanged, word of Stilicho's designs, if not of the two men's actual meeting, leaked. Arcadius's advisers immediately expelled Stilicho from their territories. Whether by hard intelligence or pure suspicion, they almost certainly had an inkling of Stilicho's plot and, to thwart it, countered Stilicho's offer. The eastern palace was ready to promote Alaric to general. Alaric accepted.

There was a story passed around Stilicho's circles in those days. In a remote time in Roman history, two military men found themselves in a standoff. Every child in Stilicho's day knew their names: Marius and Sulla. Dead for five centuries, they lived under the Roman Republic when the crises facing the government were much different. Small-town Italians who had helped Rome expand its territory were demanding citizenship rights for having served the people of the great capital even though they lived outside Rome's walls. Never before had the Senate been forced to consider amending its own hallowed legal traditions to make new citizens.

Their demands triggered a political firestorm. Romans and Italians fought a nearly four-year war to resolve the dispute, the Social War of the first century B.C. Roman soldiers largely crushed their opponents on the battlefield, but upon the cessation of hostilities, in order to ensure a lasting peace, it was stipulated that all adult males in Italy would forever hold the status of Roman citizens. The Romans always talked about that revolutionary time by recalling the lives of its two most outspoken generals, Marius and Sulla.

"The Roman Marius used to call his rival Sulla two wild beasts in one," the story went. General Sulla could be vicious, merciless, and savage one day but careful, cunning, and sly the next. As a rival, Marius said, the man was both a lion and a fox, and Marius "feared the fox more." The lesson, one a savvy soldier like Stilicho would have heard, was that your most dangerous adversary could often be two things at once.

CHAPTER EIGHT

Into the Labyrinth

To the fight / which lies before me now I go with Justice.
—EURIPIDES

In 397 Arcadius's men appointed Alaric general of Illyricum. He had a salary, his own staff, and probably a small office with a transom window, expensive marble paneling, and an expertly laid herringbone brick floor whose occasional dampness could always be covered with a nice rug. It speaks to the paradoxes of the Roman Empire that, during these difficult years when many Gothic immigrants performed menial labor in Roman villas and others experienced the soul-crushing realities of slavery, Alaric began enjoying his first promotion and all the perks that came with it.

By the late fourth century, thirty thousand Goths called the city of Rome their home; many more had scattered throughout the empire. Some lived as free people and partook in the luxuries of urban living their cities offered. But others, brought into the empire by slave traders, worked as butlers, cooks, and errand runners, and their quality of life depended on the personality and the morals of their masters. Alaric's rapid, nearly stratospheric rise meant that he now policed towns, delegated instructions, and answered petitions in collaboration with the praetorian prefect and the *dux,* respectively the senior civilian and military authorities of Illyricum.

The leaders of Rome's four imperial prefectures oversaw a small empire of their own. They collected tariffs, supervised construction projects, and protected the postal service. The military played a supportive role in these endeavors, and a range of both stimulating and tedious tasks likely consumed Alaric's days. Illyricum had the most jig-sawed jurisdiction of the four. Officially, Constantinople superintended its affairs, but the land was a rather in-between place where powerful people rarely lingered. Unlike the other prefectures, whose names more obviously corresponded to their locations—Gaul, the East, and the pre-fecture of Italy-Africa, the latter of whose economies were so tightly bound that the Romans administered the cross-continental area as a single unit—Illyricum managed the nearly impossible feat of touching both the Danube River and the Mediterranean Sea. It was known for its munitions factories and its Adriatic ports, the advantages Stilicho had proposed wresting away from Arcadius's men.

The real reward for Alaric, as he settled into his new role, may have come from his emotional connection to the land. Illyricum's northern border was the western extension of the Danube. He was both near to and far from his childhood home and its attendant memories, and as he ascended in the Roman ranks, it is clear that he remained grounded in Gothic values, a balancing act that attests to his charismatic leadership, his strong sense of Gothic identity, and his personal priorities.

It was a honeymoon on two accounts. By then, he also very likely had wed a Gothic bride. Ancient sources never give his wife's name, not even Jordanes, the sympathetic Gothic historian. The only surviving detail about her comes from the unflattering poetry of Claudian, who por-trayed her as a woman of insatiable greed: a "shrill" Gothic wife with expensive taste in jewelry, which she had hoped her husband would steal for her from Roman aristocrats.

As Alaric settled into his new roles, as government appointee and husband, many other Goths joined him in Illyricum, never abandon-ing the man who had fought for their basic necessities in Greece. Schol-ars looking at these years traditionally style his loyal companions the "Visigoths" to distinguish them from other Goths located across the empire, but the word, which means "West Goths," didn't exist in the late fourth century. It was a creation of the sixth century, when it functioned as a handy tool for distinguishing the Visigoths from the Ostrogoths, or

"East Goths," who would come to govern Italy after the fall of the last emperor. Still, undeniable bonds formed during Alaric's Illyricum years among the men later called Visigoths, even if much of that fellowship came as a result of hardship and adversity.

Jealous Romans distrusted foreigners who earned promotions. A "barbarian by extraction" might be incapable of restraining his "cruel and violent disposition," the fiery Christian bishop Synesius said, if he were handed more authority. The Gothic people, he maintained, were a fearsome, ferocious, and animalistic race, and the government should "admit no fellowship with these foreigners" but, rather, would do better to "disown their participation" in public life. Even the talented ones were little more than animal-skin savages who brought embarrassment to real "men who wear the Roman general's cloak." The whole history of the republic was teetering on a "razor's edge" because of the immigrant crisis, and politicians had to crack down, he said: "The shepherd must not mix wolves with his dogs, even if, caught as whelps, they may seem to be tamed." The more bitter Romans imagined that immigrants made decisions based solely on their own ethnic allegiances, accusing Gainas, Alaric's mentor and now a general stationed in the eastern Mediterranean, of awarding "the principal commissions in the army to his relations."

A Goth in Alaric's post would not have gone unnoticed. During his Illyricum years, Bishop Synesius, motivated by an increasing number of Gothic promotions, published an allegory calling for the defense of Roman culture against foreigners. Set in ancient Egypt, Synesius's story, called "An Egyptian Fable," involved two brothers who were fighting for control of the government. The good brother wanted to protect Egypt from the influence of the malevolent "Scythians," a tribe who hailed from frigid northern lands and whose questionable moral character had overtaken his evil brother's judgment. (In Roman literature, Scythians were regularly used as a cipher for Goths because they shared a northern origin.) Whether Synesius intended his story to be read as a polemic against Alaric specifically, "An Egyptian Fable" found an audience among Romans who already held immigrants in contempt.

Other Romans twisted chapter and verse of the well-nigh sacred text of Homer to fit their bigotry. In order for the Roman Empire to recover its military might, the government should prohibit foreigners from advancement, they said, and the emperors should act aggressively to "drive out these ill-omened dogs." In Homer's *Iliad* the off-color phrase is attributed to the Trojan prince Hector, who uses this animal imagery to rally his troops against the Greek invaders. Homer used Hector's monologue to inflame the passions of his own Greek audience, who would have been appalled by its basic lack of decency.

But recalcitrant Romans in Alaric's day didn't care whether they accurately understood Homer's scene. Any quotation, from any historic author, that could support their anti-immigrant view was a legitimate weapon in these debates except, oddly, Jesus's words. In the Gospels, Jesus had said, "I was a stranger and you welcomed me." But Roman Christians conspicuously never mentioned that line during the intense immigration debates of the early fifth century. And by 399, the hard-liners had their sights set on their next target, an Armenian immigrant named Eutropius who had become a high-profile politician in Constantinople.

Eutropius had followed an unconventional path to the halls of Roman power, although his parents may have planned for their boy's career as a political adviser by arranging for his early castration. Court eunuchs were invaluable counselors and liaisons in Persia and Rome, where politicians considered them trustworthy, a highly desirable trait in the scheming corridors of any palace. Politicians' wives regularly confided in them. Yet misfortune ultimately thwarted Eutropius's parents' plans, when slave traders on the Roman Empire's eastern border captured their castrated boy and sold him into bondage before he reached adolescence. Later, with the financial help of a generous owner, he was allowed to buy his freedom. Lucky Roman slaves often could do so, and—although the point is controversial—he probably did earn Roman citizenship through his manumission. Eventually, he settled in Constantinople, drawn to the enchanting city by its mix of foreign diplomats, government officials, and cultural sophistication. He leapt onto the political scene.

With language skills, a knowledge of geography, and an international fluency that few Romans possessed, Eutropius quickly proved a capable adviser to Emperor Arcadius. From the emperor he earned an appointment as consul, or chief executive, of Constantinople, an unprecedented advancement for an Armenian-born immigrant.

Partisans jeered at this "ape" in fancy clothes. It would have been less shameful "if a woman were in charge," they said. (Women, who were otherwise permitted a range of liberties, such as managing their own financial affairs and serving as public priestesses, were, nevertheless, forbidden from holding the office of consul.) At least the flamboyantly Gothic Rufinus had been a real man, others griped. This one could barely act the part. Mercilessly, the opposition hit Eutropius with rounds of tactless questions no other Roman politician had to answer: How many owners did he recall having? How many slave catalogs had he been listed in? The questions came from rich, well-placed members of the establishment to whom nothing was more unnerving, as the poet Claudian put it, "than a poor man who stumbles into prosperity."

"I dare you to find, onstage or off, a man who inspires more laughter than a comedy or more sorrow than a tragic play," Claudian dared his readers, in a pamphlet he called *Against Eutropius*. Audiences laughed at the poet's cartoon version of the hardworking Roman consul. But by the year's end, a faction in Constantinople had forced Eutropius from power. In 399, they executed him.

In this poisonous atmosphere, even a eunuch's acquaintances did not escape unharmed. Eutropius's opponents mocked his friends and allies for indulging in lavish dinner parties of exotic peacock, parrot, and expensive varieties of fish. "Not the Aegean, not deep Propontis, not Maeotis's lake afar can sate their appetites," Claudian said. Ordinarily, a politico's dinner menus would never have deserved public scrutiny because it was naturally assumed that every officeholder acted this way. But these were a band of profligates who flaunted traditional values, the partisans insisted. If the empire were ever attacked, if savage Huns ever stormed the city's gates, Eutropius's staff would surely fail to protect the people, they said. How could any of them be entrusted with the empire's security when their loyalties were tarnished by mere association with such a questionable man? The critics concluded: "Rome, they despise."

The situation turned vile, and not just for Armenians. While Claudian stridently compared immigrants to "a pestilence" devouring "our land," other minority groups inside the empire, like Roman Jews, watched helplessly as civic society unraveled. After Rome's three Jewish Wars, which devastated the Jewish populations of Judaea and Egypt during the first and second centuries A.D., the idea of an open Jewish resistance to the empire had lost its appeal. As the painful memories of war faded, Jewish communities had proudly grown more visible. They raised money to repair synagogues, buried their dead in brightly painted tombs, and put important symbols on their buildings, like the menorah, the lampstand that was a powerful reminder of the lost Temple in Jerusalem. With an identity forged in hardship, they were among the many communities to benefit from the milestone Edict of Milan.

During Arcadius and Honorius's administration, quiet discrimination and open violence threatened to overturn those hard-won triumphs. On April 11, 399, the emperors declared the Jewish faith, while technically still legal, an "unworthy superstition," and they ordered the Jewish patriarch, the ancient community's spiritual leader, to cease collecting financial contributions from local synagogues. "We are appropriating [this money] and [have] abolished the practice," the law announced. Anti-Jewish incidents were on the rise, with both verbal and physical attacks warranting public comment from the palace.

Jews should be left alone in their synagogues, Arcadius wrote to the governor of Illyricum in 397. Since a large part of the anti-Jewish sentiment was disseminated from the empire's pulpits, where Christian preachers planted seeds of suspicion of Jews in the minds of their unsuspecting congregations, it's not improbable to imagine that Alaric, who was then settling into his new position in Illyricum, saw one or two perpetrators walk out of a local church.

The situation reached historic lows in the empire's cultural capital, Rome. Two years after Arcadius's imperial directive aimed to stop attacks on Jews in the towns of Illyricum, further legislation forbid residents of Rome from wearing two items of clothing, *tzangae* and *bracchae,* which sounded as strange in Latin as they looked foreign on people strolling the city's streets of volcanic cobblestones: "boots" and "pants." It is unlikely that the emperors intended the legislation to police Roman citizens for embracing the latest fashion trends. The ban on foreign clothes, a flagrant betrayal of Rome's usually permissive cultural mores, instead fell heavily on immigrants who wore their own ethnic dress.

In truth, many Romans were deeply concerned about the possibility of foreign customs invading their lives, and they pressed the boy emperors to wall off these outside influences. Claudian profiled one of these panicked constituents, a hardworking anonymous farmer from northern Italy. He was perhaps in his fifties or sixties when Claudian spoke with him, and he was proud to have known only the dusty roads around his hometown of Verona. Fame, politics, and the fancier accoutrements of urban living were other people's prerogative, he told the poet. He dreamed of simple comforts, as Claudian made clear in his short profile of the man:

> Happy is the one at home.
> The farmhouse watches him grow;
> counts the ages with a stick
> in dirt he crawled. Commotion
> never rocked his future.

> Never someone's guest,
> or experienced the sea,
> heard the soldier's trumpet,
> suffered shouting in the forum.
> Unteachable, unconcerned,

he took it in, not a care—
tracks years by crops, not consuls;
sees fall in its apples, spring
in its flowers. Suns come and
go; the world in a day for

a simple man, who knows the
acorn in his oak tree.
Farther than bright India is
Verona; Lake Garda, like
the Red Sea. Now he's a
grandfather, trunks for arms.

Let someone else wander
the ends of the earth. There are
many ways to enjoy life,
not all of them on the road.

Claudian's poem reminded many Romans about the deep contradictions at the heart of their society and expressed a "simple man's" nos-
talgia for a Roman way of life that long predated the complexities of
the world around him. While the empire's cities drew people of every
race and ethnicity, many citizens still hesitated to welcome people from
beyond the borders. Newness brought anxiety with it and, as the farmer
hinted, an unnecessary level of "commotion." Yet by the early fifth century, those isolationist sentiments had been driving Rome's immigration policies for decades, and neither the citizens who affirmed those
views nor the emperors who encouraged them showed any willingness
to reverse course.

The brutal reality of Roman bigotry in these years almost certainly
led to the death of Alaric's mentor, Gainas. As foreigners achieved more
political successes and a discontent with immigrants grew widespread,

many Goths considered the government's response inadequate. Entire communities of Gothic immigrants needed land, food, and work and lacked protections commensurate with those for Roman citizens, such as laws against capture by slave hunters, which the emperors and the Senate were disinclined to consider or incapable of providing. By the late 390s, the plight of Gothic communities in Asia Minor, specifically, had become an urgent issue. In their desperation, Goths nominated a man named Tribigild to raise alarm and champion their cause. After he began causing disturbances in nearby cities, the Roman government ordered Gainas to intervene.

Instead of reaching a resolution, Gainas joined the revolt. A lack of opportunity to advance his own career, after Rufinus's assassination, may have convinced him to support Tribigild's protests. Inspired by their passionate demonstrations, Gainas met the rebellious Gothic leader, and they formulated a plan. Gainas wrote to Arcadius's palace and demanded, on behalf of the movement, the immediate dismissal of several anti-Gothic politicians from the emperor's inner circle. Surprisingly, Arcadius's men consented, and at the start of 400, Gainas returned to Constantinople, believing that he and Tribigild had achieved some measure of change. Tribigild died within the year. But with most of Constantinople's more objectionable leaders sent off to early retirement, Gainas assumed that the Goths' fate would improve. It did not.

Members of the establishment did not view Gainas's return to Constantinople so charitably. Whether from malice or ignorance, by early 400, they were circulating rumors that his homecoming would lead to an imminent attack. Socrates of Constantinople, a contemporary church writer, said Gainas had come back to the city "for the purpose of burning down the palace." The brutish Goth hoped to turn the city into a tomb for the Christian souls who did not yet know they were going to die. Panic gripped the citizens.

After a rogue group of Goths killed the city's gate patrol one night in late spring or early summer of that year, unconfirmed talk spread that Goths had been trying to smuggle weapons into the city. People also mentioned a plot to rob Constantinople's bankers. Neither piece of gossip was ever substantiated. In all likelihood, it's just as probable that the guards who blocked the Goths from entering the city based their decision on nothing but their own stubborn prejudices, and that the violence erupted in a tense moment of mutual distrust.

Whatever happened, Arcadius quickly moved to assert control and declared Gainas an enemy of the state. Constantinople's residents, already alarmed by the murdered guards, turned into a frenzied mob at the news and chased the city's Gothic residents from their homes. Many Goths fled to their local church. On July 12, 400, an angry band of Roman citizens came to its wooden doors carrying torches and "burnt it to the ground." Seven thousand Gothic Christians reportedly lost their lives in the inferno.

Gainas had no more options. The emperor had publicly denounced him, the eastern capital was a smoldering Gothic pyre, and his onetime ally, Tribigild, was dead. In a moment that must have mixed resignation with the reality of defeat, he hastened northward to Gothia, thinking he could escape by returning home. The ruthless Gothic soldier Fravitta, whose sword thrust at a state dinner party decades ago had launched his successful career, went in pursuit. Perhaps unbeknownst to Gainas, Hunnish warlords—they had devastated Gothia in recent years—already occupied the other side of the Danube. There was no escape. Whether apprehended on Roman land or in Gothic territory, by early in the year of 401, Gainas was dead. Fravitta marched through the streets of Constantinople carrying his head, "seasoned with salt." Three years later, death would finally overtake even Gainas's shameless captor in Constantinople, where Fravitta was swept up in another outbreak of violence targeting foreigners.

The young Arcadius wasted no time in demanding a tribute for himself to honor the successful suppression of Gainas' revolt. Artisans were instructed to carve reliefs for a victory monument to be modeled after Trajan's Column in Rome. On its winding panels, they depicted every episode in the hunt for Gainas, from his flight to his dismemberment:

Romans gathered in the streets of Constantinople to cheer for Fravitta's success; naked tribesmen in Gothia quaking at the sight of the arrival of Fravitta's Roman army. Other scenes showed the admirals of the Roman navy stationed at the Hellespont, ready to thwart Gainas's attempt to flee by sea. And at the column's crown was placed a statue of Arcadius and his brother, embracing in the widely recognized personification of *concordia,* or "harmony." Their silhouette against the horizon consummated a bond between eastern and western territories that would have made their father proud. When it was completed in the 420s, Arcadius's monument reprised the jingoism familiar from an earlier age of Roman conquests and towered pompously over Constantinople, a triumph of what the Romans considered art.

The pagan senator Symmachus once remarked in the heat of Rome's battle for religious freedom, "The truth of why things happen is hidden at the end of a multiplicity of roads and pathways." He was referring to the mysterious *ratio,* or reason, that lay behind the sometimes inexplicable events that shake our lives. Symmachus's outlook was humble, open-minded, and spiritually transcendent. But these were not ideas his uncompromising political opponents cared to hear. Many Christians at the time espoused more rigid ideologies, embracing partisanship and intolerance, among their own stubborn convictions.

The Christian poet Prudentius, for example, refused to let the pagan senator have the final word on matters of faith. In his fifties by the time Gainas was killed, Prudentius, who had dedicated a lifetime to writing, had grown convinced that the senator's tolerance for other religious beliefs was fundamentally dangerous for their times. Christians should not be given choices about what to believe. "The windings of the labyrinth offer little but doubtful corners and the promise of more uncertainty," Prudentius said in a sharp retort to the senator, a poem he released titled *Against Symmachus.*

Prudentius knew that people had choices and that, at some point in their lives, everyone faced difficult decisions. "I don't deny that the fork in the road can take our human affairs in two directions," he confessed. But when it came to religion, the most important choice a Roman faced was whether to believe in the Christian God or the pagan gods. For Prudentius, there was one and only one path toward understanding God, and he communicated the urgency of that message to hordes of Christian readers, who fawned over his spiritual epic, the *Psychomachia* ("The Battle of the Souls"), a poem that remained popular among Christians well into the Middle Ages.

As a Roman set in his ways, Prudentius disregarded the plight of Gothic immigrants. And as a man of faith, raised to see the world as locked in a spiritual war, he believed that his version of Christianity offered the only path to salvation. But as a human and as a writer, Prudentius also realized something profound: that everyone, in everything they did, at least had the freedom to make their own futures.

The reason why events turned out *this* way, not *that* way, was a perennial topic of conversation in Rome's philosophical, scientific, and literary salons. Speculation about the natural world, about the origins of matter and what kinds of realities might exist beyond our perception of it, led to important debates about how we derive our moral principles—topics that had fascinated the Romans and Greeks for hundreds of years. In a poem Claudian wrote during the early months of Arcadius and Honorius's reign, he, too, paused to reflect on the origins of the universe and described the frustration of not knowing our ultimate place in it.

My mind wavers between
two options: Does someone
guide our world, or does it
lack a captain and we
float on by chance?

Earth and sky have signed a
treaty. Land and sea share

a border. Years pass. Sun and moon
rise and set, ratified
by a deity who

has made it all happen:
stars to move, crops to grow,
Phoebe to be lit by
a distant fire, Sol
to burn on his own.

But then I saw the fog
covering today's world.
Criminals are heroes,
Decent men, harassed. God,
it tempted me with that

other road: where atoms
charge in empty space and
we owe life to chance, not
design—vague gods, no gods,
or yet, none who care.

Claudian was summarizing the allure of a philosophical system called
Epicureanism, named for a Hellenistic philosopher and early scientific
thinker who believed that "atoms" constituted the foundation of the
natural world. Romans of the republic, like the poet Lucretius, author
of *On the Nature of Things,* had warmed to Epicurus's ideas because
they underscored how much of our own lives we owe to chance and, by
extension, how needlessly we worry about the future. For in a universe
made of indestructible particles and "empty space," as Claudian says,
correctly recapitulating the core Epicurean teachings, our fear of pain
or death should amount to nothing. With no gods to punish us and no
hope of afterlife, we pass our lives, and then we return to dust.

As men like Prudentius and Claudian waxed poetic, it was Alaric, stuck in the no-man's-land of Illyricum, who faced his own set of difficult choices. It was a Roman general's business to stay informed of events and to know what was happening outside his camp. The manuals encouraged military leaders to be "watchful, sober, and discreet." Usually, that meant keeping an eye on "the habits of the enemy." But Gainas had been a friend, a fellow soldier, and a Goth. And the shocking report of his murder, along with descriptions of his seasoned skull, would have been delivered to Illyricum quickly in early 401.

The news that Gainas was dead marked the start of Alaric's terrible spring. Tense situations demanded vigilance, and the military handbooks offered some guidance as well, recommending "caution and prudence." Above all, reliable intelligence in the cloud of war was essential. It was paramount for a Roman general "to find out everything from intelligent men, from men of rank, and those who know the localities, individually." The goal was "to put together the truth from a number of witnesses."

Alaric likely filled his anxious summer doing just that. With the recent church arson in Constantinople, the mass murder of the city's Gothic community, and the spectacular parade of anti-Gothic sentiment after Gainas's capture, it was obvious that a Goth could no longer be safe on the streets of many Roman cities. No immigrant could feel welcome standing underneath Arcadius's horrendous column, even in its half-finished state. But if the Goths were expecting Alaric to use his position to speak on their behalf or craft a plan, there were few good options. Returning to Gothia, as Gainas had done, was too dangerous, and staying in Illyricum too uncertain. Doing nothing, however, would have been the least satisfying alternative of all, and while Alaric would have been trying to make that very decision, more upsetting news arrived.

Without any explanation, Alaric's command in Illyricum was terminated. Scholars surmise that Arcadius's advisers, looking to tighten their emperor's hold on power, had decided to redraw the boundaries of provinces within the prefecture, reallocate their military and financial resources, and better defend the lands closer to Constantinople. Because Alaric no longer fell inside the jurisdiction of their capital, he was told that he had been let go. Whether Arcadius's men were disingenuous about their reasons is unclear, but almost as quickly as they had promoted him, they had manipulated him out of his first and only real job. Just as many Gothic families had begun to respect him as their "king," Alaric's dream of a career in the government came to an end. Alaric would have passed a frantic autumn contemplating how best to help the people dependent on him.

It was said during the highly divisive years of Eutropius's administration that "universal contempt is sometimes a boon." That is, a man who was free of every expectation could always bank on the element of surprise for his next move. For Alaric, a path to justice may not have been clear at this moment, but experienced generals were always said to have a backup plan. And for a consummate strategist, that meant knowing when to pause and regroup.

Let's imagine Alaric calling for his maps, as any cornered general in his position well might. Sometimes, an ancient military "map" was nothing but a raw table of numbers that listed the distances between landmarks and towns. "The more conscientious generals," Vegetius said, "reportedly had itineraries of the provinces . . . not just annotated but illustrated as well," suggesting a high degree of surveying and draftsmanship. Although none of these drawings survives from Alaric's time, written descriptions of them suggest that they showed an extensive network of roads and cities, which helped field generals ensure a basic level of preparedness for war. The military's maps not only told "the distances between places in terms of the number of miles and the quality of roads" but also had "short-cuts, by-ways, mountains, and rivers, accurately described." Studying the topographical features of a prospective military theater on a table in one's own tent was an obvious advantage when it came to ancient warfare. Within two decades of Alaric's death, a team of talented cartographers boasted to the emperor that they had miniaturized these drawings, making them more convenient for an army on the move.

There was always a danger in consulting these devices. A spy could interpret a general's thoughtful brow, as he peered into the crevices of a papyrus scroll, as unauthorized war planning or, worse, the beginning of a usurpation. Military operations were easily exposed in the most inconsequential ways, as when news leaked in "a drunkard's babbling." Military men were expected to keep their plans hidden from all but the most essential eyes and ears. "The safest policy on expeditions is deemed to be keeping people ignorant of what one is going to do," noted Vegetius. If there was a tried-and-true lesson of war planning, it was the desire to protect confidentiality at all times. "The most important thing to be careful about," Vegetius wrote, "is to preserve secrecy concerning the places and routes by which the army is to proceed."

The need for strict security motivated the Romans to paint a drawing of the Minotaur on their army's standards. According to legend, the famous monster, half man and half bull, of Greek myth dwelled at the center of an ingenious labyrinth, from which he could never escape. Roman soldiers recognized the image of the beast and the maze as a metaphor for tight operational planning. "Just as he is said to have been hidden away in the innermost and most secret labyrinth," Vegetius explained, "so the general's plan should always be kept secret."

On November 18, 401, Alaric crossed into Italy with his followers, entering through the peninsula's Alpine wall near the harbor city of Aquileia. The mountains, which had once marked Rome's earliest frontier border, serving as an imposing defensive wall against the hostile Gauls, were no longer much of an obstacle. The land on both sides of them belonged to the empire, and there were no guards protecting its passes, the way there were at the customs towers outside Rome, Constantinople, and other large cities. Alaric and his Gothic men would have easily slipped onto the northern Italian roads. The Adriatic port gave easy access to the old Roman road, the Via Postumia, which led directly to the epicenter of western power, Milan. Smaller cities with large attractions—like Verona, with its impressive stone amphitheater—lay on or near this road, which stretched for miles across Italy's Po Valley. A branch of it, the Via Aemelia, led south to Rimini, where it merged with the Via Flaminia and, farther on, the Via Salaria, the Salt Road.

Over the next six to nine months, there were reports of Gothic attacks up and down the northern Italian roads. With the Goths' precarious predicament in Illyricum, their "king" unable to provide them with more than words of encouragement, and the eastern palace indifferent, if not hostile, to the Goths' troubles, Alaric had come west to solicit help. In one of his first acts upon entering Italy, he contacted Honorius. According to Jordanes's account of their correspondence, Alaric asked the young emperor to "permit the Goths to settle peaceably in Italy." If Honorius agreed to the terms, Alaric stipulated that the Goths "would live with the Romans in a way that others might believe them both to be one people."

Unfortunately, Jordanes's story of what transpired late in 401 is confused. Allegedly, Honorius was so eager for a settlement with the tribes harassing the provinces of western Europe, among them the Sueves, the Vandals, and the Franks, that he immediately granted the Goths farmland in Spain and Gaul. "For at this time," Jordanes wrote, "the empire had almost lost [these lands]."

None of that is true. While towns in those distant regions had witnessed a rise in tribal disturbances, the threat of the empire's losing whole swaths of its territory was unrealistic, and there was no negotiation between Honorius, Alaric, and the Goths—at least none that was ever witnessed and recorded by any Roman writer in 401. Alaric's anger would not have been so easily appeased. In truth, Jordanes probably invented the exchange based on facts that everyone knew by then. During that brief period of unrest in Italy, from late winter to the following spring, many Roman townspeople spotted Alaric and the Goths along the road to Gaul and Spain, the Via Postumia. Alaric famously faced Stilicho there, outside a small Italian village in the Piedmont called Pollentia.

On a rolling stretch of wide open farmland near that northern Italian city, on Easter Sunday, April 6, 402, Alaric and his band of Gothic supporters faced the Roman army sent to stop him—a confrontation Alaric almost avoided because it fell on a religious holiday, which he had initially planned to observe. Instead of engaging, he had called for a retreat "in respect for religion," one Roman contemporary, the Latin historian Orosius, explained. General Stilicho harbored no such scruples. He forced a fight and, in doing so, Orosius said, violated one of "the most revered days of the year." Stilicho's performance at the Battle of Pollentia may have persuaded Alaric to leave Italy, convincing him that he could not risk leading the Goths farther south. But the fact that the battle was fought on an important religious holiday distressed many Romans, who lamented that their empire had sacrificed their own Christian values to secure an easy victory.

Armed conflict filled the months after Alaric's march into Italy. He and Stilicho fought again at Verona, at several towns outside Milan, and near small villages in the northwestern hills of Italy, as far away as Asti. The fast-paced narratives and impressionistic histories that were written at the time by Oly, Philostorgius, and Orosius place Alaric all over the map of northern Italy, without narrating the events in chronological order. Later writers, among them, Socrates of Constantinople, Sozomen, Jordanes, and Zosimus, never corrected their predecessors' errors or found their structure perfectly satisfying. As a result, precision is lacking, and dates differ. In Jordanes's Gothic account, Alaric wins the Battle of Pollentia. In Claudian, he loses it. One modern scholar has called it a "draw." Ancient audiences may not have given much thought to this chronological and geographical jumble. Impressionistic storytelling was expected. In the practice of history, names and dates were always "full of errors and contradictions," Eunapius observed, and hashing out the details of who did what, when, and why always led to spirited disagreements. Even a polite gathering of learned people, Eunapius admitted, could devolve into "an un-chaired meeting."

But by 403 Stilicho had prevailed, and a defeated Alaric fled Italy that year, with nothing to show for his violent demonstrations. Rome's politicians rejoiced. Almost immediately, Claudian wove the current events into a story about Roman supremacy and Stilicho's military prowess.

Aristotle once said, "Poetry is the work of a gifted person, or of a maniac." Claudian, the fifth-century's insatiable dramatist, might have been both. No writer of the time surpassed Claudian for his sense of character. The two poems he wrote that retell the history of these years, although they have largely left the exact details of what happened hard to reconstruct, do succeed in putting a human face on a confusing sequence of events. A dearth of reliable facts never dismayed the partisan poet, and Claudian filled in the historical gaps with his own voice and ideas, bringing Rome's archenemy to life.

Claudian finished his penultimate poem, titled *The Gothic Attack,* as hostilities calmed down after the Battle of Pollentia. Educated Romans who attended its debut at the emperor's court endured the litany of Stilicho's accomplishments. They heard of terrible times in northern Italy, of savage invaders, and of the dejected morale of the group's foreign organizer. They also learned about Alaric's wife and her expensive tastes. But what Claudian captured best was the state of relief among the senators, the palace, and the emperor at knowing that Alaric had been routed.

A savage warrior, an avaricious upstart hunting for conquest, and a cocky soldier sure that he would prevail against the lesser man, Stilicho: Claudian's Alaric entranced Roman audiences. With thoughts, feelings, and motivations invented entirely by the Latin poet, the man from Pine Tree Island, as Claudian styled him to emphasize his backwater beginnings, conjured up a memorable villain for Romans, who were more accustomed to the silent Gothic slaves in their homes. In a dramatic monologue that would have been suitable for the Athenian stage, Claudian showed Alaric at the apex of greed, surveying the rich cities of northern Italy in 401 or 402, unaware that Stilicho would ultimately defeat him:

ALARIC: A deficit of good ideas,
age robbed of its good senses,
are what my advisers bring? A
Danube man never calls it quits.
With the marshes as my witness,
why should I give up, persuaded
by cowards when it used to be
nature bowed to me: mountains crouched,
the waters trickled, Caesars quaked.
Never may the spirits of my
Gothic homeland welcome me back.
This land I'll take as king or corpse.
Cities, people, the Alps, the Po:
I've seen victory everywhere. Why
should I stop at Rome? Goths prevail
even when arms are few. But with
a fresh supply of spears and shields,
helmets forged in forced labor for
me, now is the time to strike. Fate
compels me. The Romans, weakened
year after year, will be made my
slaves. It's time to pull the iron
from the fire. The gods urge it,
not as a dream or paths of birds.
I heard a voice in a grove, saying,
"Don't delay. If you crash the Alps,
you'll reach the city this year!" The
road is clear, the path ours. Only
a fool could misread these signs.

Claudian, who wrote these lines after Alaric's defeat, knew that
Alaric had already fled Italy and played with his audience's expectations

masterfully. Here was Alaric, a dubious believer of prophecy, a gullible Goth who longed to attack Rome because he answered to some questionably prophetic "voice in a grove." The silly soldier had heard a garbled prediction, Claudian averred, and confused the city of Rome—so famous it was simply called the "City," the *Urbs*—with the name of a similar-sounding river outside Pollentia, called the Orba. Claudian's "Alaric" was a bumbling idiot, but Romans applauded their own sophistication at deciphering the linguistic puzzle.

Less than two years later, the poet returned to the same material for his last performance, a work titled *Poem to Celebrate Emperor Honorius's Sixth Consulship*. Emperors regularly held one of the two consulships in Rome as a show of collegiality and an expression of their willingness to collaborate with the occasionally recalcitrant senators, who nevertheless helped the emperors govern in an advisory role. For the emperors, the honor of being named consul, which invested them with no additional authority, was largely symbolic. But symbols mattered in a government that lacked any written constitution, like Rome's; they set expectations, generated consensus, and gave the citizenry a shared, albeit simplified, framework for understanding the power of their civic institutions, whose workings were otherwise muddled by no end of statutes and codes. Honorius had held his first consulship when he was two years old, an appointment arranged by his father, who used the occasion to launch his family's dynasty. In 404, at twenty, Honorius held his sixth consulship, an excuse for more propaganda and the subject of Claudian's last known poem.

Running to nearly seven hundred lines of Latin, it was no doubt, for some Romans, as it would be for Claudian's harsher literary critics, a tedious, rambling, and unedited mess of a poem; others likely found it a tour de force, a triumph of artistic expression, and an irresistible who's who of the day. Theodosius's ghost makes an appearance. Arcadius and Honorius feature in it. So does Claudian's hero Stilicho, as well as his wife, Serena, and their little boy, Eucherius. The personified city of

Rome speaks, delicately chiding Honorius for opting to live in Ravenna, away from the marble halls of the old palace on the Palatine Hill, where esteemed emperors once dwelled. A humble citizen, as Theodosius's son surely was, could count himself worthy of living in the halls of such great predecessors, she says. There are talking rivers, extended descriptions of the pageantry in the Circus Maximus, and scenes of young Romans perched on the city's rooftops cheering an emperor their own age.

Claudian's final poem shows Alaric at his lowest. In one of the poem's most memorable similes, Claudian compares him to a washed-up pirate of the high seas whose ship has sunk.

> No more empty threats; the city
> is safe. Togas come and go again.
> The restless Goth has taken flight.
> He knows his way ahead is hard;
> to turn back, dangerous. Fear warns
> him every road is closed; rivers
> he once scorned as small, no thought
> of crossing anymore. That's how
> pirates act, terrors to the sea,
> when they see their life of crime
> finally runs aground.

Desperation has consumed the Gothic leader, the poet goes on to intimate. Alaric's formerly powerful magnetism fails him, and he has nowhere left to go, although it's hard to say at this point whether Claudian wanted his audiences to condemn Alaric or empathize with him. As the literary critic in Aristotle knew, good poets always excelled at achieving a maddening level of ambiguity. Here is how Claudian portrayed the disgraced Goth as he stands at the Alpine wall around 403, looking back into Italian territory, reflecting on his failures, and ruing his final confrontation with Stilicho.

ALARIC: Foul kingdom, that Goths are taxed
                 for sinister signs unheeded!
                 Fortune's wave brought me here; a stern
                 judge breathes down my neck to leave it.
                 I am exiled though I admit
                 mistakes were made: Pollentia
                 lost and treasure taken, chance or
                 destiny we can debate. But
                 I had my troops, and they had their
                 horses when we spied the tumbling
                 Apennines, sund'ring Italy
                 in two from Liguria to
                 Sicily, and faced a choice. Was
                 there a world beyond the borders
                 of my anger? Could a greater
                 prize await? I would have seen you
                 Rome, seen you then, if I had kept
                 on south through your fields, to make my
                 hunter earn his Pyrrhic victory.
                 But I couldn't risk the loss of
                 lives. Stilicho laid a skillful
                 trap, his peace be cursed, its terms
                 more dreaded than bondage. My own
                 death I pledged to him in defeat.
                 My people forfeited their hope.
                 Where will the weary find comfort
                 or counsel now, surrounded by
                 enemies? If only I had
                 lost it all in that dreadful war!
                 The loser of any hard-fought
                 contest will always be my hero,
                 death by a valiant sword better
                 than watching friends suffer wounded

trust. Where are they, my followers?
Are none left? My men despise me.
I must haul this wreckage somewhere,
but might will follow. And I will
never outrun Stilicho's name.

By the time the script was written for him, Alaric had already returned
to Illyricum, and Romans were speculating that he was dead.

CHAPTER NINE

The Crash

Who could believe that Rome, after being raised up by victories
over the whole world, should come crashing down and become
at once the mother and the grave of her peoples?

—JEROME OF BETHLEHEM

It was Stilicho's last act. As his onetime ward, Emperor Honorius,
publicly celebrated the Goths' expulsion from Italy, behind the palace curtains, the mood darkened. Honorius's advisers had expected
General Stilicho to end this Gothic problem years ago. When it had not
been wrapped up—first in Greece, now again in Italy—the palace man-
darins grew suspicious. It was twice that this Vandal had let Alaric slip
away, was it not? While the insinuations of treason wormed their way
through the members of the court, another invasion rocked Italy. An
audacious tribal leader named Radagaisus, arising from the middle
Danube and possibly a Goth, had stormed the river, evaded the border
army, and inexplicably reached the outskirts of Florence before Stilicho
stopped him. The gross security lapse confirmed the western establishment's profound mistrust of Serena's husband.

Hoping perhaps to take control of a situation quickly turning against
him, and with the memory of Radagaisus's unprecedented invasion still
fresh in people's minds, Stilicho reached out to broker a partnership
with Alaric. The two men met, or perhaps corresponded. Alaric agreed
to respond to other rising border threats, as needed, and to help Stilicho bring the entire prefecture of Illyricum under western control at
last—not just the individual territories Arcadius's men had divested five
years earlier, when Alaric had lost his appointment. The two men came
to their informal arrangement sometime around 406. Alaric would stay

in Epirus until Stilicho called. There would be the prospect of payment at last, money Alaric and his followers desperately needed.

Neither the orders nor any money came. Despondent again, Alaric packed, headed toward Italy, and composed a letter to Stilicho en route. Would Stilicho please forward payment at his nearest convenience for the time Alaric had spent waiting in Epirus? Zosimus only summarizes this letter, but a certain degree of politesse on Alaric's part might have been warranted, coming from a fiercely proud immigrant and loyal public servant who wanted to mask his crushing financial situation. Not only was he not drawing a salary at the time, but he and his followers owned no land, and everyone in the community feared for their security inside the empire.

As the year 408 opened, Stilicho convened a meeting of the senators in Rome and raised the issue of reimbursing Alaric. The men were outraged at mere mention of the laughable idea of using government funds to subsidize a mutinous Goth. One politician, Senator Lampadius, opposed the plan by quoting one of Cicero's old tirades against Marc Antony. *"Non est ista pax sed pactio servitutis!"* "This is not a pact of peace but the price of slavery!" The self-important elite always leapt at the opportunity to spring a literary allusion on their peers; Latin word games were easier than addressing real people's problems.

As the hardworking Vandal, Serena's devoted husband and the proud guardian of Theodosius's grown children, left the Senate meeting without any guarantee of money for Alaric, the whispers began in earnest that he must be a mole. Only a traitor, it was said, would undermine Rome's security by undertaking such a questionable arrangement. According to Oly, there was also a quiet fear that Stilicho wanted to put his son on the throne. On August 22, 408, a band of renegades from Honorius's palace ambushed Stilicho outside Ravenna and murdered him. They pursued his son, Eucherius, to Rome, and there they murdered the boy, as well. Whether they planned the family assassination with the expressed or tacit permission of the young emperor is unclear. But Serena, for the moment, survived.

The ancient world may not have been fair to Serena, but her maneuverings as a powerful woman veer history away from the hypermasculine world of the Roman battlefield and reveal how gender roles and family life shaped people's values on the eve of the Middle Ages. A Roman emperor's wife or daughter was expected to perform a role; throughout her marriage to Stilicho, Serena had funneled information, taken senators' suggestions, and carried gossip between her network and her husband's. A thoughtful wife could also bring a touch of humanity to the acts of a tyrant. Theodosius's first wife, Flacilla, had ministered to patients in hospitals, serving soup, handing out bread, dispensing medicine, and washing dirty bowls. Theodosius gave her the eminent title *Augusta,* effectively making her a co-ruler before she died. At her funeral, she was remembered for her unassuming compassion.

Serena doubtless understood the delicate balancing act Rome's conservative society required of her but had been clever at subverting it. There were tendencies a Roman woman could never show in public, like inclining toward innovation or risk-taking. Roman men avoided those dangerous traits, too, but in a Roman woman, any hint of progressivism was downright scandalous. During their ten years of marriage, Arcadius's wife, Eudoxia, gained a reputation for such fierce self-assertion that she became the target of frequent political attacks from church pulpits. But she preserved her own authority at home by bearing her husband multiple sons, one of whom, Theodosius the Second—named for his revolutionary grandfather—would become Honorius's partner in governing Rome the very year Stilicho was killed.

Confidently marching at the front of imperial processions, Serena also dared to be bold. During one of Theodosius's victory parades, she had ripped an expensive necklace, a prayerful Roman's dedication, from a pagan goddess's statue. The theft earned her an immediate rebuke from an elderly eyewitness, but her religious vandalism endeared her to her uncle. He was, after all, celebrating the end of the pagan cults. A woman in Serena's position did not need to fear using her voice.

Modesty was more becoming to her after her uncle's death. For nearly

twenty-five years, she played Stilicho's supportive wife well, and her
Vandal husband must have been grateful for her faith in him. She was,
and there is no doubt about it, her husband's most valuable confidant and
most vocal champion. Together, the couple served Theodosius and protected his sons, even when the responsibilities taxed their own family.
While Stilicho was on a campaign, they settled into a routine of living
apart. Because both husband and wife traveled, they sometimes found
themselves thousands of miles away from each other in two entirely different cities from their home. They threw an extravagant state party to
celebrate the wedding of their daughter Maria to the young Honorius,
which Claudian recorded in flattering verses as though it were a visit
from the Olympian gods. Romans showered the young ruling family "in
a mist of purple blossoms," and the prince gave his bride an heirloom,
the empress Livia's four-hundred-year-old jewels. Stilicho and Serena
had wound themselves even more inextricably into the workings of
imperial power.

Of all the Roman souls in all the taverns of the empire that might
have instantly reminded Alaric of himself—had they ever met—it might
have been Serena's. She was Alaric's age, and the two were cursed for
being inopportunely born. As a Roman woman, she knew what it was
like to be overlooked; as a Gothic man, he knew what it was like to be
ignored. History never gave Serena a chance to stand on equal footing
with her uncle's male heirs, Arcadius and Honorius. And Alaric was
given his opportunity to serve, but never anything more. Recogniz-
ing the parallels in their lives is not modern psychology. The Romans
intuited their connection. Among Oly's pile of "material for history" is
found this one provocative note: Serena "was thought to be the reason
for Alaric's march on Rome."

How such a claim could be true is almost impossible to figure out in
hindsight. What could Stilicho's wife have done or said to inspire Alaric's attack? And when? There is no recorded meeting between the two of
them ever, but Oly scribbled this note down. Zosimus did not trust the
account; but if the observation is even remotely true, one guesses that

Serena saw in Alaric what she saw in her husband: an outsider whose career had gone as far as the unjust system would allow, an eminently capable man who, through no fault of his own, would be denied further success, without her own expert hand.

It's remarkable how one single line of history can be so absorbing that it brings out all the maybes. Maybe Alaric and Serena did meet. Maybe Zosimus was wrong to doubt Oly's remark. Maybe Alaric did benefit, even at a distance, from a strong Roman woman's vote of support. Serena left no records of her own, but there is no mistaking her power. History lets us picture her fondling that stolen necklace of hers, in crucial moments when she considered if and how to use her authority.

⟩☜

In the days that followed Stilicho's death, the empire witnessed the outbreak of a violent anti-immigrant sentiment on its streets. Emboldened by the public killing of a Vandal, Romans pent up with anger at foreigners openly turned their rage against them. In the city of Rome, they attacked Gothic men, women, and children indiscriminately. In response, thirty thousand Goths, almost the entire Gothic population of the historical capital, poured into the streets to protest the brutality and to demand political changes. Comfortably isolated in the marshes of the northern Adriatic Sea, Emperor Honorius never heard their voices.

As the weeks passed, Honorius's government, opposed to any corrective course of action, hunkered down, hoping that the anger in the streets would dissipate. With the onset of autumn, tempers subsided, and the Romans returned to their usual routines. But not for long. The winter of 408 ushered in first weeks, then months without food.

From the senatorial elite to the lowly street sweeper, everyone in the city felt the hunger pains. The customary "workman's lunch," an already "insipid" plate of Romans beets, was served without its usual finishing touches of wine and pepper. There were no elegant holiday food gifts this year for Roman lawyers: no frankincense, no Lucanian sausages, no Libyan figs. The boxwood pepper mills in the kitchens of wealthier villas

were ground bone-dry. Romans experienced an abrupt return to a simpler time, an age before their empire's rise, when, as Pliny put it, there
had been "no demand for Indian pepper and the luxuries that we import
from overseas." In those days, Rome's hills were a collection of humble
neighborhoods where modest families picked herbs from tiny gardens
outside their windows and a knocked-over flower pot was the extent
of a neighborhood disturbance. But every Roman cupboard had at least
some seasoning on hand. Nothing was more dreadful to the Roman pal-
ate throughout the city's long history than food of "dismal uniformity."

In 408, more than salt, wine, and delicacies went missing from the
tables. There was no grain with which to bake bread, no olive oil or
pork—staples that normally arrived in regular shipments from the farms
of northern Africa. No dust storm in Africa or early frost in southern
Italy's fertile fields had provided advance warning of any drought. The
city itself had an extensive supply of emergency food stored in sophisticated brick vaults, which engineers had designed to be elevated, to protect those supplies from mildew and mold. But the *horrea*, the massive
warehouses at the harbors of Portus and Ostia, remained mysteriously
locked. Captains were met near the lighthouse and told to turn their
ships around, regardless of their cargo. There would be no disembarking.

Frustration at the political inaction had at last brought Alaric and
his men to Rome's riverbanks, where they stopped all boats and barges
from entering the capital. "Anger and indignation" were two of the most
effective weapons in a general's arsenal, and Alaric surely put them to
effective use as he rallied his men for their coordinated assault on the
harbor. "Say anything by which the soldiers' minds may be provoked
to hatred of their adversaries by arousing their anger and indignation,"
the military handbooks instructed—and that winter he did. When news
reached the Gothic camps that Romans were marshaling local forces
to break the blockade, Alaric is alleged by Zosimus to have reacted
with maniacal delight. "Thicker grass is easier to mow than thinner,"
he quipped. Armed Gothic guards kept the Portus warehouses on lock-
down for months.

Basic training had taught Alaric that a famine would always be "more terrible than the sword" because it threw unsuspecting populations into "irrecoverable confusion." Oly says that Alaric blockaded Rome because of "Stilicho's execution."

By late November or early December, the public's general bewilderment at the food shortage turned to panic as people asked what was happening and when it would end. Who was this "pepper-sharp" burglar (as literary Romans styled fast-handed thieves) holding up their deliveries? Public officials, more interested in finding scapegoats than in alleviating the growing starvation, accused Serena of orchestrating the famine with the enemy—an unsupported charge that, nevertheless, may have prompted Oly's note about how she "was thought to be the reason for Alaric's march on Rome." While Alaric choked the harbor, a death squad from Honorius's palace went to her villa. They strangled Serena that winter.

She had outlived nearly everyone who had been close to her: her crusading emperor uncle; her young daughter Maria, whom she had wed to the imperial family and whose early death must have broken her heart; her little boy, Eucherius, who fell for no other reason than his father's supposed treachery. And she had lived through the murder of her own husband, Stilicho, a restless man whose ambitions were ultimately checked by forces beyond his control. Serena died four months after her husband's untimely death as the year changed to 409. She was survived by her younger daughter, Thermantia, whom Honorius had taken as his second wife after Maria's sudden passing.

Claudian, in the opening lines of his last poem, had described what it was like to search for fulfillment. People are always hounded by their obsessions, he said: from the tasks of their daily life to their hopes for a different future. But sometimes, the graying poet wrote, we are trapped by our deepest desires:

The hunter who reclines returns
in his mind to the woods and bogs.

Judges relive their court cases.
Drivers, they dream of the chariot—
hear the hooves, muscle horses
around the posts. Lovers smile when
they steal the memory of a love.
Shopkeepers give change in their sleep;
the penniless wish for riches.
But not even night's magic will
bring a cool drink to the thirsty.

Even poets, Claudian admitted, were pursued at night by rhythms and beats. When writers slept, they dreamed of seeing perfection on the page. But when they were awake, they followed the daily drudge to the sludge of the inkwell and prayed for the right words to come, longing, just like everyone else, to recognize happiness.

What drove Alaric to leave Illyricum again, to enter Italy again, and to attack Rome? Many Romans, if they were asked in those years, would have given pat responses to these complex questions. Goths didn't know any better, they would have said; his people were barbarians. Some Christians would have explained that he had been driven to his heinous act by evil.

Christians of the day understood abstract, spiritual, and cosmic motivations. Sozomen, the author of a popular book titled *Church History,* told his readers the story of a monk who, encountering Alaric on his way to Rome, pleaded with him not to take the city hostage. Alaric confessed that he was doing so reluctantly but that "something deeply troubling" motivated him, and he "fulfilled it by going [to the city of Rome]." Although the story is probably fictional, told after the fact to soothe the spiritual nerves of Christians and to absolve them of their own political indifference, it would have sounded perfectly plausible to many Romans; for them, it was easier to attribute Alaric's attack to a vague sense of "something deeply troubling" rather than to confront the inequalities of their present world.

For three decades, Gothic families had been forced to live without the legal protections afforded their Roman neighbors. Some, we can assume, found work and settled down. Others, like the majority of Alaric's followers, seem to have shuffled temporarily between cities where they might be fortunate to receive some generous handouts of food. But regardless of their own individual success stories, every Goth lived precariously, their property and their person subject to seizure at the government's whim, and everyone was told to be content with second-tier legal categories as Rome took no action to address their plight.

Yet political paralysis was not a natural feature of the ancient world. Even judging conservatively, Rome had extended citizenship to foreigners a minimum of three times throughout its history: first to the Italians after the Social War, then to the residents of the colonies during the age of expansion, and finally to the people of the Mediterranean during Emperor Caracalla's day. Even in Alaric's time, a loss of citizenship was one of the stiffest penalties a Roman judge could hand down to a Roman defendant. The emperors themselves passed laws during these very years to ensure that the citizen status of any Roman prisoners of war would be quickly restored, if and when they returned to Rome. References to being a "citizen" were manifest in every aspect of popular culture, including love poetry, Claudian's propaganda, philosophical reflections on free will, Bishop Ambrose's eulogy for Theodosius, and the letters delivered to the wives of lost soldiers. Still, no new Caracalla rose to defend the Goths, and according to Roman law, throughout the fifth century it remained easier to grant citizenship to enslaved people than to immigrants. The Romans obstinately refused to address this patent inequality.

Alaric shouldered that effort. For most of his forty years, he fought to be a part of Rome, often giving people the impression that he was "more like a Roman" than a Goth, and what he and the Goths wanted was straightforward. They desired, as Alaric had supposedly proposed to Honorius, to "live with the Romans [so] that men might believe them both to be of one family or people."

In the Romans' minds, however, every immigrant was expected to make a series of cultural compromises if they wanted to earn acceptance. They should hide their native languages, shelve their native dress, and bury their ethnic pride—requirements that were as unrealistic in the fifth-century Roman Empire as they sound deeply discriminatory centuries later. Like many Roman immigrants, Goths esteemed their own language, were proud of their culture, and had fond connections to their homeland. They did not want to forfeit their heritage to be a part of Rome. Alaric's actions forced a difficult, long-overdue conversation about acceptance, belonging, and the rights of immigrant communities. He was, in this respect, a bona fide gate-crasher.

❧

Through the cold months of January and February 409, Roman families turned to their stockrooms for sustenance while the charitable widow and mother-in-law of Emperor Gratian lightened some of the public's hunger pains. A group of sympathetic senators, meanwhile, contacted Alaric and agreed to listen to his grievances. Goths needed to be paid, Alaric told them. Their families needed to be fed. Adults and children lacked decent clothes. The diplomatic men reassured him that they would offer their assistance if he agreed to lift the blockade.

Alaric asked for five thousand pounds of gold, thirty thousand pounds of silver, four thousand silk tunics, three thousand scarlet-colored cloaks, and three thousand pounds of pepper. The last request was probably a sign that many Goths longed for a taste of home; Black Sea traders delivered boxes of the spice to Gothia's shores. In the spring, Alaric relented. At least some of the requested supplies must have been delivered within weeks, if not days, as a sign of Roman good faith. The senators promised that they would collaborate with the emperor to address any lingering hardships. Relations thawed as the next round of diplomacy opened. Alaric agreed to meet with Honorius.

In April, the young emperor traveled south to face the man who had caused the sudden panic. Alaric came north and prepared his presentation. The two leaders could not have been more different: one entering middle age, living temporarily in a canvas tent; the other, twenty-five, who traveled on a golden couch. They met at the Adriatic coastal town of Rimini, joined by their entourages and their go-betweens. Prominent among them was an amicable Roman from Honorius's court named Jovius, whom Alaric had befriended during his temporary posting in the prefecture of Illyricum. During his brief tenure, Jovius had learned about and taken an interest in the Goths' grievances and Alaric's cause.

Before the deliberations began, Jovius pressed the emperor to make a bold and magnanimous opening move. Honorius, he suggested, should restore Alaric's rank to general, the position he had held in Illyricum, before Arcadius had stripped him of it. The emperor should also consider enlisting the services of Alaric's brother-in-law, a reliable field commander named Athaulf who had looked after many Gothic families during their years in Illyricum. The conscientious soldier might be good to have on retainer. The offer would be seen as a token of goodwill and might immediately diffuse any lingering hostility between Goths and Romans at the start of the negotiations.

Honorius, adamant that no higher rank be conferred on Alaric or on any member of Alaric's family, summarily rejected Jovius's idea.

Jovius was with Alaric in his tent when the news of Honorius's obstinacy was delivered, and he watched as Alaric grew indignant. Jovius reported back that a resolution with Alaric under these circumstances did not look possible, even as Alaric himself, after his anger subsided, convinced himself to hold out hope. He contacted Jovius one last time, conveying his own willingness to compromise, and made two demands of the emperor. Alaric wanted "a moderate amount of food" and "permission to live on Roman land."

Statecraft in antiquity hinged on precise words and phrases, but the two men who reported what Alaric said, Jordanes and Zosimus, were not dedicated foreign service officers sensitive to government nuance. They fancied themselves stylish historians. Understanding what happened at the Rimini conference requires a closer, critical look at their own words.

Alaric's first request, for food, would have been fairly reasonable. Without money, their own farms, or stable employment, the Goths undeniably needed government assistance to survive. Asking for an immediate supply of grain or pork would have made sense, and the ancient writers were probably accurate in reporting it. But they certainly misrepresented Alaric's second request, "permission to live on Roman land," because neither Alaric nor the Goths needed legal permission to do so. When and if they survived the border crossing—a hazardous proposition at the militarized Danube, where the impluses of the Roman soldiers controlled a refugee's fate—immigrants could and did live wherever they wished; Rome's borders were technically always open.

More likely, Alaric requested a legally protected way of living on Roman land, the kind that would have been associated with Roman citizenship. Zosimus, even though he was writing in the sixth century, grasped this important subtext. Alaric was searching for "a home," he explained to his Greek readers, a "place to dwell." And for a Goth to have a "home" inside Rome's borders meant having a right to live peacefully without harassment, the same as any citizen.

Honorius refused both demands. No immigrant had ever demanded these rights from the Roman government. The negotiations collapsed.

In December, for the second time in his life, Alaric stood before the imposing brick walls of Rome. A decade earlier, the government, having decided that the city could use a set of new defenses, had commissioned civil engineers to calculate the wall's perimeter, with the goal being to double its height and add newer towers to the gates. They calculated its length rather sloppily, giving a final measurement of twenty-one miles. (In reality, Rome's walls measure about twelve miles.) But the construction plans advanced, with bricks baked, cement mixed, and marble quarried for the facing of the towers. When they were finished, the new city walls stood fifty-feet high, paid for by Honorius's government. They still measure that height in many places around the city.

Because of the senate's generosity the previous year, Alaric returned to Rome to ask the senators for their help in brokering the current impasse with Honorius. The man in charge of securing Rome's streets, a well-liked politician named Priscus Attalus, proposed an ingeniously simple solution with far-reaching implications. If he, Attalus, took the emperorship, and Alaric supported him, would that remedy the Goths' problems?

Attalus, a pragmatic intellectual, was not a man to propose a dramatic military intervention lightly. Before managing Rome's streets, he had tried his hand at architecture and successfully designed the baths for his own villa, which earned him a nod of approval from a discerning colleague. Then he became prefect of the city, a position that gave him responsibility for managing the city's fourteen regions and an invaluable political platform. It is a testament to Attalus's moral character that, even as a product of Rome's traditional education system, with its systemic biases against foreigners, and even as a resident of Rome, with its sizable but often overlooked population of Gothic slaves, he sensed an urgent need to address the present injustices.

Over the following weeks and months, Alaric, Attalus, and Attalus's like-minded colleagues drafted a plan of action. The august group of senators and Roman politicians would announce their intent to appoint a new emperor in a daring play designed to force Honorius to capitulate. It was almost certain that Honorius and his advisers would not react well to the formation of a new resistance. Testy letters traveled up and down the Via Flaminia that winter. As exhaustion settled upon Roman homes following the January 1 New Year celebrations and the calendar eased into the year 410, the plan went into effect, and Attalus took office. Alaric was promoted, and the members of their alliance, notwithstanding a few unresolved logistical questions, braced for a confrontation with Ravenna. Earlier, Attalus had proposed they use the moment to implement a more ambitious scheme of returning Egypt's governance to Italy, wresting it from Constantinople's bureaucrats. Alaric had demurred, suggesting that if they were to open a second front, the alliance should focus on securing Africa, where Honorius was said to have pockets of loyalists in powerful positions.

The strategic disagreements did nothing to prevent the two men from moving forward, and Alaric spent the following weeks running a door-to-door campaign across northern Italy to rally Romans to Attalus's side. As boots hit the ground in a now-urgent campaign to drum up support against the reigning emperor, Athaulf was invited to Rome and promised a government salary. The alliance drafted its ultimatum for Honorius. The emperor could agree to retire to an island of his choosing, or he was going to be removed.

The palace rushed to protect its favored son. The generals were ordered to draw up plans to counter any imminent assault on the emperor's seaside palace at Ravenna, and within the first few months of 410, Alaric attacked. If reinforcements hadn't arrived from the Adriatic Sea, and if General Sarus, a Goth, hadn't brilliantly foiled Alaric in the late stages of his offensive, the emperor might not have survived. The defeat devastated the rebels: Attalus, Alaric, the Goths, and the senators who supported them. They had tried to gain too much too soon. Second-guessing had divided them. In Rome, their hastily formed partnership crumbled. After the shock of seeing a Goth defend the emperor, Alaric was "enraged."

That summer, cooks in Rome visited the neighborhood markets to stock their pantries with necessities, like beans, sausages, honey, and bread. Backgammon players perched on stools outside the taverns, where they could nod at the neighborhood's regular faces and cast sidelong views down Rome's alleyways. The Goths with Alaric set up their tents in the northeastern district of the city, off the busy Salt Road. Gothic husbands and wives, sons and daughters came and went through the city's Salt Gate. No one reported seeing Alaric.

The usual summer swelter soaked Rome that August. Romans called it a "torrid" month. The unbearableness of the heat was manifested in numerous ways, but one of the most pleasant and anticipated was the month-long holiday. Romans adored civic festivities. During the early empire, the calendar was filled with seventy-seven days of entertainment on which Romans could expect to find chariot races, gladiator games, aquatic battles, and parades passing below their windows. Businesses closed, sometimes for days. By Alaric's time, those seventy-seven holidays had swollen to a hundred and seventy-seven. Intellectuals perennially grumbled about the amount of time the Roman people wasted watching sports, but the stadium offered the only place a citizen regularly saw their ruler.

August's circuit of festivals had a particular theme: avoiding the heat. Peacock-feather fans were the fashionable accessory. The month's celebrations were devoted to honoring the sun, the fire god Vulcan, the river ports, the icy-cool mountain-fed Tiber, the start of the fall harvest, and the first autumn wine. In manuscript illustrations of August, designed in the fourth century and copied through the Middle Ages, Romans are always depicted stripped bare—their clothes, like their cares, tossed to the wind.

There were sixteen main gates in and out of Rome's city walls, thirteen on the city's eastern side, three to the west of the Tiber. A villain planning to attack the city would have gathered intelligence about all of them. A seasoned Roman commander would do the same if he were attacking a walled city, with access to field manuals, personal reconnaissance, and a lifetime of experience to help devise a plan for how to breech a city's defenses. By this point in his life, of course, Alaric had all of the above.

To see a wall in the ancient world was to be put in awe of habitation and culture, what the Romans thought of as "civilization." Not everyone was so fortunate as to live in such sophisticated settings. "The wild and uncivilized life of man at the beginning of time was first separated from communion with dumb animals and beasts by the founding of cities," Vegetius wrote. Urban living kept those "animals" at bay, and walls created a superficial sense of community. Every night, Rome's gates were locked as a reminder to keep hostile forces out.

Brick and mortar and months of manual labor may not seem like cutting-edge technology, but with it, Rome's engineers had been able to provide a formidable set of defenses. The walls Alaric faced were jagged, laid out in "sinuous windings," zigzag patterns that may have stymied an accurate measurement of their perimeter. They angled in and out of neighborhoods, as military experts suggested, so soldiers could be stationed on top and be able to surveil every direction. The walls were also deceptively simple-looking. Two parallel courses joined at the ramparts, so that an enemy who rammed through one was exhausted before discovering the second. They were batter-proof and arrow-proof, with "double-thickness cloaks and goat's hair mats" hung on the front to absorb any impact.

If Rome's walls had one weakness, it was its gates. There were three different kinds. The most recognizable were the broad marble archways that decorated the most important roads. One gate welcomed the arriving traffic and the other ushered traffic out. Each passageway could be closed with a portcullis, a large iron grill dropped into place by soldiers manning towers on either side. The Appian Road, Ostian Road, Flaminian Road, and Portus Road—three of them on the south side of the city alone—offered grand entrances to the historic city. There were also two smaller types of gates: a modest rounded stone archway spacious enough for a carriage or two, and a simple brick-framed passage whose wooden door could be bolted at night, like the Salt Gate.

Roman generals who had seen other cities' walls, as in Persia, knew how to plan an attack against them and could easily anticipate what kinds of countermeasures an enemy might deploy. A "mobile tower" of ladders and ropes, built on casters, might be rolled up to an enemy's fortifications to lower soldiers into the streets from drawbridges, anticipating aerial warfare in a premodern age. But they took costly time to build. Trees had to be felled. Yards of cords had to be unwound, cut, and retied, as the army carpenters labored quickly to keep pace with a general's war plans.

Targeted tunneling also worked, as did brute ramming, but one had to be careful, depending on the enemy's technological capabilities. Persians, at the sight of battering rams, poured pitch onto soldiers and filled underground tunnels with bitumen and sulfur, igniting them to create sulfur dioxide, which gassed the enemy, as they had done to a Roman army at the Battle for Dura-Europus. Other opponents stood on the ramparts and dropped oversized wooden wheels onto attacking armies, which, as they acquired velocity, flattened both men and horses. Of all the options familiar to a Goth with Roman military training, however, the most conservative approach was precision, not bluster, as Vegetius explained:

> The most essential part of the art of war, not only in sieges, but in every other branch, is to study and endeavor to be thoroughly acquainted with the customs of the enemy. It will be impossible to find opportunities of laying snares for them unless you know their hours of repose and the times when they are least on their guard. These opportunities offer [themselves] sometimes at noon, sometimes in the evening, or night, when the soldiers of both sides are at their meals or dispersed for the necessary purposes of rest or refreshment.

Careful observation of comings and goings at the Salt Gate and of soldiers' habits in the towers—could that be how Alaric passed his July and August, patiently logging hours of reconnaissance on a series of nightly watches? If so, it was textbook planning for what military men feared most, the "surprise attack." And the night of August 24, 410, if anything, was expertly, meticulously timed. By the twenty-fourth, vacation was just ending, and businesses were focused on the work of reopening. Life must have felt untroubled.

At a dangerous hour called "the dead of night," which Romans knew was "no time suitable for conducting business," a rich matron prepared to leave her house. Proba belonged to the Anicii, titans of Roman industry, a family with a reputation for eloquence and influence, with estates on three continents. Proba's grandmother, after whom she was named, had shot to the public's attention as a literary virtuoso after she seamlessly weaved snippets of Virgil's poetry into a repurposed set of verses about Jesus's life—a difficult enough task for the Latin-speaking men who dominated Rome's literary scene and an unheard-of accomplishment for a female poet. The men of the house had lucrative businesses in olives, oil, and ceramics. Proba, when she was younger, had given birth to three boys, all of whom had become successful politicians. On the night of August 24, we can imagine her closing her jewelry boxes, donning a simple tunic to mask her aristocratic pedigree, and slipping through the doors of her villa to enter the dark streets. She advanced to the Salt Gate.

Without disturbing the night watchman, and with all the self-confidence of a woman in her privileged position, Proba unbolted the door, cracked the gate, then hurried home. Alaric crept in. The lone ancient writer who tells this intriguing vignette, Procopius of Caesarea, lived a century after 410 and loathed Proba's family, making the details of his version of what happened that night extremely doubtful. But his memory was accurate in other ways. A Gothic pariah, like Alaric was, could have dedicated supporters in Rome, men and women like Proba who—whether driven by their ideals, their personal aspirations, or some ulterior motive—were willing to help immigrants, even at a great cost to themselves, because they likely thought that such an act would better Rome. A gate-crasher did not need to be loud to make noise.

⤞

What happened next can look in our historical imagination like a reel of images pulled from a Hollywood disaster movie. Wild-haired, leather-clad barbarians maraud through the streets. Wealthy citizens hoard their coins and jewelry as they stare at the realities of future financial ruin. Privileged senators, scared for their lives, dirty their white togas as they run to escape the devastation. An attack by foreigners causes the end of ancient civilization. Yet much in this apocalyptic scenario has been assembled from inference and speculation, reconstructed from charred ruins in the city's archaeological record and from the upsetting news, preserved in a chance letter from Saint Jerome, about the death of the elderly Marcella.

One surprising description about what happened during those seventy-two hours, however, preserved in the accounts of the contemporary Latin writer Orosius of Spain, upends the disaster narrative. As the Goths raided Rome in the days that followed, Alaric made it clear that he would spare Romans who sought refuge in a church, extending that protection to every resident of the city, regardless of their faith or creed. "He also told his men," Orosius said, "that as far as possible, they must refrain from shedding blood in their hunger for booty."

Many Goths obeyed Alaric's command to the letter. When one soldier encountered an elderly Roman woman gathering precious vessels from St. Peter's Basilica to safeguard them, he "was moved to religious awe through his fear of God" and communicated to Alaric, who "immediately ordered that all the vessels should be taken back, just as they had been found, to the basilica of the Apostle [Peter]." The woman was allowed to return to her home unharmed. After the tension of the encounter was defused, the heavy gold and silver objects—an assemblage of lamps, cups, and plates used for Holy Mass—were paraded through Rome's streets in thanksgiving. Gothic men, armed with "drawn swords," policed the solemn procession. Romans and Goths "joined together in singing openly a hymn of praise to God." It was a stunning moment of accord for two groups usually said to loathe each other, enacted by citizens and immigrants alike during a time when the Roman government had failed both.

CHAPTER TEN

Alaric's Dying Ambitions

T he magnitude of the shock, as it crossed continents by word of mouth, unsettled many of the empire's churchmen, who used their pulpits and their extensive networks of like-minded Christians to frame Alaric's attack in biblical terms. Already in the years leading up to the attack, an obsessive preoccupation with the end of the world had beguiled many Christians, taught to believe that one evil age must necessarily come to an end before a new, pure age could begin. Two spiritual leaders of the day—in particular, Jerome in Bethlehem and Augustine in North Africa—gradually shaped many of history's lasting perceptions of 410.

Jerome was working in a monastery in the Holy Land when he heard the news. "Day and night I could think of nothing else but of everyone's safety," he later wrote. At the time, he had returned to his books, closed the door to his cell, and reread the Hebrew prophet Ezekiel for solace. He confessed that he could never claim to have seen the "sea of smoke," the ominous cloud that engulfed Rome's orange-tiled roofs, which others told him about. He had visited Rome in his youth and mingled with Romans in its tight-knit coterie of Christian salons, where he remembered meeting Marcella. At the wise age of sixty-three, in the wake of the attack, Jerome was sensitive to people's suffering. He wrote a commentary on Ezekiel's book, guiding readers through the prophet's words to soften their "tears and moans" and perhaps to remind distraught

Christians about what they could learn from painful periods of earlier Jewish history.

Ezekiel had spoken of suffering, punishment, and hope during the days of King Nebuchadnezzar, when the Neo-Babylonian Empire was on the rise in the sixth century B.C. Long before the Roman Empire, before Alexander the Great conquered the first Persian Empire, Jews faced the challenge of finding their place in this changing world. In 586 B.C., the Babylonian army had sacked the holy city of Jerusalem, destroyed the Temple, and exiled many of the city's Jewish residents. Some writers, like Ezekiel, interpreted the catastrophe as divine retribution for an unspecified "abomination" among his own community, one that threatened their covenant with Yahweh. Eager to make sense of the senseless attack, the prophet in his writing told of a comforting vision he had seen: of desiccated bones, strewn across an arid Judaean valley, which God would restore to life. "I will put my spirit within you, and you shall live, and I will place you on your own soil," Ezekiel wrote, giving his listeners hope for a return to Jerusalem.

Inspired by the story of the historic city's capture, Jerome drafted his own lament about the sack of Rome, which he also presented as a spiritual disaster. "The city that once captured the hearts and minds of the world has been captured," he wrote, referring to Rome, in his commentary on Ezekiel's book. He went on to explain that Alaric had extinguished "the bright light of all the world," so that it appeared as if the head of the world had been cut off.

Jerome adapted this vivid image from the Christian book of Revelation, authored by an enigmatic man named John of Patmos in the first century A.D., who drew on motifs from the Jewish book of Daniel. Both the Christian and Jewish Scriptures had told of four kingdoms that would rule the earth before the end of time. In the book of Daniel, written in the second century B.C., after the death of Alexander the Great, the Jewish community wrestled with the effect of living through a period of intense change, as Alexander's successors fought bitterly for control of his kingdom and pagan Greek customs began pouring into

Jerusalem. Daniel's vision of the "fourth kingdom" cast the second century B.C. as an age of evil, where foreign beliefs and culture threatened to upset the established Jewish way of life in Jerusalem. Yet this fourth kingdom would one day fall, Daniel predicted, comforting his readers with the notion that their anxieties would not last forever.

A little more than two hundred years later, John's Revelation achieved a similar effect, mesmerizing Christians by transforming the "fourth kingdom" into the Roman Empire, which John also referred to in his visions as the kingdom of "Babylon." The Christian community lived in trying times, John admitted to his readers, but the message of his highly symbolic prophetic language—of dragons and beasts and of a woman sitting atop seven hills—was that their own uncertain predicament would eventually end. Rome would not remain hostile to them forever, he said. "Fallen, fallen is Babylon the great!" John declared in a vision of the future. His predication of Rome's "fall" told audiences to persevere in their Christian faith.

After 410, many Christians drew upon these and other apocalyptic ideas in a literal way to persuade themselves that the end of the world really was growing nearer. The more outspoken, radical believers claimed that God had punished Rome for its wicked ways, just as he had condemned other profligate cities. As early as September 410, Christians had started to compare Alaric's attack to the destruction of Sodom and Gomorrah and strained to provide biblical justifications for the misfortunes of their day. A line in the book of Ezekiel that warned the Jewish people about the coming of an apocalyptic villain named Gog was interpreted as a reference to "the Goths." Other Bible readers, convinced that the literal word of God held an unchallenged authority, turned Ezekiel's reference to Gog and his place of origin, Magog, into a pair of evils, which they used to stir up fear of other ethnic groups, more widely. Throughout the Middle Ages and beyond, Christian preachers instinctively invoked this demonic duo, Gog and Magog, in times of sudden cultural upheaval, as when the Huns came to Europe from the north, when Muslims came from the south, and when Mongols came from the east. No longer tied to the Goths, "Gog and Magog" frightened generations of Christians into thinking that the next wave of foreigners was heralding the end of the world.

Other Christians, in the wake of 410, used the fear of another pending attack to fight for their own political priorities. During these years, the bishop of a small town in North Africa, Augustine of Hippo, published the first five books of his epic twenty-two-volume manifesto—part pastoral letter, part rant against Roman society's evils—called *The City of God*. As a young boy raised by parents of modest means, Augustine had left North Africa with the help of a well-placed patron and had studied in Rome and Milan, with the dream of becoming a successful lawyer. But his conversion to Christianity in a garden outside Milan disrupted his plans, and by 410, he had abandoned a lucrative career to become the bishop of the North African village, Hippo, a small town that lay beyond the outskirts of the sprawling suburbs of Carthage.

Well-traveled Romans stumbled into a coastal town like Hippo; they did not choose it as their destination. But over the next two decades, from his desk in the quiet village, Augustine made his name, brawling by letter, teaching by sermon, and cementing his intellectual heritage with extensive theological treatises. It was a healthy literary output for—as he presented himself in his autobiography, *Confessions*—a boy who had supposedly given up a life in politics and high culture.

After 410, the bishop's key concern was to foreclose any return to the pagan past. As Augustine knew, nearly twenty edicts against paganism alone had been published in the last two decades of the fourth century, during Theodosius's rise, and Augustine did not want to allow Rome's moderate Christian party to overturn them. The risk of compromise was real. During Alaric's blockade in late 408, the city's worried pagan community had consulted with the city's chief priest and bishop, Pope Innocent I, about their desire to perform a pagan sacrifice—illegal in Theodosius's Rome. A return to tradition might be appropriate in Rome's time of need, they argued. Innocent, to many zealous Christians' shock, had granted their request, "preferring," as Zosimus explained, "the preservation of the city to his own private opinion [about matters of faith]."

Appalled by such public acts of religious compromise, Augustine used *The City of God*—at a crucial time when Rome might have returned to its roots as a tolerant empire—to argue for a more unyielding set of values. He defended the legacy of Theodosius against charges that the emperor's fanaticism had ruined Rome and blamed Alaric's attack on the pagans and Christians alike who had resisted Theodosius's policies. Twisting the events of 410 to suit his own agenda, Augustine insisted that Christianity remain the empire's official religion by implying that Rome risked further catastrophe if it did not. Secular thinkers later labored for hundreds of years to disentangle the power of the Christian church from the workings of the state, which Augustine's thinking had helped graft together.

With the razor-edged partisanship popular among churchmen of his day, Augustine, through *The City of God*, taught Christians to believe that pagan Rome had been a spiritually bankrupt place, a land of false gods whose cities were ruled by demons. Writing for many of the wealthier citizens who fled Rome after the attack, and who had "managed to reach Carthage as refugees," he articulated a vision of the church as a community to which all men and women were urgently called. It was time to leave behind the "moral disease" of Roman culture, he explained; even in the early fifth century, it was not uncommon to find sympathetic magistrates who allowed pagans to parade their sacred statues through the streets on holy days. Until those corrupting influences could be removed once and for all, Augustine said, Christians would have to dwell in an imperfect land.

From this argument Augustine developed his famous theory of the two "cities." One was the Roman Empire, located on Earth, filled with a diverse population of pagans, Christians, and Jews, where the messiness of culture made life confusing for devout Christians. The other was heaven, a glorious new Holy Jerusalem, where the true believers would finally gather in each other's comfort after Jesus's Second Coming. Until then, Augustine encouraged all Christians to replace their spiritual anxieties with aspirations of becoming *cives futuros,* or "future citizens," in the heavenly church, a theory he had been mulling for years in sermons and letters while crafting the ideas that became *The City of God.* Yet even as Christian readers began to encounter Augustine's spiritual notion of "future citizenship" throughout the fifth century, no Roman ever extrapolated from those ideas to articulate the need to extend "future citizenship" to their present political context.

⁂

On August 28, three full days after they stormed Rome, the Goths collected their belongings, both personal and pirated, packed their tents, and began to walk south, along the length of the Italian peninsula. The city had nothing more to give them. Alaric told them to dream of a wider continent, of fields of grain in a milder climate and a land they would lay eyes on soon. It would provide them with food and respite from their uprooted existence. His intention was to lead them to "the quiet land of Africa."

Frustrations mounted. Many Goths were unhappy with the succession of recent failures, and desperation gnawed at their Gothic pride. At the time, disgruntled men, including Alaric's brother-in-law, wanted, according to Orosius, "to obliterate the name of Rome and make the Romans' land the Goths' empire in both word and deed." Rumor quickly spread that the Goths were regrouping with the hope of establishing "a Gothia where there had once been a Roman state."

Alaric's brother-in-law, Athaulf, pressed Alaric to escalate the conflict. Despite the punishing symbolism of the August attack, many were unsatisfied. Even if Alaric entertained their opinions, or at least sympathized with them, in the end he overruled them. He had a border child's faith in Rome and an undying belief in the decency of the Roman people. Roman Africa would be a place for the Goths to regain their composure. Carthage was said to awe people with its "ancient wealth," and perhaps the Goths' good fortune lay there, in the empire's agricultural heartland.

In the governmental corridors of Carthage, Goths could negotiate with slippery but important officials, some of whom were increasingly candid about their own disagreements with Emperor Honorius. There was an outside chance to find powerful allies, as well. A renegade general and loose supporter of Honorius, named Heraclian, had recently held the state fleet at the harbor and prevented grain from sailing to Rome—a spiteful attempt by a political appointee to humiliate his own rival, the prefect of the city of Rome, Priscus Attalus, for supporting Alaric. Whether he fully intended it or not, Heraclian's actions in 409 or early 410 temporarily starved the people of Rome, shocking the city's residents almost as much as Alaric's own, earlier blockade.

The Goths left Rome on the Queen of Roads, the Via Appia, following the route most southern travelers took. Their wagons jostled across the road's volcanic stones as they steered past aqueducts in the countryside, underneath Latium's stone pines—old enough to have opened into their iconic umbrellas—and past numerous churches and catacombs. As the excavated ruins tell us, they left everything intact, no doubt as much from exhaustion as from deference to the dead. Just outside of the city were the cemeteries where the Romans buried their loved ones and celebrated their lives with family picnics.

Behind them, the gates of the city became smaller, while over the horizon, small southern towns wondered whether the "cloud of grim war" was coming to them. The south of Italy had largely been spared the decade of disturbance, but the marching Goths threw their security into doubt. The citizens of the small city of Nola, outside Naples, prayed to their local saint, Felix. The archaeology of their town neither confirms nor denies whether their prayers saved them.

It was said in Alaric's time that studying history was like watching an itinerant roadshow, one filled with a bedraggled cast of characters who filled the streets with their cacophony of odd musical sounds. Men and women sang together, high-pitched notes complemented low ones, and everyone had different timbres. But the joy in learning about the past, the writer Macrobius said, ultimately arose from seeing how a complicated series of events might come together in a meaningful way, not unlike listening to the sound of a caravan harmonizing along a country road.

It's hard to know how many families and wagons joined Alaric on that southward march. Anyone could have fallen in line, and not just a Goth, which makes it equally impossible to hazard a guess about their group's ethnic composition. Over time, though, they found their voice, like good troupes did, and developed a tight-knit identity; Jordanes called them the Visigoths.

Whatever they called themselves, Alaric's followers needed at least some rudimentary sense of solidarity in the years to come. Some people in antiquity didn't need much to be content. A little farm, a view of the sea, and a steady income would do. "I want to glide in my little boat by the shore of a peaceful coast," one Roman of the sixth century said, and "to gather little fishes from the pools." He intended the image to be a metaphor for the life of the mind. The lesson was that wisdom came with every moment of studied concentration, just like casting a fly. But such tranquility was a dream others never attained.

Late that year, as the Goths departed the mainland for Carthage, a storm broke and capsized several of their hired ships. Many died at sea. Captains ordered the rest back to land, where they were told that Africa would have to wait. As the fall turned to winter, Alaric, among those still waiting for passage, suddenly died.

Oly says Alaric died of "sickness," Jordanes that his passing was "untimely." Without any body to exhume, every written report naturally demands a healthy degree of suspicion. Some scientists have proposed malaria caused by *Plasmodium falciparum* as the likely killer, based on knowledge of the boggy climate in southern Italy, which could have fostered the parasitic disease. But the same Greek word Oly used for "sickness," *nosos,* evoked a range of ailments, and not all of them the purview of antiquity's medical professionals.

According to the archaic Greek poet Hesiod, *nosos* was an "affliction" that pecked at a tormented soul. People who obsessed about their wounded honor were said to suffer from it, the moody playwright Sophocles noted, like a "disease." *Nosos* was the "madness" that came from loving something or someone too much, Euripides explained. Given that Alaric suffered from all three of these ailments—personal anguish, hurt pride, and an unfailing love for his people—it might be better to say that he died from "complications."

That winter, Jordanes said, the Goths mourned Alaric "with utmost affection." Late in the year in ancient Cosentia, now Cosenza, a small town in the Calabrian region of southern Italy, they buried him in an unusual rite. Gothic leaders ordered several enslaved men to dam the waters of the Busento, so that Alaric's body could be laid in the riverbed, where it would be covered with mud and enveloped by the rushing stream. It was a custom known from Dacia, although no Goth after Alaric is ever said to have requested it. The passing of their highly respected leader left the Goths rudderless. They had experienced long periods of migration, starvation, and poverty in the years since hitching their fortunes to Alaric's ideals. Men had died in battle to secure a better future for their families, one that never came. Women and children struggled every day to survive, but no one could go on like this indefinitely.

During the recent conflicts, Emperor Honorius's half sister, Galla, had joined the Gothic march, a remarkable turn of events so unbelievable to Romans they claimed she had been captured. Perhaps she went of her own volition, her own moral commitments inspiring her to ally against her brother's causes. The possibility of sexual violence against a woman in wartime also lurks disturbingly beneath the surface of the Roman and Gothic presentation of events. Whether by choice or force, by 414, Theodosius's only surviving daughter had wed Alaric's brother-in-law, Athaulf, in an extravagant ceremony at a villa in Narbonne, near the Mediterranean coast in Roman Gaul. The fortyish-year-old Goth, who only four years earlier had tried to convince Alaric "to obliterate the name of Rome" and had returned to Rome himself after Alaric's death to strip it "bare like locusts," stood at his bride's side dressed smartly in a

Roman soldier's white formal wear. The former prefect of the city, short-lived emperor of Rome, and man of eclectic talents, Priscus Attalus, helped compose the wedding poetry, a standard element for a classical occasion meant to honor the bride and groom. Honorius did not attend.

By 418 or 419, Galla's husband, who had returned to war to fight against Vandals in Gaul and Spain, was dead—killed, Orosius says, "by the treachery . . . of his own men." But Galla remained deeply connected to the Gothic community. Political reconciliation between the Roman government and the Gothic community at last seemed possible.

Honorius, now in his mid-thirties, convinced that a true and proper Gothic state was the surest way to avoid future attacks, had ordered his advisers to scrutinize the empire's maps for Roman territory to divest. They settled on the Roman province of Aquitaine, nestled on the Bay of Biscay. The pleasant Garonne River, which emptied into the blustery Atlantic, made communication among inland towns easy, and the land around the larger cities, like Bordeaux and Toulouse, teemed with fertile soils that would provide the Gothic settlers with ample food. Due to the recent border wars against the local Franks and Burgundians, as well as the Vandals, many citizens had already evacuated their estates. The Goths could farm as much as they liked here and could govern themselves as they wished.

The borders of this new Gothic kingdom were hazy in the fifth century, as borders usually were, and the precise legal arrangements that secured its creation remain, centuries later, unclear. But the Roman emperors ceded their rights to the land, and their decision to forfeit Aquitaine was the first move in the dissolution of the once-united Roman Empire. Gothic monarchs ruled this corner of western Europe for three centuries and shaped the history of the continent—actual kings, not men with honorary titles. King Euric established a law code that incorporated long-respected Roman legal principles, encouraging Gothic lawyers to borrow what they needed from Rome's law books, including the need to protect private property, to establish the power of the courts, and to preserve the ancient right of the paterfamilias, the

ability of a Roman father to manage the affairs of his extended household. Gothic legal scholars added what they needed from their own customs, too, such as the Goths' practice of punishing legal infractions with
fines, which they applied even to the loss of life, as when a pregnant
woman miscarried through an act of household violence. According
to Visigothic law, a man guilty of killing a woman carrying a "formed
fetus" was required to pay 150 *solidi;* if the fetus was "unformed," the
penalty was 100 *solidi.* The desire of jurists to distinguish an early-stage
pregnancy from a later one not only demonstrates, in the estimation of
one scholar, the Visigoths' "pragmatic and relatively compassionate"
approach toward reproductive health and justice; it also finds no parallel in the Roman world, which, after Theodosius's revolution, increasingly often chose to enforce orthodox canon law.

In the sixth century, Alaric II, traditionally identified as Alaric's
great-grandson, codified all these laws in a collection called the

*As a Gothic golden age
settled upon Europe, an artist
fashioned this evocative
sapphire gem with an
unmistakable echo of the
Gothic past. The surrounding
text, carved in reverse so that
its owner could use the gem
as a seal, reads, "Alaric, King
of the Goths." The portrait is
likely that of King Alaric II.*

Breviary of Alaric II and, in yet another move that reaffirmed the Goths' commitment to building a religiously neutral public space, denied Christian priests the privilege of sitting as judges in civil matters, a right they maintained in contemporary Roman law. These and other moderate Gothic ideas, interwoven with selected Roman precedents, formed the basis of legal culture in medieval Spain.

The Roman Empire did not fare as well. As it had with Dacia in the third century, Rome's government abandoned England in the fifth century because of difficulties securing the island's towns. Franks unseated Rome's government in northern Gaul, and by the 430s, less than a decade after Honorius's death, the Vandals had commandeered the great port city of Carthage, where they installed their own government and halted grain shipments to Italy. Romans, raised to expect an unending supply of cheap, state-subsidized food, were forced for the first time in hundreds of years to pay full market price for their grain and olive oil. Rome's population thinned as people decided to take their families elsewhere. Estimates put the loss to Rome at around a half million residents over the course of the fifth century.

Two generations later, as the Goths solidified their kingdom in Aquitaine, the Roman Empire crumbled. Without the engine of the cross-continental economy to inject money into its cities, people couldn't afford the same luxury array of spices, clothes, and even mass-manufactured building materials as before. Standards of living dropped in the western Roman territories. As urban investments declined, houses shrank into huts again. Italian families set out modest handmade dinnerware on their tables, no longer the fancy wheel-spun imports from Alaric's time. Neighborhoods contracted, and unused land devolved into private urban farms.

By 476, when a northern warlord, named Odoacer, seized control of the Roman government by forcing the western emperor to abdicate, residents of the city of Rome no longer lived within the borders of their own empire. All that remained of the Roman world was the territory governed by the eastern emperor, Zeno—a horseshoe-shaped state that followed the coast of the Mediterranean from the Aegean Sea to Egypt. While the empire's citizens and its leaders remained oblivious to the fortunes of those on its borders, Constantinople led this greatly diminished Roman Empire into its next millennium from one capital, not two, with two imperial prefectures, not four, and with a collection of semiautonomous territories. But the torch of *Romanitas* would be picked up and carried forward from surprising directions during these centuries of change, as it was by another Gothic boy from the Danube River, a lad named Theoderic.

"A youth of tall stature but very poorly clad" when he started his first job in the eastern Roman Empire in the late fifth century, Theoderic studied hard, won the emperor's trust, and was promoted to high office in Constantinople. Theoderic served the emperor loyally on the battlefield and in civil service during those years, even as the hardships and misfortunes of the Goths who had settled in Illyricum weighed heavily on him. It seemed heartless, Theoderic told the Roman emperor Zeno, "to enjoy the advantages of the Roman Empire in luxurious ease while his tribe lived in want."

The receptive Roman emperor, keen to keep the rising Goth at a safe distance, answered with a proposal: Theoderic should take his followers, organize a Gothic army, and march westward to Italy. If they successfully deposed the warlord Odoacer, who had forced the western emperor into recent retirement, Theoderic could keep the old Roman territory as his personal reward and govern it as he wished. In 493, the victorious Goths acclaimed Theoderic king of Italy, and his reign inaugurated a Gothic golden age. The Ostrogoths of Italy and the Visigoths of southern Gaul and Spain united their kingdoms such that, in the sixth century, a Goth could sail down the Tiber River, head to the Atlantic Ocean, and still be in this new "Gothia."

Under Theoderic's leadership, religious pluralism reigned, with the king's family serving as its model. Theoderic's mother recited the Nicene Creed, while her son the king recited Arius's. State money was used to repair Italian churches and synagogues alike. When Theoderic visited St. Peter's Basilica, people said that he had done so "with as much reverence as if he himself were a Catholic." His concern for religious moderation and justice impressed many, it was said at the time, and "won the good-will of the neighboring nations."

A healthy economy returned to Italy after decades of mismanagement by the Roman emperors. The Gothic king, who discovered the state's finances "nothing but a haystack," quickly replenished the treasury by raising taxes. He brought a welcome transparency to government, reinvested in public works, and repaired Italy's aqueducts and the grand bath halls of Rome, Ostia, Verona, Ravenna, and Pavia. Streets were swept; public announcements were posted in highly trafficked areas so that everyone could read "the words of the promise" the king had made to his people. In a move that would have raised eyebrows among Gothic partisans in Alaric's time, Italians acclaimed this successful boy from the Danube as a new Emperor Trajan.

Highly traditional Christians, many of whom, in the sixth century, remained as fearful of the Goths as ever, endeavored to lead an exodus from society during these years. Hoping to lure like-minded Christians to protected islands of self-imposed isolation, men like Benedict of Nursia established Europe's first monasteries as the Ostrogoths came to power. Day and night, Benedict's monks copied old Greek and Roman manuscripts, prayed, and engaged in self-reflection. The activities kept their anxious minds off the new realities of life beyond their cloistered walls, where Goths and Romans lived side by side in cities and "the two groups of people were governing as one"—*duas gentes in uno,* people quipped in Latin. The idea seems to have been an aspirational motto for many Goths, harking back to the days when the aged Judge Athanaric had toured Constantinople on a state visit and marveled at the Roman city's many waters flowing into one.

A sense of civic community came back to Italy; it could be seen in the camaraderie between Romans and Goths at the stadium, in public marketplaces, and on holy days. People attended Arian churches, Catholic churches, and synagogues in the same city. As the powerful rays of *civilitas* returned, the clouds of fear lifted. "Everyone could carry on his business at whatever hour he chose, as if it were in daylight," people boasted. The king from the Danube was so committed to bringing back ancient Roman civic ideals that "he gave no city a gate. And where there were already gates, they were never shut." An open door was probably all Alaric had ever wanted.

✒

While Theoderic's Ostrogothic kingdom flourished, Visigothic kings successfully protected their people from outside threats, and they fought off invasions for most of the fifth century, until Alaric's great-grandson, Alaric II, lost a major battle at Vouillé in 507. The defeat forced the Visigoths to leave Aquitaine in disgrace, and they fled to Barcelona, transforming the old Roman town into a vibrant Gothic harbor. Other ancient cities across the Iberian Peninsula, like Mérida, Seville, Córdoba, and Toledo, were reborn under Gothic leadership, until the last Visigothic king, Roderic, lost his crown to a conquering army of Muslim Arabs and Moors, in 711. Roderic's memory would be preserved in an unexpected place.

The Islamic caliph's small stone lodge sat in a bright moonscape of rocks and wadis in the Jordanian desert, a seemingly unimpressive location for a ruler of a young but rapidly growing empire. By the time al-Walid II occupied the lodge at Qusayr 'Amra, Jordan, Islamic forces had already taken Syria, Egypt, and northwestern Africa, including the port at Carthage. From there, they conquered Europe's southwestern corner, the Iberian peninsula. The proud caliph wanted to impress his desert guests with his knowledge of the wonders of this expanding globe, so he commissioned a series of portraits for his lodge. On the walls of this luxurious space, which included a private bathhouse fed by a nearby cistern, al-Walid commissioned artists to paint a series of human figures: the emperor of Constantinople, the shah of Persia, the king of Axum (in Ethiopia), the emperor of China, and the ruler of Sogdiana, a rich trading community along the Silk Road. Joining the gallery of distinguished rulers on the walls was the last king of the Visigoths, Roderic.

It is a safe bet that Alaric would never have imagined that a Gothic face would one day be painted on the walls of a Muslim lodge in the Middle East. But in many ways, it was Muslims who helped preserve the Goths' story, not the narrow-minded churchmen of Europe or the secular humanists of the Renaissance. It was Muslims who challenged medieval Europe to incorporate Gothic history into an emerging sense of world history. The Islamic governors of al-Andalus—to use the medieval name for the lands of the Visigothic kingdom—drove this new conversation.

In order to foster a society built on coexistence, Muslim rulers of Visigothic Spain decided to research how Rome's empire fell apart and began by collecting evidence for their histories of the Goths. The Arabic writer Ibn Habib al-Ilbiri told his audience that *al-Qut,* as the Goths were called, had migrated from Persia. Others erroneously claimed that the Visigoths had lived in Spain "for a thousand years." One explained that the Arabs had conquered Spain by displacing *al-Rum,* the Romans. There's a delightful irony in seeing a Muslim writer mistake the Goths for the Romans, given Alaric's long quest for unity and Rome's hard-fought battle to oppose it.

All these early Islamic history books were based on a mix of misheard words, oral stories, and foreign authors who were read in translation. But the Muslim effort to gather this material was in many ways more important than the outcome. Islamic scholars taught themselves Latin, so that they could read the history of the later Roman Empire, and they hunted for other books to fill in the gaps in their knowledge of the time. During the ninth and tenth centuries, Arabic translators made the first copies of important Latin texts they found and passed those stories down to the people of al-Andalus. Among their cherished discoveries was the Latin author Orosius of Spain.

A Roman, a Christian, a friend of Augustine's, and a pioneer in writing the history of the Roman Empire, Orosius had authored a monumental work called *Seven Books of History Against the Pagans,* which he published in the decade after Alaric's attack. One of the first works by a Latin writer to eschew the gloomy picture Jerome and Augustine had painted, the work gave Christian readers an honest account of what had happened in 410. Orosius's message was that even after serious disasters, history went on. The world did not end. Life could and did recover. Orosius's straightforward approach to 410 became essential reading for Christian realists during the Middle Ages, many of whom had tired of hearing apocalyptic sermons from their pastors about the "Fall of Rome," the downfall of society, and the immediacy of the Second Coming.

Two centuries after Orosius died, the Muslims of al-Andalus, eager to repair social relationships across a kingdom of Jews, Christians, and Muslims, sought out Latin editions of his text from libraries and marketplaces and enthusiastically recopied and translated his books. Like Virgil to Dante, Hurushiyush, as they styled Orosius in Arabic, became medieval Islam's guide to this captivating lost world. Islamic and Christian readers alike found a road map to their common future in Orosius's pages. The Muslim scholars of al-Andalus were thus intellectually a step ahead of many later Christian book hunters, most of whom lauded Cicero and the Roman Republic but scoffed at any attempt to valorize the period of the Goths or the study of the Roman Empire. The Renaissance's well-educated men, like Petrarch, Giorgio Vasari, Flavio Biondo, and their classically minded followers, regularly told others that a gloomy dark age had settled over Europe with the Goths' arrival. In their minds, Alaric and his followers were animals, just as Ovid, Prudentius, and others had said they were.

As a result of these and other self-righteous judgments, whole chapters of the later Roman Empire and, by extension, Alaric's history became unpalatable to generations of humanists. The notion of the "Gothic" as scary, weird, and a departure from the norm became Europe's bête noire. Gothic was everything the humanists hated, so Gothic became the preferred label for anything different, from letterforms to architectural forms. Still, curious people drew inspiring lessons from the Goths and valued their contributions to history. Reflecting on the excitement of 1492, after the Muslim al-Andalus had become the Christian kingdom of Ferdinand and Isabella, the sixteenth-century Spanish poet Francisco de Quevedo found it perfectly natural to think that the intrepid crews of the *Niña, Pinta,* and *Santa Maria* had set out across the Atlantic with the goal of bringing "the Goths to the unknown edge of the globe." For the king and queen's Christian subjects, as well as for an international audience, the idea of the Gothic became a hallmark of freedom and experimentation, a way to describe architecture loosened from its classical shackles, and a name for typography free of classical influences.

In the coming centuries, the Gothic came to symbolize liberty itself, a quality that was embraced by the members of the British government, who were skeptical of the heavy hand of kings and queens; they built their Houses of Parliament in the Gothic style. In novels, the Gothic replaced the syrupy atmosphere of romances with a more mysterious world of castles and counts, of telltale hearts mysteriously beating under the floorboards, and of gruesome fairy tales. To be Gothic was to be a risk-taker—maybe not a pirate exactly but a restless explorer, nonetheless.

Yet as Muslims carried the Goths' reputation east and Columbus brought it west, Alaric's reputation went nowhere. The forty-year-old had risked everything on a spectacular attack, but his name had never recovered. The earliest anyone dared to admire him came in the sixteenth century, when German writers claimed the Goths as their country's ancestors, an assertion based on the erroneous assumption that, since the Gothic language and the German language belong to the same family tree, their people must also have been related in the distant past. After this baseless suggestion won over a gullible audience, it inspired centuries of supposedly critical inquiry that sought to link the history of modern Germany to ancient stories about a virtuous race of brave, patriotic warriors who hailed from northern and eastern Europe, just as the Roman writer Tacitus had described it in his book on Germanic warrior culture, *Germania,* and as Jordanes had in his *Origins and Deeds of the Goths.* In the twentieth century, specious ideas of racial and ethnic purity in northern Europe were deployed to march history in a horrific direction. Medieval and modern Europe owes much of its complicated heritage to the life of Alaric, a bold, aggressive, outspoken, and idealistic immigrant who died a failure.

CHAPTER ELEVEN

Smoldering Ruins and a Lost Key

History aims for a truer interpretation of what happened.

—EUNAPIUS OF SARDIS

Claudian once remarked that the gods would have to rewrite "the immutable laws of the universe" to dampen the Roman people's indefatigable spirit. In the months after 410, the Roman people proved him correct. There were bodies to be buried, family members to be mourned, lost dogs and other pets to be found. The work of sweeping up broken pots and hauling away marble drums from toppled columns and other clumps of brick and mortar was a constant reminder of a deeper loss. "A wound, though deep, heals by degrees," it was said during the fifth century, and the Roman people seem to have recognized that the life-changing events they had witnessed would not be cleared away from their lives as quickly as the debris.

There was still government money in those years to repair the city. Construction workers cleared rubble from damaged lots, and tourists to the cultural capital were astonished at the progress the Roman people were making. Less than five years after the attack, it looked as if "nothing had happened," they told Orosius, who recorded their honest quip in his history book. A mix of sympathy, empathy, and curiosity motivated many to come to Rome and see for themselves. Sometime during these months and years, Rome began talking about a memorial.

For a culture with a history of spellbinding ostentation, the Roman monument to 410 proved surprisingly modest but powerful. Romans appreciated how absorbing memory could be and how it overwhelmed people when they stood in meaningful places. Experts in the art of mnemonics, or techniques to assist one's memory, had taught Romans how to improve their recollection by storing important facts in an imaginary house. By strolling the rooms of one's mind, one could more easily retrieve the necessary information. "For when we return to a place after considerable absence," Quintilian noted, "we not merely recognize the place itself but remember things that we did there."

The emotional effect of an absent building could also keep a memory alive. Many ancient people experienced that phenomenon during their visits to Athens, where the Athenians had used a mix of monuments and memory to commemorate a painful episode from their own history. In 480 B.C., the Persian king Xerxes sacked the city and burned the city's first Temple of Athena. In order to preserve the powerful moment in time when the building fell, the Athenians intentionally left the wreckage in place. Fifty years after that attack, when a new Parthenon arose under Pericles's leadership, it did so adjacent to the visible ruins of the original building. The juxtaposition of a damaged site with the brand-new temple reminded the Athenians of the horrors their city had endured. A similar calculus led to the creation of Rome's memorial to 410.

Seven addresses worthy of note—although there certainly were more—were damaged in Alaric's attack and are known explicitly from the ancient writers. Two were churches, the first a small neighborhood basilica dedicated to Mary and located in the Trastevere district. The second occupied the expansive Lateran property near the center of town. Dedicated to Saint John and the seat of Rome's powerful bishop, it had been the most important church in the fifth-century city, with impressive mosaic walls, a gilded ceiling, and dazzling clerestory windows. In both appearance and public stature, it surpassed even the reputation of St. Peter's Basilica, whose connection to the dead apostle some Romans considered tenuous at best. Poor and wealthy Christians alike attended Mass beneath its roof.

Four houses were also destroyed, most of them luxury residences: the city mansion of the rich Valerii family, Marcella's house, the house of the writer Sallust, and a villa belonging to Anicia Proba, the wealthy woman who supposedly opened the gate for Alaric. The seventh site was an open plaza in the city center called the Peace Forum, in the shadow of the Colosseum. Its trees and fountains sat near an older war memorial that commemorated the Roman conquest of Jerusalem.

Of these seven structures, the writer Sallust's house, which had always attracted sizable crowds, became the core of the memorial to the attack. Its owner, a hard-nosed political reporter, wrote the definitive history of the conspiracy of Catiline, a crisis that had almost unraveled the republic in the first century B.C. Back then, Sallust lived in a pleasant grove outside the city center. After his death and with the expansion of the capital, the quiet space around his property was absorbed into a large urban park, later acquired by the emperors. They enclosed the sprawling villa inside the city's expanded walls and erected a fence around the house and gardens to keep drifters away from it. To protect their privacy, generations of Caesars locked its gates, but occasionally they were thrown open to curious visitors, drawn to the villa by its charming mix of historic architecture and exquisite landscaping in a quiet corner of the city. It was a pleasant stroll from the swimming pools of Diocletian's Baths, and the property lured others off the Salt Road, which passed right by.

During the 410 attack, a large portion of the brick house collapsed in the fires. Several of its tall walls survived, a dark coat of charcoal scarring the red and yellow bricks. The ruins, perhaps because of their proximity to the sight of the breach, became a ready symbol of the attack. Although Romans never said who decided to preserve the core of the building and the surrounding rubble, they did so for more than a hundred years. The ancient writer Procopius, who visited it in the sixth century, called it "half-burned." No ancient source explains why a hollow shell of a building captivated so many people for so long when others were demolished in far less time, but the reasons are easy to deduce. Romans must have come to it looking for catharsis.

The Romans did not give up on their historic city, at least in the short term, despite the shifting political realities and the onset of economic decline. In 414, the ranks of the city's welfare program continued to swell. Astoundingly, government workers that year registered tens of thousands of new names in the local program for free or reduced-price handouts of oil, wine, pork, and bread. In one day alone, the office of the city prefect added fourteen thousand new people to the list and immediately informed Honorius that Rome's supplies "were insufficient for the city's increased population." A half million people by then still called Rome their home, although, as it soon became clear, neither the city nor its government would be able to sustain them. In 455, just forty-five years after Alaric's attack, Vandals departed from their new kingdom in North Africa and sailed to the Italian coast. With an unknown political aim, they burned the Roman harbor and proceeded to sack the city—and this raid, the second part of a devastating one-two punch from two separate groups of foreigners, was the blow from which the Roman Empire never recovered.

Almost every period in Roman history has witnessed its own version of a catastrophe: from the devastating fire of Nero's reign in A.D. 64, which destroyed ten of the city's fourteen regions, to Alaric's attack, to the Vandal destruction of the city. During the Middle Ages, the Tiber River caused perennial flooding, and the city's residents left notches on church exteriors to record the height of the waters. Some marks still astonish for their placement well above eye level. In the eleventh century, the Norman conqueror Robert Guiscard set fire to the city in a dispute with the papacy and the Holy Roman emperor. During the Renaissance, the city's most notorious raiders often originated from within the walls. Pope Urban VIII, who hailed from the aristocratic Italian Barberini family, at one point melted the Pantheon's tall bronze doors and used the raw material to redecorate the Vatican. Critics accused the freewheeling pontiff of cannibalizing what little the ancient "barbarians" had left untouched.

In the eighteenth century, Rome's urban history fascinated those who sought out artifacts of the classical past. Every episode in the city's long story tantalized them, luring them beneath the surface of the streets, underneath the stately Renaissance *palazzi* and beneath the damp shops of the city's *botteghe*. Unfortunately, many antiquarians didn't know how to distinguish Robert Guiscard's fire of 1084 from the Vandal raid of the fifth century. The ruins of Rome, to them, remained largely a romantic jumble. No one really understood what they were looking at when they descended with their torches into the dark caverns below the marble monuments. Everyone guessed. The ability to examine buildings beneath the ground and reconstruct their history through a precise sequence of time—the science of archaeology—was born in the nineteenth century.

More rigorous observation eventually became the norm. And as record keeping sharpened, the discipline of archaeology matured and inspired a generation of researchers. In Rome, one particular event opened exciting opportunities for new archaeological discovery. On September 20, 1870, an army of Italian Republicans crashed through Rome's city walls at the Porta Pia, near the Salt Gate, and forced Pope Pius IX to relinquish his control of the city, both within and outside its historic perimeter, and to cede its governance to the Italians. The besieged pope fled to his Vatican property, where his successors would establish their own small independent state. One year after Pius left, Rome became the capital of a newly united Italy.

The Italians of Rome craved knowledge about their city's ancient heritage, and many foreigners came to study its ruins in the decades following the birth of the modern country. President Woodrow Wilson stepped onto the basalt stones of the old city in 1919 as one of the first Americans to tour the impressive monuments of the Roman Forum, but it was a woman of Italian-American heritage named Marcella, the daughter of parents who were pioneers in the archaeology of Rome, who watched some of the most significant discoveries take place.

Very little is known about Marcella's mother, Mary Ellen Rhodes of Providence, Rhode Island. But about Marcella's father, Rodolfo, scholars have written volumes. He was an Italian who studied to become an engineer, later worked as an archaeologist, and was among the first

Pictured at right is Rodolfo Lanciani, the Italian archaeologist who spent decades excavating Rome, including the House of the Vestal Virgins in the Forum, as well as edifices on the Aventine Hill. At center, archivists believe, is his American wife, Mary Ellen. The two are joined by their driver, left. The couple generated transatlantic interest in the story of the ancient Romans.

to bring expert draftsmanship and mapmaking to the study of ancient Rome. A tireless excavator, he sometimes sported a pate of fuzzy hair, a neatly trimmed white walrus mustache, and giant herringbone topcoat. Rodolfo and Mary Ellen collaborated for many years. She translated his discoveries into English and sent bulletins to the United States, which appeared under her husband's name in the *New York Times*. Together, they introduced generations of readers to life in ancient Rome.

Italians have a delightfully deferential way of referring to esteemed scholars and performers. They use the definite article *il* or *la* before their last name, making them larger than life: "the" only one of their kind. To scholars, Mary Ellen's husband, Marcella's father, will always be "il Lanciani." In his eighty-four years, he celebrated professional triumphs and moments of family joy. He became an Italian senator, helped establish the new capital's National Museum of Roman Antiquity inside Diocletian's Baths, and arranged for museums in Chicago and Boston to acquire Roman artifacts, a decision that caused some scandal.

Names were important to Rodolfo and Mary Ellen Lanciani, both of whom adored the history of Rome, and in many ways, the professor made his own name by excavating the city's Aventine Hill, the site where an eighty-year-old reader had been sitting quietly with her books in the late summer of 410, before she was abruptly taken from it. The modern couple who devoted so much of their energy to resurrecting the ancient past gave their daughter that distant woman's name. Two residents of Rome, each named Marcella, born hundreds of years apart, would share a connection to Alaric's story.

Gates of Rome—Porta Salaria, Honorius, a.d. 400.

Carlo Baldassarre Simelli, a nineteenth-century photographer with an eye for landscapes, made this albumen print of Rome's Salt Gate, with its simple archway and wooden door, sometime between 1864 and 1866, before the monument was demolished.

Rome's ruins spoke to Lanciani. Whenever he descended beneath the city, he said, he "felt more than ever the vast difference between reading Roman history in books, and studying it from its monuments, in the presence of its leading actors; and I realized once more what a privilege it is to live in a city where discoveries of such importance occur frequently." Ancient Rome's sordid stories enthralled him. "I wish I could tell my readers that my hands did actually touch the bones of those murdered patricians," he explained on one expedition, referring to the evidence he hoped to find for those who had been killed by Emperor Claudius's murderous wife, Messalina. His discoveries that day were more typical of an archaeologist's unsensational work: broken slabs of marble, empty funerary urns, and piles of unidentifiable bones.

As a scientist, Lanciani knew how hard it would be to find traces of Alaric's Rome in this rising European capital. Great parts of antiquity intruded into contemporary life—for instance, Honorius's walls, which corral the same area today as they did in the fifth century. But he also knew that most of the city's ancient stones had been rearranged to form the modern city, and a good detective would need the testimony of an eyewitness if he hoped to locate any Gothic crime scene in this confusing heap of evidence.

Lanciani had seven clues. These were the seven addresses, known from the ancient writers who had described some aspect of the attack. One of the most promising pieces of testimony was the letter Jerome wrote from the Holy Land and sent to Principia, the young girl who was with Marcella at the time of her kidnapping. The letter gave Lanciani the idea to excavate the Aventine Hill. By the time he finished, in 1899, the picture he had assembled was frightful.

I have witnessed excavations made in the Vigna Torlonia, among the remains of the Thermae Decianae [the Baths of the Emperor Decius] and of the house of Trajan; in the Vigna Maciochhi, among the ruins of the palace of Annia Cornificia Faustina, younger sister of Marcus Aurelius and wife of Ummidius Quadratus; in the garden of [Saint] Anselmo, where the palace of the Pactumcii was discovered in 1892; and in the garden of [Saint] Sabina, once occupied by the houses of Cosmus, Minister of Finance under Marcus Aurelius, and of Marcella and Principia, the friends of St. Jerome.

In watching these excavations, I was struck by the fact that these beautiful places must have perished towards the beginning of the fifth century of our era, and all from the same cause. The signs of destruction are everywhere the same: traces of flames which blackened the red ground of the frescoes, and caused the roofs to fall on the mosaic or marble pavements of the ground floor; coins scattered among the ruins, belonging, with rare exception, to the fourth century; statues that had been restored over and over again; marbles stolen from pagan buildings, mostly from sepulchral monuments, and utilized for hurried restorations; and Christian symbols on lamps and domestic utensils. These indications fix the period and point to the same historical event—the capture and pillage of Rome by the Goths in August, 410.

The Aventine paid dearly for the partiality shown for it by the noble and wealthy. The treasures accumulated in its palaces roused the cupidity of the invaders, and led them to excesses of plunder and destruction such as were spared to more humble districts of the City.

If one scholar was responsible for influencing people's perceptions of Alaric's attack, it was Lanciani. But despite the richness of his writing and the authority that undergirds his description, not everything he thought he saw has been confirmed by later scholars.

The problem has stemmed from the list of sources Lanciani used. None of the writers was present in Rome on August 24, 410, and it is entirely possible that they exaggerated or distorted the extent of Alaric's "destruction" because they were describing what they themselves had not seen. The information on the damage that befell Rome's four churches comes from an anonymous sixth-century biography of the popes. Procopius mentioned looting at the Peace Forum, but how he cataloged it in the sixth century remains unclear. Even the location of some buildings mentioned in the list is doubtful. Jerome's letter to Principia, from which scholars infer what happened the night Marcella was kidnapped, refers to the elderly woman's residence but lacks an actual address. Notwithstanding Lanciani's insistence that he saw it as it was excavated, the property could be anywhere on the Aventine Hill, perhaps still underground. Similar difficulties arise in locating Anicia Proba's house and the Valerii estate.

A skeptical approach to the written and archaeological evidence did not concern Lanciani. Alaric's men were "bigoted Christians," Lanciani explained in his book *The Destruction of Ancient Rome*. They had ransacked the precious cultural heritage of "Roman civilization," a beloved though highly problematic Eurocentric concept in Lanciani's day. By the time he died, in 1929, almost every broken pot in the city had become, under his influence, proof of the crimes pinned on Goths. The evidence was always circumstantial, but archaeologists and historians were undeterred and used it to fit a predetermined narrative about Gothic "barbarity."

Examples of Gothic destruction soon proliferated, even when the ancient sources never mentioned seeing Goths in a specific neighborhood of the city, like near the Roman Forum. Because a fire ravaged the great law courts there in the early fifth century, and a later papal biographer suggested that they had burned "in the Gothic attack," scholars pinned the destruction on Alaric's men. Yet the most recent study of a key damaged monument, the Basilica Aemelia, cautions that, although such reconstruction of events might be possible, "it cannot clearly be documented."

Not every scholar or even antiquarian has always zealously prosecuted the Goths, as Lanciani did. Ennio Quirinio Visconti, an antiquities hunter who worked for Pope Pius VI in the eighteenth century, stood out among his time for hesitating to make such blanket statements. When Visconti's team unearthed a cache of silver on the city's Esquiline Hill, pieces that belonged to a Roman politician from the 360s A.D., they were careful to present the discovery in neutral terms. The remarkable "Esquiline Treasure," as it came to be known, comprised two candlesticks, five plates, four bowls, a washbasin, lamps, cups, forks, and spoons. To Visconti, the reason why the owner buried the items was unclear. Nothing about the scene incriminated the Goths.

Centuries later, however, Lanciani imagined for his readers the terrifying circumstances that had led to the burial of the silver collection during Alaric's attack. "We are not far ... from the date of the sack of 410," he explained, brushing away five decades of intervening history. He was certain that Alaric was implicated in the loss of the treasure.

Much more work still needs to be done to separate our assumptions from the facts, but it is clear that the apocalyptic imagery used by Christian writers, including Augustine and Jerome, to describe 410 has distorted history's picture of what happened in Rome. In fact, when archaeologists do find signs of fire or ruin in excavations today, the scientific evidence overwhelmingly points to an event in the middle of the fifth century, around the year 455. The ancient apartments on a little road called the Vicus Caprarius, buried beneath Rome's Trevi Fountain, collapsed around that time, probably because of a Vandal attack. Scholars have also proposed various overlooked geological causes, like earthquakes, to explain noticeable damage from the early fifth century. One such quake ruptured the pipes in Marcella's local neighborhood baths, the Baths of the Emperor Decius, around 408. Lanciani blamed that complex's destruction, too, on Alaric.

In the end, although 410 left an indelible mark on the Roman psyche, the traces of that attack are not really visible anymore. As one Italian scholar has noted, when it comes to finding Alaric's Rome, the ruins tell us *"quasi nulla,"* almost nothing, about those seventy-two hours. A chance event, however, does occasionally pull modern Rome back into the fifth century. In 2006, engineers from the Italian natural gas company Italgas wanted to install underground pipes in the center of the still largely residential and still very delightful Aventine Hill. Before they could proceed, they called a team of archaeologists to the site. Instances like these are referred to as "rescue excavations" and offer opportunities for scholars to collaborate with industry. The archaeologists are usually the happier group, because, for once, a wealthy sponsor wants to dig under Rome. The bargain is that the scholars have to proceed with their usual fastidiousness but also with the clock ticking, as when a four-story 1930s ocher condominium with pleasant balconies and climbing ivy needed urgent repairs to its gas line.

A twenty-first-century rescue excavation is not easy. Six meters of earth and rubble—twenty feet, or almost two stories—can separate the city's modern cobblestones from the ancient streets. Few experts can predict what they will find when they dig. In one of Lanciani's first attempts to reach ancient levels on the Aventine, he stumbled upon a seventeenth-century Jesuit school buried underneath an open plaza, a surprising discovery that told him to go deeper. The team in 2006, led by archaeologist Paola Quaranta, dug until they came upon the familiar pattern of an ancient Roman floor, a recognizable mix of crushed ceramics stirred into cement and poured on the ground. Italian archaeologists call it a *cocciopesto* surface, from the *cocci,* or ceramics, ground into a paste. The ancient Romans laid surfaces like it to protect the ground from repeated wear and tear, the way a craftsman might throw sand on a workroom floor.

The archaeologists had discovered an ancient house. As they cleared the surface of debris from the tiny corner of the workroom, an object in the corner startled them. It was a melted but still identifiable ball of glass beakers, metal cups, and tools that had been welded together— *"semifusi,"* as the excavators said. These were the telltale signs of a fire. Farther on, in a second room, the only other space the archaeologists explored before refilling their trench, they made another remarkable discovery. It was a bronze padlock, still tightly bound to an iron chain, the kind of puzzling prop an audience member might inspect after a magician escapes from his shackles. The device, locked in antiquity, remained locked centuries later. And it was missing its key.

To the smart excavators of La Quaranta's team, a simple explanation presented itself. The workshop had housed the ancient owner's safe deposit chest, which had been fashioned from perishable wood. After a fire broke out in the workroom, the flames fused together the disparate objects on the floor and incinerated the chest, leaving its chain and lock intact. According to remarkably precise evidence collected at the site, in the form of stamped Roman coins, the scholars concluded that this fire had ravaged the property a year or two after 408. Unlike the situation witnessed at the nearby baths, whose walls were shaken by an earthquake and eventually restored, the rubble was never cleared from these rooms. Over time, as the months and years passed and its owner—whoever he or she was—never came home, the vacant house on the Aventine fell into a permanent state of disrepair.

It is easy to fall into the trap of thinking that a single key unlocks the meaning of historical events, just as it is to judge the Romans for their unwillingness to extend citizenship to the Goths. The Romans themselves knew that the history of what caused the raid of 410 could not be reduced to such a simple explanation. "It is obvious that the capture of so great a city as Rome must have been attended with many remarkable circumstances," Sozomen said in his *Church History*. Yet many at least endeavored to wrestle with the causes of what had happened and to understand it. Some turned to their faith and saw Alaric's attack as a "punishment for God's wrath." Socrates preferred to scrutinize the action of his government, convinced that the horror of 410 had stemmed from the "casual disregard and complete inattention to the situation between citizens and foreigners."

The ancient Romans were smarter than is sometimes recognized. They may not have articulated clear strategies for improving racial and ethnic tensions across their society, but they found creative ways to build a multicultural society across three continents. They did not have the words to describe what it meant to identify as a religious moderate, but many pagans, Christians, and Jews demonstrated a noble commitment to moderation in their beliefs and their everyday actions. And although the Romans lived under strong-willed, occasionally tyrannical emperors, many of them were highly motivated, politically attuned men and women who could band together, when necessary, to accomplish common goals for their society. The Romans achieved all these things despite living in a world of terrible discrimination, fanatical religious intolerance, and a restricted access to political power.

Alaric's quest for change, motivated by decades of encounters with bigotry and xenophobia, challenge hysterical notions about this pivotal moment in ancient history. His decision to attack the city, while admittedly extreme, was his last and perhaps most effective weapon for gaining the attention of a government that refused to make him its full partner or his people full citizens. The fact remains that the Romans could have extended citizenship to the Goths, but they did not, and the Roman people could have used 410 to demand changes from their leaders, championing the rise of a new Caracalla or advocating a retreat from Theodosius's single-party Christian state. Instead, Rome fomented its policies of intolerance and settled for the status quo.

Epilogue

To weep with them that weep does ease some deal
But sorrow flouted at is double death.

—SHAKESPEARE, *Titus Andronicus*

C uriosity has pushed many people to go to the modern Italian town of Cosenza, in Calabria, to look for Alaric's tomb. Some take Jordanes's history book and follow it like a map to a buried treasure. Gibbon called the burial Cosenza's "secret spot," and Jordanes does say that Alaric was buried in the Busento River "with many treasures," before its waters, obstructed for the ceremony, finally swallowed him up. Among the riches he allegedly took with him were a collection of Jewish Temple objects that the Romans had stolen during the sack of Jerusalem, in A.D. 70, and kept for centuries in Rome's Peace Forum until Alaric pillaged it.

The dream of seizing the ancient Temple menorah has lit a crazed fire in many eyes over the years. But everyone who has hunted for it has gone home disappointed, including the Nazis, who went to Cosenza in the 1930s and returned to Berlin empty-handed. Alaric's death still shapes life in Italy, with many children taught to see him as the "barbarian" who attacked the empire. But after sixteen hundred years, that legacy might be changing.

In 2013, Cosenza's enterprising mayor, Mario Occhiuto, floated plans to build a museum to one of Roman history's much-maligned figures. Convinced that Alaric's connection to the town deserved to be more widely publicized, he began fund-raising for an exhibition hall to be called the Museum of the Treasure of Alaric. The attraction would be constructed at the city's riverbank and would complement the collection of largely

A bronze sculpture of Alaric, titled Alarico *and constructed by Paolo Grassino, was unveiled in Cosenza in 2016. It stands at the confluence of the Crati and Busento Rivers, where Alaric's body was supposedly interred.*

indigenous artifacts—simple cups and bronze pins—already housed in Cosenza's more prestigious Museum of the Bretti and Enotri, named for two of the local populations of the area in ancient times. Clearly, the mayor hoped that a second cultural institution would lure even more visitors to this sleepy corner of Calabria. Not everyone was supportive, and the detractors included leading archaeological authorities in Rome, who lost no time in objecting that there were no artifacts to put on display in such an ill-conceived "museum." Plans have stalled indefinitely. Cosenza holds the memory of Alaric's death, but nothing more.

A lack of a tangible connection to Alaric has not stopped the southern Italian city from claiming its part in history in other creative ways. On November 5, 2016, the city's officials invited journalists and local dignitaries to a ceremony at the Busento River, where they unveiled their latest effort to put Cosenza on the tourist map: an avant-garde equestrian statue of the town's most notorious visitor, sculpted by the artist Paolo Grassino. Depicting a full-sized naked warrior in a king's crown perched strangely on the horse's head, Grassino's bronze disorients the casual observer, who might be stumped by the artist's choices. But there's no mistaking King Alaric's elegiac look, as he gazes beneath him at the place where the town's two bodies of water, the Busento and the Crati Rivers, meet as one.

ACKNOWLEDGMENTS

The Roman historian Eunapius once told his readers, in one of the many fragments he left behind, how difficult it was to make a realistic portrait of another person. One wrong stroke could spoil an entire life, and it was incumbent on the writer or artist to capture the tiniest details—from "a deep furrow on the brow" to an individual's "prominent sideburns"—to do justice to one's subject. I'm grateful to the following individuals for sharing their time and expertise as I gathered the many puzzle pieces that constituted Alaric's life.

At the Palazzo Traversa in Bra, Italy, Marco Dellarocca guided me through the material from ancient Pollentia. At Cosenza, thank you to Dr. Maria Cerzoso for welcoming me to the Museo dei Brettii e degli Enotri and sharing her perspectives on the collection. In Rome, my thanks to Dr. Angela D'Amelio and the staff at the Archivio Fotografico di Museo di Roma for helping me develop a mental picture of nineteenth- and twentieth-century Rome; to Alessandra Giovenco, archivist at the British School at Rome; and to Dr. John Ochsendorf, director of the American Academy in Rome, whose institution hosted me for two weeks in October 2018 while I was finishing a draft of this book. Special thanks to Stephen Kay, Letizia Ceccarelli, Robert Coates-Stephens, Roberta Bernabei, Jonathan Levi, Katie Parla, Darius Arya, Barry Strauss, and Crystal King for making Rome even friendlier. The staff at La Rinascente near Piazza Fiume deserves acknowledgment for permitting me to study the remains of the Porta Salaria from their terrace.

In Athens, I owe a debt to Dr. Jorunn Økland, director of the Norwegian Institute, and to her family, who were expert guides to the city, its monuments, and its people.

Special thanks to Ilse Jung at the Kunsthistorisches Museum in Vienna.

This project was supported by a Mellon Faculty Development Grant from Saint Louis University, a Summer Research Award in the Humanities from Saint Louis University, and support from the Saint Louis University College of Arts and Sciences. I would like to thank the dean of the College of Arts and Sciences, Christopher Duncan, and associate dean Donna LaVoie for their support; the chair of the History Department, Charles Parker; Jamie Emery in the Saint Louis University libraries; and our administrators, Chris Pudlowski and Kelly Goersch. I am also grateful to my graduate research assistant, Robert Olsen; to the undergraduate students in my fall 2018 Historian's Craft class; to the graduate students in my Late Antique Cities course; and to my undergraduate research assistant Jiaqi Chen for thoughtfully commenting on the manuscript.

In Austin, I would like to express my thanks to the staff at Austin Central Library, to Shiela Winchester at the Perry-Castañeda Library at the University of Texas, and to Dr. Lesley Dean-Jones of UT Austin's Department of Classics for facilitating my research. I owe three other scholars a note of thanks for the support they have showed me over the years: Michele Salzman and Noel Lenski in the United States and, in Budapest, Marianne Sághy, who passed away during the writing of this project.

Various people read drafts of this manuscript and offered feedback. I'd like to thank Ike Krumenacher, who read the project in its early stages, and Shakira Christodoulou and Holly Rubino for their suggestions at the end. I feel lucky to have had such thoughtful listeners: Nathaniel Jones, Sara Ryu, Adrian Ossi, and Lisa Çakmak; the graduate students in the ancient Mediterranean program at the University of Chicago; Sean Leatherbury; and Adam Levine at the Toledo Museum of Art.

Karl Galinsky, Michael White, Hendrik Dey, Adam Rabinowitz, Lorri Glover, Torrie Hester, Silvana Siddali, Claire Gilbert, Fabien Montcher, Thorsten Fögen, and Peter Ginna heard about the work and shaped it in important ways. My thanks also to Shawn Bose, Taylor Bose, Sally Quinn, and Jon Meacham for their encouragement and to Mo Crist, Bonnie Thompson, Ingsu Liu, and the entire Norton production team for their dedication to details.

I couldn't imagine having undertaken this project without the guidance of two professionals whose instincts and insight I deeply trust: Alane Mason at Norton and Ayesha Pande at Ayesha Pande Literary. Alaric's story would never have come to life had it not been for their encouragement, and I'm grateful for the patience they extended to me, and the wisdom they imparted, during these past four years.

Finally, thank you especially to Gardiner. You always help me hear which notes to strike.

NOTES

Source Abbreviations

I chose the translations of the works of ancient authors largely based on their literary appeal, so some texts are listed with more than one translator. Chapters and line numbers refer to modern publications or, where I am the translator, to the ancient texts. Most of the translations of Claudian, including the text of Alaric's two monologues, are my own, since the standard English version of Claudian's poetry remains Maurice Platnauer's stodgy prose edition from 1922—and I suspect that an opinionated artist like Claudian, had he ever been asked, would have insisted that his audience listen to his performance in verse.

AM	*Ammianus Marcellinus: The Later Roman Empire (A.D. 354–378)*, translated by W. Hamilton (London: Penguin Books, 1986); and *Ammianus Marcellinus* by J. Rolfe (Cambridge, MA: Harvard University Press, 1935–39).
Augustine	*CG = The City of God Against the Pagans*, translated by H. Bettenson (London: Penguin Books, 1972).
	R = Sermon on the Destruction of the City of Rome, translated by M. V. O'Reilly (Washington, DC: Catholic University of America Press, 1955).
	S = Sermons
Claudian	*E = Poem Against Eutropius*
	F = The Farmer from Verona
	G = The Gothic Attack
	H3 = Poem for Emperor Honorius on Celebrating His Third Consulship, in 396
	H4 = Poem for Emperor Honorius on Celebrating His Fourth Consulship, in 398
	H6 = Poem for Emperor Honorius on Celebrating His Sixth Consulship, in 404

R = *Poem Against Rufinus*

S = *In Praise of Serena*

W = *Wedding Poem for Maria and Honorius*

All translations are by the author or have been adapted from M. Platnauer, *Claudian* (Cambridge, MA: Harvard University Press, 1922).

Eunapius   Fr. = Fragments in *The Fragmentary Classicising Historians of the Later Roman Empire*, edited and translated by R. Blockley, volume 2 (Liverpool: Cairns, 1983).

Lives = *Lives of the Philosophers*, translated by W. Wright (Cambridge, MA: Harvard University Press, 1921).

EV   The anonymous sixth-century "Excerpta Valesiana," in *Ammianus Marcellinus: History*, vol. 3, *Books 27–31 and Excerpta Valesiana*, translated by J. Rolfe (Cambridge, MA: Harvard University Press, 1939).

J   Jordanes's *The Origins and Deeds of the Goths* in C. Mierow, *The Gothic History of Jordanes* (Princeton, NJ: Princeton University Press, 1908).

Jerome   L = Letters, found in *NPNF* 6, translated by W. Fremantle, G. Lewis, and W. Martley, 1890.

Ez. = *Commentary on Ezekiel*, translated by Thomas P. Scheck (New York: Newman Press, 2016).

M   Macrobius, *Saturnalia*, 3 vols., edited and translated by Robert A. Kaster (Cambridge, MA: Harvard University Press, 2011).

Oly.   Olympiodorus's Fr. = Fragments in *The Fragmentary Classicising Historians of the Later Roman Empire*, edited and translated by R. Blockley, vol. 2 (Liverpool: Cairns, 1983).

Orosius   *Seven Books of History Against the Pagans*, translated by A. T. Fear (Liverpool: Liverpool University Press, 2010); and *The Seven Books of History Against the Pagans: The Apology of Paulus Orosius*, translated by I. Raymond (New York: Columbia University Press, 1936).

Ovid   *Poems from the Black Sea*, in *Tristia: Ex Ponto*, translated by A. Wheeler, revised by G. Goold (Cambridge, MA: Harvard University Press, 1924).

Philostorgius   *Philostorgius: Church History*, by P. Amidon (Atlanta: Society of Biblical Literature, 2007).

Procopius   H = *History of the Wars*, vol. 2, *Books 3–4: Vandalic War*, translated by H. Dewing (Cambridge, MA: Harvard University Press, 1916).

Prudentius   S = *Two Poems Against Senator Symmachus*, in *Prudentius*, 2 vols., translated by H. Thompson (Cambridge, MA: Harvard University Press, 1949 and 1953).

Saba   In *The Goths in the Fourth Century*, by P. Heather and J. Matthews (Liverpool: Liverpool University Press, 1991).

Socrates   Socrates of Constantinople, *Church History*, found in *NPNF* 2, translated by A. Zenos, 1890.

Sozomen   *Church History,* found in *NPNF* 2, translated by A. Zenos, 1890.

Synesius   *On Kingship,* translation by A. Fitzgerald, in *The Essays and Hymns of Synesius of Cyrene* (Oxford: Oxford University Press, 1930).

Theodoret   *Church History,* found in *NPNF* 3, translated by B. Jackson, 1890.

V   *Vegetius: Epitome of Military Science,* translated by N. Milner (Liverpool: University of Liverpool, 2001); also quite literary is *The Military Institutions of the Romans,* translated by J. Clarke (Harrisburg: Military Service Publishing Company, 1944).

Z   *Zosimus: Historia Nova; The Decline of Rome,* translated by J. Buchanan and H. Davis (San Antonio: Trinity University Press, 1967); and from the edition prepared for W. Green and T. Chaplin (London, 1814).

Other Abbreviations

CIL   The collection of Latin inscriptions published as *Corpus Inscriptionum Latinarum* (Berlin: Walter de Gruyter, 1973–).

NPNF   *The Nicene and Post-Nicene Fathers,* edited by P. Schaff and H. Wace. 2nd ser., 14 vols. (Peabody, MA: Hendrickson Publishers, 1994–).

ThC   *The Theodosian Code and Novels and the Sirmondian Constitutions,* translation with commentary by Clyde Pharr with Theresa Sherrer Davidson and Mary Brown Pharr (Princeton, NJ: Princeton University Press, 1952).

PLRE   The lives of the people of the later Roman Empire, published as *The Prosopography of the Later Roman Empire,* vol. 1 (A.D. 260–395), edited by A.H.M. Jones, J. Martindale, and J. Morris; vol. 2 (A.D. 395–527), edited by J. Martindale (Cambridge University Press, 1971–1980).

SoR   *The Sack of Rome in 410 AD: The Event, Its Context and Its Impact,* edited by J. Lipps, C. Machado, and P. von Rummel (Wiesbaden: Reichert Verlag, 2013).

Chapter One: Seventy-Two Hours

1   **"Whoever attacks one city":** Libanius, *Selected Orations,* vol. 2 (Cambridge, MA: Harvard University Press 1977), 20.49, my translation.

1   **the forty-second man:** Based on the count by Orosius 7.35.

1   **Marcella's library:** The details of Marcella's life have been collected in *PLRE,* vol. 1, 542–43. From Jerome we learn that she was an avid reader and how she "often quoted with approval Plato's saying that philosophy consists in meditating on death" (Jerome *L* 127.6), an idea that is discussed at length in Plato's *Phaedo* along with the ideas of goodness and justice.

2   **"one thousand one hundred and sixty-four years . . .":** Orosius 7.40.1, translation by Fear, slightly modified.

3   **grabbed her from her bedroom:** Jerome *L* 127; "the most celebrated figures" is at 127.1.

3   **church outside the city walls:** The basilica dedicated to Saint Paul, built outside the Ostian Gate (Jerome *L* 127.13).

4   **"savage barbarians":** Augustine *CG* 1.1, my translation.

4   **"The city that once captured":** Jerome *L* 127.12.

4   **preachers like Timothy Aelurus:** Edward Watts, "Interpreting Catastrophe: Disasters in the Works of Pseudo-Joshua the Stylite, Socrates Scholasticus, Philostorgius, and Timothy Aelurus," *Journal of Late Antiquity* 2 (2009): 92–96.

4   **"in the farthest parts of the earth":** Augustine *CG* 1.33, along with "days of public grief" and the flight to second homes, at 1.32.

4   **"Choosing a night when there was a faint glimmer":** Livy, *The History of Rome from the Founding of the City* 5.47, translated by Canon Roberts (New York: E. P. Dutton, 1912).

5   **"sanctuary for refugees":** Plutarch, *Romulus* 9.3, translated by Bernadotte Perrin in *Lives,* vol. 1 (Cambridge, MA: Harvard University Press, 1914), adapted.

5   **the virtues of being a "cosmopolitan":** Ralph Mathisen, *"Peregrini, Barbari, and Cives Romani*: Concepts of Citizenship and the Legal Identity of Barbarians in the Later Roman Empire," *American Historical Review* 111 (2006): 1011–40, at p. 1012.

5   **Superstitious beliefs about geography:** Ptolemy, *Tetrabiblos* 2.2, in Rebecca Kennedy, C. Sydnor Roy, and Max Goldman, *Race and Ethnicity in the Classical World: An Anthology of Primary Sources in Translation* (Indianapolis: Hackett Publishing, 2013), 49–51.

6   **"Here merchant vessels arrive":** Aelius Aristides, *Oration 26*, translated by James Oliver in *The Ruling Power* (Philadelphia: American Philosophical Society, 1953), 896–97.

6   **"What one does not see here, does not exist":** Aelius Aristides, *Oration 26*, translation adapted from C. Behr, *The Complete Works of P. Aelius Aristides, 2* vols. (Leiden: Brill, 1981–86).

7–8 **"gowns of lustrous, imported silk":** Jerome *L* 127.3.

8   **frittered away their fortunes:** Oly. Fr. 41.2.

8   **a medium-sized city:** Oly. Fr. 41.1.

8   **"No other city":** Claudian, *H6,* lines 39–40, translated by Platnauer.

8   **recipe for a popular herbed cheese spread:** M 3.18.12.

9   **"Everyone insults the immigrant":** Claudian *H6*, lines 199–200, translated by Platnauer.

9   **dinner companions who sparred:** M 1.4.5.

9   **"I am a citizen of Bordeaux":** Ausonius, "The Order of Famous Cities," in *Ausonius,* vol. 1, *Books 1–17* (Cambridge, MA: Harvard University Press, 1919), 285, my translation.

10   **"always been dependent on the help of these same foreigners":** AM 28.4.32, translated by Hamilton.

10   **short, sometimes alliterative lists:** "On Peoples' Qualities," discussed and translated by Andrew Gillett, "The Mirror of Jordanes: Concepts of the Barbarian, Then and Now," in *A Companion to Late Antiquity*, edited by P. Rousseau (Malden, MA: Wiley, 2009), 393–94.

10   **"no end in space or time":** Translation adapted from *The Aeneid*, translated by Robert Fagles (New York: Penguin, 2006), 56.

12   **the prospect of "terror":** Claudian *H6*, lines 133–46.

Chapter Two: The Trailblazer

13   **"Be bold, so that someone of future generations":** Eunapius Fr. 34.

15   **"metamorphosed":** Ovid 1.1, with "barbarian land" at 5.2; "Privacy and ease" and "pine planks" at 1.4; and a "state of mourning" at 5.1.

16   **knives "fastened to their sides":** Ovid 5.7 for this and other quotations in the paragraph.

16   **"Peace there is at times":** Ovid 5.2.

18   **workers in the city of Roșia-Montană:** Teodor Sambrian, "La *mancipatio* nei trittici della Transilvania," *Diritto e storia* 4 (2005), published online at http://www.dirittoestoria.it/4/Tradizione-Romana/Sambrian-Mancipatio-trittici-Transilvania.htm.

19   **"Maximus son of Bato":** Dated 17 March 139, in *Inscripțiile Daciei romane*, edited by D. Pippidi and I. Russu (Bucharest: Editura Academiei Române, 1975), wax tablet number 6, 212–17, my translation. On the sale, see Elizabeth Mayer, *Legitimacy and Law in the Roman World: Tabulae in Roman Belief and Practice* (Cambridge: Cambridge University Press, 2004), 56–57.

19   **"There was hardly a region":** *The Writers of the Augustan History*, "Life of Claudius the Second" 9.5, translated by David Magie (Cambridge, MA: Harvard University Press, 1932), 169, slightly modified.

19   **"the price [for slaves] is right":** Symmachus, *Letters* 2.78, discussed in Kyle Harper, "Slave Prices in Late Antiquity (and in the Very Long Term)," *Historia* 59 (2010): 223–24.

19   **"for sale in all parts, without distinction of status":** AM 22.7.7, translated by Hamilton.

19   **Every Roman home in Alaric's day:** Synesius 15.2.

20   **purchased homes:** *Inscripțiile Daciei romane*, edited by D. Pippidi and I. Russu (Bucharest: Editura Academiei Române, 1975), 226–31, with some English translations in *History of Rome Through the Fifth Century: The Empire*, edited by A.H.M. Jones (Boston: Palgrave Macmillan, 1970), 261.

20   **business partnerships:** *CIL* 3, 934–35, 950–51.

20 **spelling was frequently poor:** *L'année épigraphique* 1972, 523; 1972, 524 (husbands); 2004, 1271 (parents).

22 **"Italian rights":** Adrian Sherwin-White, *The Roman Citizenship,* 2nd ed. (Oxford: Clarendon Press, 1973), although it is virtually unreadable to a layman, with extensive passages of untranslated Latin and Greek and often opaque English.

22 **five largest towns of Dacia:** Ulpian *Digest* 50.15.1.8–9. The status also exempted them from paying property taxes to the governor.

23 **"Recently we have been settled by veteran soldiers":** Apuleius, *Apology,* translated in R. Kennedy, C. Roy, and M. Goldman, *Race and Ethnicity in the Classical World: An Anthology of Primary Sources in Translation* (Indianapolis: Hackett Publishing, 2013), 49.

23 **"Let someone see whether he can follow":** *CIL* 3.3676, translated by Jo-Ann Shelton in *As the Romans Did,* 2nd ed. (Oxford: Oxford University Press, 1998), 266–67.

24 **Max's parents:** J 15 for this detail and other quotations from Maximinus's life.

25 **Sexual assault:** Quintilian, *The Lesser Declamations,* vol. 1, edited and translated by D. Shackleton Bailey (Cambridge, MA: Harvard University Press, 2006), nos. 245, 247, and 270.

26 **"Cyclops!":** Jason Moralee, "Maximinus Thrax and the Politics of Race in Late Antiquity," *Greece & Rome* 55 (2008): 55–82.

26 **"by luck" rather than talent:** Herodian 7.1.2, translated by Edward Echols in *Herodian of Antioch's History of the Roman Empire from the Death of Marcus Aurelius to the Accession of Gordian III* (Berkeley: University of California Press, 1961), slightly modified.

26 **"lowly origin":** Herodian 7.1.2, translated by Echols, slightly modified.

27 **the drinking habits of their emperors:** Galerius's staff regularly ignored the emperor's afternoon dictations because everyone in the palace knew he imbibed too much at lunch (EV 4.11).

27 **his favorite bird, named Rome:** Procopius *H* 3.2

27 **"formidable chin and jaw":** The quote is from C. Sutherland, "What Is Meant by 'Style' in Coinage? *American Numismatic Society: Museum Notes* 4–5 (1950): 6.

27 **"exposed to the birds and dogs":** Herodian 8.5.9, translated by Echols.

28 **fallen to a lethal arrow:** J 18.103.

28 **"that the province could be retained":** From the "Life of Aurelian," in *Historia Augusta,* vol. 3, 39.7, translated by David Magie (Cambridge, MA: Harvard University Press, 1932).

Chapter Three: Stolen Childhoods

30 **"It is slow speech that brings the greatest wisdom":** Euripides's *The Phoenician Women,* line 453, translated by Elizabeth Wyckoff in *Euripides IV: The*

Complete Greek Tragedies, 3rd ed., edited by D. Grene, R. Lattimore, M. Griffith, and G. Most (Chicago: University of Chicago Press, 2013).

30 **Gothiscandza:** J 17; "five kings," the mooing cows, and the bridge are at J 4.

31 **the Balthi, or the "Bolds":** J 29.

31 **"quaking bogs":** J 4.

31 **Rugged outcroppings at the river's mouth:** Andrew Poulter, "The Transition to Late Antiquity," in *The Transition to Late Antiquity on the Danube and Beyond,* edited by A. Poulter (Oxford: Oxford University Press, 2007), 30.

32 **"Communities" of plants:** M. Petrescu, V. Cuzic, V. Panait, M. Cuzic, A. M. Rădulescu, and C. Dinu, eds., *Danube Delta 5: Studies and Research of Natural Sciences and Museology* (Tulcea: Gavrilă Simion Eco-Museum Research Institute, 2014).

33 **"suitable homes and pleasant places":** J 4.

33 **Pine Tree Island:** G. Romanescu, O. Bounegru, C. Stoleriu, A. Mihu-Pintilie, C. Ionut Nicu, A. Enea, and C. Oana Stan, "The Ancient Legendary Island of Peuce: Myth or Reality?," *Journal of Archaeological Science* 53 (2105): 521–35.

34 **women labored at the hearth:** Saba 5.3.

34 **freewheeling, tattooed adventuresses:** Adrienne Mayor, *The Amazons: Lives and Legends of Warrior Women Across the Ancient World* (Princeton, NJ: Princeton University Press, 2014), 95–116, with the quotation from Pliny at p. 104.

34 **"swamps and forests":** J 5.

34 **pioneering but now-nameless ancestors:** J 11.

34 **"sweet and fit to drink":** J 5 for this and other quotations.

35 **wingspan of a vulture:** C. Johnstone, "A Short Report on the Preliminary Results from the Study of the Mammal and Bird Bone Assemblages from Dichin," in *The Transition to Late Antiquity on the Danube and Beyond,* edited by A. Poulter (Oxford: Oxford University Press, 2007), 288–89.

35 **"a great rushing sound":** J 55.

36 **Charietto:** Z 3.7, from which the quotations are taken, and AM 17.10.

36 **strumming of a cithara:** J 4–5.

36 **excavated tombs across central and eastern Romania:** Kulikowski 2007, 67–68.

37 **the despondent Gothic chief:** AM 31.4.

37 **a refugee, a *profugus*:** Servius's *Commentary on* The Aeneid *of Virgil,* line 2, edited by G. Thilo and H. Hagan (Leipzig: Tuebner, 1881).

38 **"life's necessities":** AM 31.5.1, translated by Hamilton.

38 **sold second-rate dog meat:** J 26.

38 **wild animals who had escaped from their cages:** AM 31.8, Eunapius Fr. 42.

38 **Dinner invitations were extended:** Lenski 2003, 328, with pp. 178–81 for Pap. Quotations are from the Armenian *Epic Histories Attributed to P'awstos Buzand,* translated by N. Garsoïan (Cambridge, MA: Harvard University Press, 1989), 5.2.

39 **"better to lose liberty than life":** J 26.

39 **"Even if they were the judges of their own case":** AM 31.4, translated by Rolfe.

39 **handouts of food:** AM 31.4.

39 **for his "compassion":** Socrates 4.34.

39 **pledging "faithfulness":** Z 4.26 for this and "insurrection."

40 **"who were too young for war":** Eunapius Fr. 42, which also has the detail of "a fair and pretty boy" and discussion of "hostages."

40 **suitable holding pens for the children:** AM 31.16.

41 **One version of the incident:** AM knew both (31.13), as did Socrates 4.38. See the discussion in Lenski 2003, 338–41.

41 **to exonerate his people:** J 26.

41 **Julius:** Z 4.26 for quotations in this paragraph.

42 **buried this episode in a brief aside:** Michael Speidel, "The Slaughter of Gothic Hostages After Adrianople," *Hermes* 126 (1998): 503–06.

42 **praised Julius's "wise plan":** AM 31.16.

43 **guilty of embellishment:** François Paschoud, *Zosime: Histoire nouvelle*, vol. 2, part 2 (Paris: Les Belles Lettres, 1979), 390.

Chapter Four: Opportunity

44 **"All of us, beginning with himself":** Plutarch, "On Exile," in *Moralia*, vol. 7, translated by P. De Lacy (Cambridge, MA: Harvard University Press, 1959), 569.

44 **"transferred to river barges and transported":** Z 4.10, translated by Buchanan and Davis 1967.

45 **In 2014, a team of Romanian workmen:** F. Topoleanu and L. Chrzanovski, "O descoperire arheologică unică la Noviodunum: Arhetipuri, tipare şi producerea traiţelor," *Peuce* 14 (2016): 145–58.

47 **"sweet and pleasant" and "bitter and pungent":** Plutarch, "On Exile," translated by De Lacy 1959, 523; "happiness," 571; "boundless aether," 529; the moon, 533.

48 **"Rome wasn't built in a day":** *Li proverbe au Vilain*, edited by A. Tobler (Leipzig: Verlag von S. Hirzel, 1895), 43.

49 **boorish and unrefined:** Lenski 2003, 84–97.

50 **a good *cervesia*:** Balsdon 1979, 222.

50 **pigs in Judaea:** Balsdon 1979, 223.

50 **Both Goths and Romans enlisted:** J. Bury, *History of the Later Roman Empire: From the Death of Theodosius I to the Death of Justinian I* (New York: St. Martin's, 1958), 38–54; A. D. Lee, *War in Late Antiquity: A Sourcebook* (Malden, MA: Blackwell, 2007); and Hugh Elton, *Warfare in Roman Europe, AD 350–425* (Oxford: Clarendon Press, 1996).

51   **"enduring the sun, careless of shade":** V 1.3, translated by Milner.

51   **"simple-souled, content with a little":** V 1.3, translated by Milner.

51   **twenty-five or thirty *solidi* a year:** The lower number is the amount known to have been owed by wealthy landowners who did not want to furnish recruits; the higher one, paid out to a soldier. Both are discussed at Bury 1958, 50. See also Warren Treadgold, "Paying the Army in the Theodosian Period," in *Production and Prosperity in the Theodosian Period*, edited by Ine Jacobs (Leuven: Peeters, 2014), 303–18.

51   **a full spread:** Numbers are based on the value of a *nummus* between 375 and 410, in K. Harl, *Coinage in the Roman Economy, 300 B.C. to A.D. 700* (Baltimore: Johns Hopkins University Press, 1996), 168, at table 7.3.

52   **"the same privilege":** *ThC* 7.20.4.3, with tax exemptions at 7.20.4.1, 7.20.8, 7.20.11, and basic equipment at 7.20.3.

52   **All retired military personnel received:** Mathisen 2006, 1026.

53   **"Hailing from beyond the Thracian frontier":** Claudian, *H6*, lines 108–09, my translation. Eunapius mentions the "Macedonian marshes" (Fr. 55).

53   **"a magnet attracts iron":** Eunapius Fr. 43.

54   **"the coming and going of the ships":** J 28 for this and other quotations.

55   **"Bad water is a kind of poison":** V 3.1, translated by Clarke, with "snow," "sacks," and "marksmen" at 1.10–19.

55   **"alert eyes, a straight neck":** V 1.4, translated by Milner; also "When you see these points."

55   **"more quickly imbibed" and "stiffened by age":** V 1.4, translated by Clarke.

56   **cooks and pastry chefs:** V 1.7.

56   **"be content with crackers":** *Augustan History,* "Life of Emperor Pescennius," 10.5, my translation.

57   **Quintus Sulpicius Maximus:** M. Boatwright, *Peoples of the Roman World* (New York: Cambridge University Press, 2012), 92–95.

57   **"yowling wolves, roaring lions, grunting bears":** Nonnos of Panopolis, *Dionysiaca* 2.250–56, translated by W. Rouse (Cambridge, MA: Harvard University Press, 1940), slightly modified.

58   **"babel of screaming sounds":** Nonnos, *Dionysiaca* 2.250–56, translated by W. Rouse.

58   **responsible for bestowing citizenship:** Suetonius, *Grammarians* 22.1, discussed by Robert Kaster, *Guardians of Language: The Grammarian and Society in Late Antiquity* (Berkeley: University of California Press, 1997), 17–18; resistance to linguistic change, p. 29.

58   **"Letters are the greatest beginning in understanding":** Flavius Kollouthos, quoted and translated by Raffaella Cribiore, *Writing, Teachers, and Students in Graeco-Roman Egypt* (Atlanta: Scholars Press, 1996), 33 and 211, no. 160.

58   **"from Greece to Rome, from Rome to Constantinople":** Aurelius Harpocra-

tion, preserved on a papyrus in Cologne (P. Köln 4533), quoted and translated by Kaster 1997, 22 n. 35.

58   **"All arts and trades are brought to perfection":** V 3.10, translated by Clarke.

58   **Two Gothic churchmen:** Sunnia and Frithila's letter does not survive, but the answer they received is Jerome *L* 106, translated by M. Metlen, "Letter of St. Jerome to the Gothic Clergymen Sunnia and Friþila concerning Places in Their Copy of the Psalter Which Had Been Corrupted from the Septuagint," *Journal of English and Germanic Philology* 36 (1937): 515–42.

59   **"Who should believe that the barbarous language":** Jerome *L* 106, translated by Metlen 1937, 515.

59   **"The word 'water' should be plural":** Jerome *L* 106 for this and other quotations; stars and daggers, at 106.7, refers to a copy of Scripture Jerome has emended.

60   **"Would that many of our people":** Gregory of Nazianzus, *Letter* 136, quoted and translated at Lee 2007, 162.

60   **"There was no process by which a foreigner":** Mathisen 2006, 1037.

61   **"on a barman's honor":** Sozomen 7.25, my translation; see also S. Doležal, "Rethinking a Massacre: What Really Happened in Thessalonica and Milan in 390?," *Eirene: Studia Graeca et Latina* 50 (2014): 89–107.

61   **Butheric was eventually killed by a mob:** Theodoret 5.17.

61   **"Great enterprises are always left to the free choice":** Jerome *L* 66.8.

62   **"Let [the soldier] set up ambushes":** V 3.10, translated by Milner.

Chapter Five: The Mystery of Conversion

63   **"Nature leaves us free and untrammeled":** Plutarch, "On Exile," in *Moralia,* vol. 7, translated by P. De Lacy (Cambridge, MA: Harvard University Press, 1959), 533, slightly modified.

63   **Sweet "Cleopatra":** AM 28.4.

64   **falsified their ancient pedigrees:** Julia Hillner, "*Domus,* Family, and Inheritance: The Senatorial Family House in Late Antique Rome," *Journal of Roman Studies* 93 (2003): 129–45.

64   **"bringing up the rear of an army":** AM 28.4, translated by Hamilton, for these and the following descriptions.

65   **"Burn here, burn there":** Quoted and translated at Alan Cameron, *Circus Factions: Blues and Greens at Rome and Byzantium* (Oxford: Clarendon Press, 1976), 91.

66   **Gibbon summarizes Ammianus's episodes:** Gibbon 1970 (originally 1781), chapter 31, in his narrative on the year A.D. 408.

68   **Theodosius's father had had a promising career:** *PLRE,* vol. 1, 902–04.

68   **wore his helmet even in the scorching heat:** Claudian *H4,* line 27.

68   **The best kind of leader:** AM 28.4.

69   **dispersal of emergency food to needy Romans:** Z 5.39.

69   **"like a youth who is heir to new wealth":** Eunapius Fr. 46.1.

70   **"He traded jokes with the people":** Claudian *H6,* line 60, quoted at Cameron 1976, 166.

70   **"sailed up to them in large and strong ships":** Z 4.39.

72   **In 388, after Christians burned a synagogue:** For religious events in the later fourth century, see D. Boin, *Coming Out Christian in the Roman World* (New York: Bloomsbury, 2015), 129–33.

72–73 **"high reputation for eloquence":** Eunapius Fr. 58.2.

73   **a cautious academic:** Philostorgius 11.2, Socrates 5.25, and Z 4.54.

74   **"unused to the blast of war":** Eunapius Fr. 60, with permission to share authority at 58.2.

74   **"We gave to Christians and to all people":** This excerpt from Constantine's and Licinius's "Edict of Toleration" is from Boin 2015, 94.

75   **Christian wives were told to obey their husbands:** Boin 2015, 25.

75   **celebrating Rome's dead emperors:** D. Boin, "The Memory of 'Peter' (1 Peter 2.17) in Fourth-Century Rome: Church, Mausoleum, and Jupiter on the Via Praenestina," in *The Art of Empire: Christian Art in its Imperial Context,* edited by Robin Jensen and Lee Jefferson (Minneapolis: Fortress Press, 2015), 87–114.

75   **to create bigger worship spaces:** L. M. White, *The Social Origins of Christian Architecture,* 2 vols. (Valley Forge: Trinity International Press, 1997).

76   **"No one after lighting a lamp":** Matthew 5.15, NRSV translation.

77   **hand over their Bibles and empty their church coffers:** Eusebius, *Church History* 8.2, with reference to Christians' "freedom."

79   *Deliri,* **Lactantius wrote:** Boin 2015, 110–50.

80   **divisions spread across the Roman-Gothic border:** N. Lenski, "The Gothic Civil War and the Date of the Gothic Conversion," *Greek and Roman Byzantine Studies* 36 (1995): 51–87; E. Thompson, *The Visigoths in the Time of Ulfila,* 2nd ed. (London: Duckworth, 2008), 164.

80   **he carefully selected a set of Greek and Latin letterforms:** J 51.

81   **a reputation as the Gothic Moses:** Philostorgius 2.5.

81   **"needed its aggressiveness curbed":** Philostorgius 2.5.

83   **"If anyone eats of that meat":** Saba 3.4. The Gothic word for "fool," although not used in the story of Saba's death, is known from Little Wolf's translation of the Bible.

83   **"Over there, on the other side of the river":** Saba 7.4.

83   **Around meals of boiled game:** A number of avian bones found at Nicopolis suggest that wildfowl was boiled over "a temperate fire, as traces of burning are extremely rare," as explained by Mark Beech, "The Environmental Archaeology Research Programme at Nicopolis: Methodology and Results," in *The Transition to Late Antiquity on the Danube and Beyond,* edited by A. Poulter (Oxford:

Oxford University Press, 2007), 233. Most Goths who lived in this area drank milk, says J 51.

83   **"temperate, self-controlled in all things":** Saba 2.2.

84   **"Each tribe had brought along from home":** Eunapius Fr. 48.2.

84   **"fiction and sham designed to fool their enemies":** Eunapius Fr. 48.2.

85   **the "Atta Unsar":** Matthew 6.9, in Gothic at Saba p. 172.

85   **criminalizing nearly every aspect of pagan worship:** *ThC* 16.10.10.

Chapter Six: Love, War, and an Awakening

87   **"But this is slavery":** Euripides's *Phoenician Women*, line 392, translated by Wyckoff.

87   **"kept on pursuing with the javelin still embedded":** Procopius *H* 6.2, translated at Lee 2007, 128–29.

87   **"in the blood of their comrades":** AM 16.12, quoted at Lee 2007, 126, along with "without being wounded" and discussion of sneak attacks.

88   *fortissimi, nobilissimi, devotissimi:* Sources collected Lee 2007, 62–63, my translations.

88   **ranging in age from their twenties to their forties:** Lee 2007, 77. A field army could comprise between fifteen and thirty thousand men (Lee 2007, 76).

89   **surpassed only in the modern age:** Eero Saarinen holds that honor for his stainless steel Gateway Arch in St. Louis, Missouri.

90   **"the middle of the earth":** Cosmas Indicopleustes, *A Christian Map of the World*, 2.137, translated by J. McCrindle in *The Christian Topography of Cosmas, an Egyptian Monk* (London: Hakluyt Society, 1897).

90   **"stiff clay and marshy ground":** Z 3.16, "ships for the maintenance" at 3.18, the zoo at 3.23.

90   **"lions with long manes, bristly wild boars":** AM 24.5, describing a similar Persian collection, quoted at M. Canepa, *The Two Eyes of the Earth: Art and Ritual of Kingship Between Rome and Sasanian Iran* (Berkeley: University of California Press, 2009), 176.

91   **constructed scaffolding to hoist troops:** Z 3.22, with tunneling and the Persian kitchen; melted bolts at 2.50.

91   **Hormizd's wife conspired to release him:** Z 2.27, AM 16.10.

91   **the charge of "Traitor!":** Inferred from AM 24.5.

92   **two Gothic men, Fravitta and Eriulf:** Eunapius Fr. 59, preferred over Z 4.56–57; discussion at Heather 1991, 189–91.

94   **September 6, 394:** Rufinus, *Church History*, 11.32–33, Sozomen 7.22, Socrates 5.25, Theodoret 5.24.

94   **ten thousand Gothic soldiers:** Orosius 7.35.19.

94 **impaled his head on a stick:** Eunapius Fr. 60.

94 **"to look out a little through the mist":** John Chrysostom, *Letter to a Young Widow,* section 3, translated by W. Stephens, *NPNF,* vol. 9.

94 **painted pictures set up at the racetrack:** Eunapius Fr. 68.

95 **Emperors put "Victor" in their signatures:** See Lee 2007, 39, 42–47 for Victory's images.

95 **"Be not disturbed, O brethren":** Theophanes, *Chronicle,* quoted at Lee 2007, 129.

97 **the loss of Gothic lives that day:** Orosius 7.35.

97 **"the morale of the living":** Pseudo-Maurice, *Strategy,* quoted at Lee 2007, 129.

97 **like a thunderbolt:** John Chrysostom, *Letter to a Young Widow,* translated by W. Stephens, *NPNF,* vol. 9, for this and other quotations.

98 **Roman law required widows to wait:** The law, from the 330s, was preserved in the Code of Justinian (5.17.7).

98 **Euphemia:** F. Burkitt, *Euphemia and the Goth with the Acts of Martyrdom of the Confessors of Edessa* (Oxford: Williams and Norgate, 1913), 129–53, for all quotations. The story is set in 396 (*Euphemia and the Goth,* section 4) but is thought to have been written a century later, as pointed out by Lee 2007, 150.

98–99 **no Roman laws that forbid:** Ralph Mathisen, "Provinciales, Gentiles, and Marriages between Romans and Barbarians in the Late Roman Empire," *Journal of Roman Studies* 99 (2009): 140–55.

99 **"Don't be shocked if I, as a foreigner":** Attributed to Philostratus the Elder, *Letter 8,* lines 1–5, in *Alciphron, Aelian, and Philostratus: The Letters,* edited by A. Benner and F. Fobes (Cambridge, MA: Harvard University Press, 1949).

99 **"If you want someone who will stay faithful":** Philostratus the Elder, *Letter 8,* lines 22–24, my translation.

100 **His second wife:** "Galla 2" in *PLRE* 1, p. 382.

100 **"Theodosius mourned the dead Empress":** Eunapius Fr. 60.2.

100 **"dropsy":** Philostorgius 11.2.

101 **the horrible massacre at Thessaloniki:** Ambrose, *On the Death of Theodosius,* translated by J. Liebeschuetz with Carole Hill, in *Ambrose of Milan: Political Letters and Speeches* (Liverpool: Liverpool University Press, 2005), 189–90.

101 **"the horse returns to the stable":** Ambrose, *On the Death of Theodosius,* translated by Liebeschuetz with Hill 2005, 190, with "citizen of paradise" at p. 203.

102 **the corpse of a wealthy Roman woman:** C. Papageorgopoulou, N. Xirotiris, P. Iten, M. Baumgartner, M. Schmid, and F. Ruehli, "Indications of Embalming in Roman Greece by Physical, Chemical and Histological Analysis," *Journal of Archaeological Science* 36 (2009): 35–42.

102 **Church of the Holy Apostles:** M. Johnson, *The Roman Imperial Mausoleum in Late Antiquity* (New York: Cambridge University Press, 2009), 119–28.

Chapter Seven: The Lion and the Fox

103   **"The designs of a general should always be impenetrable":** V 3.6, translated by Clarke.

104   **Confrontation with the Roman government:** Passions in scholarly opinion about this point in Alaric's life expose the long-standing bias against him, with Thomas Burns insisting that Alaric was just a "Gothic upstart" (*Barbarians Within the Gates of Rome: A Study of Roman Military Policy and the Barbarians, ca. 375–425 A.D.* (Bloomington: Indiana University Press, 1994, 210). Burns's assessment: there "lingers a romantic sense that for some unstated reason Alaric and his followers possessed certain noble qualities" (1994, 187).

104   **"command more soldiers":** Z 5.5, my translation.

104   **"deemed worthy of Roman honor":** Socrates 7.10, my translation.

104   **constituted a formidable "army":** J. Liebeschuetz, "Alaric's Goths: Nation or Army?," in *Fifth-Century Gaul: A Crisis of Identity?*, ed. J. Drinkwater and H. Elton (Cambridge: Cambridge University Press, 1992), 75–83; also Halsall 2007, 194.

104   **Rufinus, one of the key advisers:** Marcellinus Comes, entry at 395, in Brian Croke, *The Chronicle of Marcellinus: A Translation and Commentary* (Leiden: Brill, 2017), 6.

105   **"in the bloom and flower of young manhood":** Prudentius *S* 2, line 7.

105   **leapt down onto the *arena*:** Theodoret 7.25–26.

105   **Honorius bowed to their zealotry:** With little immediate effect on games, as Michele Salzman explains in *On Roman Time: The Codex-Calendar of 354 and the Rhythms of Urban Life in Late Antiquity* (Berkeley: University of California Press, 1990), 237–38.

106   **"whether the ears would show themselves":** Eunapius Fr. 13.

106   **"I can't warn you often enough":** Claudian *H4*, lines 283–86, my translation.

106   **"Be a citizen and be a father":** Claudian *H4*, line 309, translated by Platnauer.

106   **"Earthly glory made these men famous":** Prudentius *S* 1, lines 280–81, with "outcasts" and "homeless strangers" at lines 45–56 and no limits to the Christian God at lines 427–29.

106   **"If we have to hand down all our ways":** Prudentius *S* 2, lines 277–84, my translation.

107   **"What is Roman and what is barbarian":** Prudentius *S* 2, lines 816–17.

107   **to patch broken pipes:** *ThC* 15.2.8–9, which includes the penalty.

108   **"Just as We forbid sacrifices":** *ThC* 16.10.15.

109   **"piggier" and "monkeyish":** Photius, in Eunapius, *Testimonia* 1, at R. Blockley, *The Fragmentary Classicising Historians of the Later Roman Empire*, 2 vols. (Liverpool: Liverpool University Press, 1983), 3.

109   **"He spoils and debases the nobility":** Photius, in Eunapius, *Testimonia* 1, quoted at Blockley 1983, 3.

109   **"hardly any human action it could not imitate":** Oly. Fr. 35, slightly modified.

109   **"buccaneering figure":** J. Matthews, "Olympiodorus of Thebes and the History of the West (A.D. 407-425)," *Journal of Roman Studies* 60 (1970): 79.

109   **"material for history":** Photius, in Oly. *Testimonia* 1, at Blockley 1983, 153.

110   **"displeased":** Z 5.5.

111   **two broadsides against Rufinus:** Alan Cameron, *Claudian: Poetry and Propaganda at the Court of Honorius* (Oxford: Clarendon Press, 1970).

111   **"Have you seen his yellow-stained pelts?":** Claudian *R* 2.78-85, my translation.

111   **conspiring to become emperor:** Eunapius Fr. 64 and Z 5.7.5.

112   **Fewer than twenty days had passed:** Socrates 6.1, with Burns 1994, 154.

112   **his family sought political asylum:** Marcellinus Comes, at 396, in Croke 2017; Z 5.8.2.

114   **"peace-bearing olive trees":** Ausonius, "The Order of Famous Cities," in *Ausonius,* vol. 1, *Books 1-17,* translated by H. Evelyn-White (Cambridge, MA: Harvard University Press, 1919), city number 15, Athens; "fields and fruits," city number 8, Capua; Arles, number 10.

114   **"It is indeed a wonderful experience":** *Tour of the Known World and Its People* 12, in "The *Expositio Totius Mundi et Gentium:* Its Geography and Its Language," by J. Woodman (master's thesis, Ohio State University, 1964), 40, with "the beauty of its Acropolis."

114   **When Alaric arrived:** Burns 1994, 183-223.

114   **spied Athena striding atop the city walls:** Z 5.6.

115   **requests a reading of Plato's *Timaeus*:** Marcel Brion, *Alaric the Goth* (New York: R. M. McBride, 1930), 57.

115   **"A destruction of such magnitude":** C. Bouras, "Alaric in Athens," Δελτίον Χριστιανικής Αρχαιολογικής Εταιρείας [*Bulletin of the Christian Archaeological Society*] 33 (2012): 4; rightly skeptical is Benjamin Anderson, "The Defacement of the Parthenon Metopes," *Greek, Roman, and Byzantine Studies* 57 (2017): 248-60.

117   **Sparta, Megara, Argos:** Z 5.5; *Eunapius: Lives of the Philosophers; Philostratus: Lives of the Sophists,* translated by W. Wright (Cambridge, MA: Harvard University Press, 1921), 436-39.

117   *katastrophe:* Z 5.5.

117   **"destroyer of the Greek people":** Claudian, *E* 2, lines 216-17, my translation.

117   **legitimate conflicts during these years:** Burns 1994, 167; Heather 1991, 199-206.

117   **"all possible civility":** Z 5.6.

118   **still quoted that Homeric scene:** Julian, *Letter* 22, 430c-31b, translated by W. Wright in *Julian,* vol. 3 (Cambridge, MA: Harvard University Press, 1923).

119   **the most read and performed Greek playwright:** R. Lauriola and K. Demetriou, eds., *Brill's Companion to the Reception of Euripides* (Leiden: Brill, 2015).

119   **Greek theaters never went dark:** P. Easterling and R. Miles, "Dramatic Identities: Tragedies in Late Antiquity," in *Constructing Identities in Late Antiquity*, edited by R. Miles (London: Routledge, 1999), 95–111; and E. Scharffenberger, "Phoenician Women," in *Brill's Companion to the Reception of Euripides*, edited by R. Lauriola and K. Demetriou (Leiden: Brill, 2015), 292–319.

119   **"Just as children have different spirits allotted to them":** The quote is attributed to the senator Symmachus at Prudentius *S* 2.71–74.

119   **Athens's antiquity was its best defense:** Z 5.5.

119   **"tribal leader," or *phylarch*:** Oly. Fr. 6.

119   **to hail Alaric as their "king":** J 29; Comes, entry at 395, with discussion at Burns 1994, 278, and Kulikowski 2007, 111, 165.

120   **General Stilicho took a huge risk:** Eunapius Fr. 64.1.

120   **arranged for her to marry his loyal Vandal chief of staff:** Oly. Fr. 1.

120   **had appointed Stilicho:** Ambrose, *On the Death of Theodosius*, translated by Liebeschuetz with Hill 2005, 179–80.

121   **A predictable level of hemming and hawing:** Events of 395 at Claudian *R* 1.174–272, with Burns 1994, 153.

121   **"effete, greedy, treasonous and sorrow-bringing race":** Orosius 7.38.

122   **the weapons factories of Illyricum:** Wolfram 1988, 143; Heather 1991, 204–05.

122   **Alaric in Epirus:** Summarized at Z 5.26 and based on a fragment of Oly, whose material starts around the year 407. Eunapius, by contrast, Z's source for the late 390s, offers no information about Stilicho's motivations in Greece, at 5.5–6. But it very probable that Stilicho expressed his desire to take Illyricum then. See Halsall 2007, 192–95; Cameron 1970, 85–86; and Burns 1994, 158.

122   **countered Stilicho's offer:** Claudian *E* 2, line 216, and *G* 535–36.

122   **Alaric accepted:** Events of 397 discussed at Heather 1991, 204; Cameron 1970, 172–80; Halsall 2007, 191; and Kulikowski 2007, 167.

123   **"The Roman Marius used to call":** Eunapius Fr. 20.4.

Chapter Eight: Into the Labyrinth

124   **"To the fight / which lies before me":** Euripides's *Phoenician Women*, lines 779–80, translated by Wyckoff.

124   **leaders of Rome's four imperial prefectures:** A. Kazhdan, "Praetorian Prefect," *The Oxford Dictionary of Byzantium* (Oxford: Oxford University Press, 2005, online edition).

125   **a "shrill" Gothic wife:** Claudian *G* 623–28.

126   **"barbarian by extraction":** Socrates 6.6, Sozomen 8.4.

126   **"cruel and violent disposition":** Theodoret 5.32.

126 **animalistic race:** Synesius 15.1.

126 **teetering on a "razor's edge":** Synesius 14–15 for this and other quotations.

126 **Gainas:** Socrates 6.5; *PLRE* 1, pp. 379–80; and Liebeschuetz 1991, 111–31, 189–94.

126 **"the principal commissions in the army to his relations":** Socrates 6.6, Sozomen 8.4, and Theodoret 5.32.

126 **"Scythians":** Peter Heather, "The Anti-Scythian Tirade of Synesius' 'De Regno,'" *Phoenix* 42 (1988): 152–72.

127 **"drive out these ill-omened dogs":** Synesius 15.12, quoting Hector's speech at *Iliad* 8, lines 523–31.

127 **"I was a stranger and you welcomed me":** Matthew 25.35, NRSV translation.

127 **sold him into bondage:** Claudian *E* 2, lines 329–31.

128 **"ape" in fancy clothes:** Claudian *E* 1, lines 303–10.

128 **"if a woman were in charge":** Claudian *E* 1, lines 323–24, my translation.

128 **This one could barely act the part:** Eunapius Fr. 65.

128 **How many slave catalogs:** Claudian *E* 1, lines 33–38.

128 **"than a poor man who stumbles into prosperity":** Claudian *E* 1, line 182, my translation.

128 **"I dare you to find, onstage or off":** Claudian *E* 1, lines 301–02, my translation.

128 **"Not the Aegean, not deep Propontis":** Claudian *E* 2, lines 307–24, translated by Platnauer.

129 **"a pestilence" devouring "our land":** Claudian *G*, lines 175–76.

129 **On April 11, 399:** *ThC* 16.8.14.

129 **"We are appropriating [this money]":** *ThC* 16.8.14.

129 **Arcadius wrote to the governor of Illyricum:** *ThC* 16.9.12.

130 *tzangae* **and** *bracchae:* *ThC* 14.10.2, with Philipp von Rummel, *Habitus Barbarus: Kleidung und Repräsentation spätantiker Eliten im 4. und 5. Jahrhundert* (Berlin: de Gruyter, 2007).

130 **"Happy is the one at home":** Claudian *F*, poem in full, my translation.

132 **Gainas joined the revolt:** Socrates 6.6, Sozomen 8.4, Theodoret 5.32, and Z 5.14–22.

132 **A lack of opportunity to advance his career:** Z 5.13.

132 **"for the purpose of burning down the palace":** Socrates 6.6.

132 **to turn the city into a tomb:** Eunapius Fr. 67.13.

132 **trying to smuggle weapons into the city:** Socrates 6.6 and Sozomen 8.4, both of whom also mention the plot to rob the bankers.

133 **Seven thousand Gothic Christians:** Z 5.19. Liebeschuetz (1991, 112) is skeptical of the number of the dead.

133 **Whether apprehended on Roman land or in Gothic territory:** Gainas killed in Roman territory: Philostorgius 11.8; Gainas killed in Gothia, Z 5.21–22.

133   **"seasoned with salt":** Philostorgius 11.8.

134   **ready to thwart Gainas's attempt to flee:** Z 5.19.

134   **Arcadius's monument:** Burns 1994, 174–75; Liebeschuetz 1991, 273–78.

134   **"The truth of why things happen":** Prudentius *S* 2, lines 843–45, my translation.

134   **"The windings of the labyrinth":** Prudentius *S* 2, lines 847–48, my translation.

135   **"I don't deny that the fork in the road":** Prudentius *S* 2, lines 847–48.

135   **"My mind wavers between":** Claudian *R* 1, lines 1–18, my translation, with the opening two lines slightly adapted from Platnauer.

136   **fear of pain or death should amount to nothing:** S. Greenblatt, *The Swerve: How the World Became Modern* (New York: W. W. Norton, 2011).

137   **"watchful, sober, and discreet":** V 3.9, translated by Milner, with "caution and prudence" at 3.6.

137   **"to find out everything from intelligent men":** V 3.6, translated by Milner.

137   **decided to redraw the boundaries of the provinces:** Burns 1994, 178–79, although I depart from his presumption of antagonism between Gainas and Alaric.

138   **"universal contempt is sometimes a boon":** Claudian, *E* 1, line 139, translated by Platnauer.

138   **"The more conscientious generals":** V 3.6, translated by Milner.

138   **a team of talented cartographers boasted:** Discussion in C. Whittaker, *Frontiers of the Roman Empire: A Social and Economic Study* (Baltimore: Johns Hopkins University Press, 1994), 19–20; and in Richard Talbert, with T. Elliott, N. Harris, G. Hubbard, D. O'Brien, G. Shepherd, and M. Steinmann, *Rome's World: The Peutinger Map Reconsidered* (Cambridge: Cambridge University Press, 2010), 138–39.

139   **"a drunkard's babbling":** Claudian *R* 2, lines 287–88, translated by Platnauer.

139   **"The safest policy on expeditions":** V 3.6, translated by Milner, along with "The most important to be careful about."

139   **"Just as he is said to have been hidden":** V 3.6, translated by Milner.

139   **November 18, 401:** Recorded in a Latin calendar, the *Fasti vindobonenses priores,* so called because it was discovered in Vienna (Vindobona) and printed in the series *Historical Records of Germania* (*Monumenta Germaniae Historica*) among the ancient sources ("Auctores Antiquissimi"), no. 9, 274–99, edited by T. Mommsen (Berlin: Wiedman, 1892), 299.

140   **"permit the Goths to settle peaceably":** J 30, my translation.

140   **"the empire had almost lost":** J 30, my translation.

141   **"in respect for religion":** Orosius 7.37.2, with reference to violating one of "the most revered days of the year."

141   **place Alaric all over the map of northern Italy:** Wolfram 1988, 150–53 (a "draw," 152); Burns 1994, 188–95; Cameron 1970, 180–81; Kulikowski 2007, 170–71; Heather 1991, 206–11; and Williams and Friell 1994, 142–58. Dating

Verona to 403 is J. Barrie Hall, "Pollentia, Verona, and the Chronology of Alaric's First Invasion of Italy," *Philologus* 132 (1988): 245–57.

141 **"full of errors and contradictions":** Eunapius Fr. 1, with "an un-chaired meeting."

142 **"Poetry is the work of a gifted person":** Aristotle, *Poetics* 17.1455a in *Aristotle, Longinus, Demetrius,* edited and translated by S. Halliwell (Cambridge, MA: Harvard University Press, 1995), 88–89.

143 **"A deficit of good ideas":** Claudian *G,* lines 525–53, my translation.

144 **called the "City," the *Urbs*:** Wolfram 1998, 152.

145 **A humble citizen:** Claudian *H6,* lines 55–78.

145 **"No more empty threats":** Claudian, *H6,* lines 133–46, my translation, with the line "terrors to the sea" modified from Platnauer's prose translation.

146 **"Foul kingdom, that Goths are taxed":** Claudian *H6,* lines 276–322, my translation.

147 **speculating that he was dead:** Z 5.27.

Chapter Nine: The Crash

148 **"Who could believe that Rome":** Jerome's *Commentary on Ezekiel,* preface to book 3, quoted by J. Pelikan, "The Two Cities: The Decline and Fall of Rome as Historical Paradigm," in *Daedalus* 111 (1982): 85–86, slightly modified.

148 **Radagaisus:** Orosius 7.37.4–7.

148 **bring the entire prefecture of Illyricum under western control:** Z 5.29.

149 **Senator Lampadius:** Z 5.29.

149 **he must be a mole:** Orosius 7.38.

149 **wanted to put his son on the throne:** Oly. Fr. 5.2.

149 **August 22, 408:** Sozomen 9.4, Orosius 7.38.5, and Z 5.34.

149 **a band of renegades from Honorius's palace:** Oly. Fr. 5.1.

149 **pursued his son, Eucherius:** Oly. Fr. 5.2, and Z 5.35.

150 **Theodosius's first wife, Flacilla:** Theodoret 5.18, with Kenneth Holum, *Theodosian Empresses: Women and Imperial Dominion in Late Antiquity* (Berkeley: University of California Press, 1982), 22–45. She died around 387 after traveling to a Thracian hot spring to tend her unnamed illness. The reference to Flacilla's eulogy is quoted by Holum at p. 23.

150 **Arcadius's wife, Eudoxia:** Philostorgius 11.6.

150 **Confidently marching at the front:** Claudian *H6,* line 552, with Julia Hillner, "A Woman's Place: Imperial Women in Late Antique Rome," *Antiquité Tardive* 25 (2017): 90.

150 **ripped an expensive necklace:** Z 5.38.

151 **"in a mist of purple blossoms":** Claudian *W,* lines 298–302.

151 **Augusta Livia's four-hundred-year-old jewels:** Claudian *W,* lines 12–13.

151   **She was Alaric's age:** *PLRE* 1 ("Serena"), p. 824.

151   **"was thought to be the reason for Alaric's march on Rome":** Oly. Fr. 7.3.

152   **Romans pent up with anger:** Z 5.35, with reference to thirty thousand Goths.

152   **"workman's lunch":** Martial, *Epigrams* 13.5, in *Martial: Epigrams,* vol 3: *Books 11–14),* translated by D. Shackleton Bailey (Cambridge, MA: Harvard University Press, 1993).

153   **"no demand for Indian pepper":** Pliny *Natural History* 19.59, in *Pliny: Natural History,* vol 5: *Books 17–19),* translated by H. Rackham (Cambridge, MA: Harvard University Press, 1950), with reference to tiny gardens.

153   **"dismal uniformity":** M 6.5.27.

153   **stopped all boats and barges:** Oly. Fr. 7.5, Sozomen 9.6–7, and Z 5.41–42.

153   **"Anger and indignation":** V 3.12, translated by Milner.

153   **"Thicker grass is easier to mow than thinner":** Z 5.40.

154   **"more terrible than the sword":** V 3.3, translated by Clarke, for the quotations.

154   **"Stilicho's execution":** Oly. Fr. 6.

154   **"pepper-sharp" burglar:** Martial, *Epigrams* 8.59.

154   **"was thought to be the reason":** Oly. Fr. 7.3.

154   **"The hunter who reclines returns":** Claudian, *H6,* lines 3–10, my translation.

155   **driven to his heinous act by evil:** Socrates 7.10 and Sozomen 9.6.

155   **"something deeply troubling":** Sozomen 9.6, my translation, along with "fulfilled it by going [to the city of Rome]"; Socrates 7.10.

156   **loss of citizenship was one of the stiffest penalties:** Mathisen 2006, 1019, discussing slaves and prisoners of war at p. 1020.

156   **"more like a Roman" than a Goth:** Orosius 7.37.

156   **"to live with the Romans [so] that men":** J 30, my translation. "Family" or "people" makes more sense than C. Mierow's translation of *gens* as "race," since it is clear that Alaric and his supporters wanted not to abandon their Gothic heritage but, rather, to bring it with them. I do not believe that Alaric was fighting for "Gothic statehood," as does Wolfram 1988, 161. An independent Gothic state was the result of Rome's inaction, not Alaric's primary aspiration.

157   **five thousand pounds of gold, thirty thousand pounds of silver:** Z 5.41.

157   **the next round of diplomacy:** Oly. Fr. 11.2.

158   **living temporarily in a canvas tent:** Oly. Fr. 8.1.

158   **Jovius pressed the emperor:** Oly. Fr. 8.1 and Z 5.48; Carlos Machado, "The Roman Aristocracy and the Imperial Court, Before and After the Sack," in *SoR,* 49–76.

158   **no higher rank be conferred:** Z 5.37–49.

158   **Jovius reported back that a resolution:** Oly. Fr. 8.1.

158   **"a moderate amount of food":** Oly. Fr. 8.1, Sozomen 9.7, my translation.

158   **"permission to live on Roman land":** Oly Fr. 8.1, Sozomen 9.7.

159   **searching for "a home":** Z 5.48.

159   **the same as any citizen:** Scholars have never addressed this issue directly. In

Heather's 1991 foundational *Goths and Romans,* Alaric is said to want "a fully recognized position for his people within the Western Empire" and to "exist as part of the western Empire" (216), but Heather never connects his analysis to the topic of Roman citizenship, an understandable omission at the time. Researchers once thought that the differences between being a Roman citizen and a non-citizen did not matter after Caracalla's reform—it was a distinction, Patrick Geary said, summarizing a widely shared view, that "meant nothing"; see P. Geary, *The Myth of Nations: The Medieval Origins of Europe* (Princeton, NJ: Princeton University Press, 2002), 59.

159 **to calculate the wall's perimeter:** Oly. Fr. 41.1 with the editor's comments at p. 220 note 78.

160 **a pragmatic intellectual:** *PLRE* 2 at pp. 180–81.

160 **Alaric was promoted:** Oly. Fr. 10.1, Z 6.7–10. And Matthews 1975, 284–306, is excellent.

161 **Athaulf was invited to Rome:** Sozomen 9.8.

161 **could agree to retire to an island:** Oly. Fr. 10.1.

161 **their hastily formed partnership crumbled:** Z 6.6–12.

161 **"enraged":** Sozomen 9.9, but see also Oly Fr. 6 and 10.2 for the sequence of events.

161 **set up their tents in the northeastern district:** Procopius *H* 3.2.

162 **seventy-seven holidays had swollen into a hundred and seventy-seven:** Alan Cameron, *Circus Factions: Blues and Greens at Rome and Byzantium* (Oxford: Clarendon Press, 1976), 175–76.

162 **August's circuit of festivals:** D. Boin, *Ostia in Late Antiquity* (New York: Cambridge University Press, 2013), 210–13.

162 **sixteen main gates:** Hendrik Dey, *The Aurelian Wall and the Refashioning of Imperial Rome, AD 271–855* (New York: Cambridge University Press, 2011), 29.

162 **"The wild and uncivilized life of man":** V 4, translated by Milner, for the following quotations.

163 **the broad marble archways:** Dey 2011, 29, with brick-framed passageways at p. 30.

163 **"mobile tower":** V 4.17, translated by Milner; drawbridges, 4.21.

164 **poured pitch onto soldiers:** AM 20.11.

164 **filled underground tunnels with bitumen and sulfur:** Simon James, "Stratagems, Combat, and 'Chemical Warfare' in the Siege Mines of Dura-Europos," *American Journal of Archaeology* 115 (2011): 94–97.

164 **dropped oversized wooden wheels:** V 4.8.

164 **"The most essential part of the art of war":** V 4.27, translated by Clarke. "Surprise attack" is from Milner's translation of the same passage (2001, 137).

164 **"the dead of night":** M 1.3.15, also described as "no time . . . for conducting business."

164 **Proba:** Procopius *H* 3.2.

165 **Alaric crept in:** Not "crashed," as in Orosius's version 7.39.

166 **spare Romans who sought refuge in a church:** Augustine *CG* 1.2, Orosius 7.39.

166 **"He also told his men":** Orosius 7.39 for this story and the following quotations.

Chapter Ten: Alaric's Dying Ambitions

167 **"Let be the past":** From the tombstone of Quintus Sulpicius Maximus, the eleven-year-old poetry champion buried at the Salt Gate, as translated at J. Raleigh Nelson, "The Boy Poet Sulpicius: A Tragedy of Roman Education," *School Review* 11 (1903): 386.

167 **"Day and night I could think of nothing else":** Jerome *Ez.: Preface to the Commentary on Book 1.*

167 **"sea of smoke":** Jerome *L* 130.7.

167 **"tears and moans":** Jerome *Ez.: Preface to the Commentary on Book 7.*

168 **"I will put my spirit within you":** *Ezekiel* 37.14, NRSV translation.

168 **"the bright light of all the world":** Jerome *Ez.: Preface to the Commentary on Book 1,* slightly modified.

169 **"Fallen, fallen is Babylon the great!":** *Revelation* 18.2, NRSV translation.

169 **the destruction of Sodom and Gomorrah:** M. O'Reilly makes this point in her commentary on Augustine *R* (81). Augustine reminded his own congregation that Rome was filled with many good, believing Christians whom God had saved. Rome was no immoral city, he said.

169 **Gog:** Ambrose, *Exposition of the Christian Faith* 2.16.137–38, found in *NPNF,* vol. 10, translated by H. de Romestin, E. de Romestin, and H. Duckworth, 1896.

169 **Huns came to Europe:** A. Anderson, *Alexander's Gate, Gog and Magog, and the Inclosed Nations* (Cambridge: Cambridge University Press, 1932), 3–14; also discussed at Christensen 2002, 44–50.

170 **his epic twenty-two-volume manifesto:** James O'Donnell, *Augustine: A New Biography* (New York: Ecco), 209–43.

170 **to foreclose any return to the pagan past:** Michele Salzman, "Memory and Meaning: Pagans and 410," in *SoR,* 295–310.

170 **twenty edicts against paganism:** The count is John O'Meara's from his introduction to *Concerning the City of God against the Pagans,* translated by H. Bettenson (London: Penguin Books, 1984), x.

171 **"preferring the preservation of the city to his own private opinion":** Z 5.41, who says that the sacrifice ultimately did not take place because many members of the pagan community feared performing the rites in public—a reasonable reservation given the chilling political climate; Geoffrey Dunn, "Innocent I, Alaric, and Honorius: Church and State in Early Fifth-Century Rome," in *Studies of Religion and Politics in the Early Christian Centuries,* edited by D.

Luckensmeyer and P. Allen (Strathfield, NSW: St. Pauls Publications, 2010), 243–62.

171   **"managed to reach Carthage as refugees":** Augustine *CG* 1.32, with "moral disease" at 1.33.

171   **theory of the two "cities":** Earlier sermons, treatises, and letters contained previews of the idea, as explained by Peter Brown, *Augustine of Hippo: A Biography*, new ed. (London: Faber and Faber, 2000), 285–96.

172   **"future citizens":** Augustine *CG* 1.35.

172   **"the quiet land of Africa":** J 30.

172   **"Gothia where there had once been a Roman state":** Orosius 7.43, slightly modified.

172   **"ancient wealth":** Ausonius, *The Order of Famous Cities*, translated by H. Evelyn-White in *Ausonius*, vol. 1, *Books 1–17* (Cambridge, MA: Harvard University Press, 1919), 269.

173   **Heraclian:** Oly. Fr. 10.1 and Orosius 7.42.

173   **the "cloud of grim war":** Paulinus of Nola, *Carmen* 21, quoted in Dennis Trout, *Paulinus of Nola: Life, Letters, and Poems* (Berkeley: University of California Press, 1999), 119.

173   **city of Nola:** Trout 1999, 120–21; Augustine *CG* 1.10.

173   **an itinerant roadshow:** M preface, 9.

174   **"glide in my little boat by the shore":** J preface, 1.

174   **capsized several of their hired ships:** Oly. Fr. 16, J 30.

174   **Alaric died of "sickness":** Oly Fr. 11.2.

174   **"untimely":** J 30.

174   ***Plasmodium falciparum:*** F. Galassi, R. Bianucci, G. Gorini, G. Paganotti, M. Habict, F. Rühli, "The Sudden Death of Alaric I (c. 370–410 AD), the Vanquisher of Rome: A Tale of Malaria and Lacking Immunity," *European Journal of Internal Medicine* 31 (2016): 84–87.

175   **a tormented soul:** Hesiod, *Theogony*, in *Theogony, Works and Days, Testimonia*, ed. and trans. G. Most (Cambridge, MA: Harvard University Press, 2007), line 527.

175   **wounded honor:** Sophocles, *Ajax*, in *Ajax, Electra, Oedipus Tyrannus*, ed. and trans. H. Lloyd-Jones (Cambridge, MA: Harvard University Press, 1994), line 185.

175   **the "madness" that came from loving:** Euripides, *Hippolytus*, in *Children of Heracles, Hippolytus, Andromache, Hecuba*, ed. and trans. D. Kovacs (Cambridge, MA: Harvard University Press, 1995), lines 764–66.

175   **"with utmost affection":** J 30.158.

175   **to dam the waters of the Busento:** J 30.

175   **a custom known from Dacia:** Dio Cassius, *Roman History*, vol. 8, *Books 61–70*, translated by E. Cary and H. Foster (Cambridge, MA: Harvard University Press, 1925), 68.14.4.

175   **sexual violence:** Victoria Leonard, "Galla Placida as 'Human Gold': Consent and Autonomy in the Sack of Rome, C.E. 410," *Gender & History* 31 (2019): 1–19.

175   **"bare like locusts":** J 31. For the wedding, Orosius 7.43. Jordanes claimed the two were married in Italy; see Hagith Sivan, *Galla Placidia: The Last Roman Empress* (Oxford: Oxford University Press, 2011), 9–36.

176   **a Roman soldier's white formal wear:** See Claudian *W,* lines 304–05.

176   **helped compose the wedding poetry:** Sivan, *Galla Placidia* 2011, 21, with Honorius's absence at p. 9.

176   **"by the treachery":** Orosius 7.43, translated by Raymond.

176   **scrutinize the empire's maps for Roman territory:** There is a range of opinion, much of it speculative, on the mechanisms by which Rome loosened its grip on its territories, from new tax laws to the divestment of land; see Halsall 2007, 425–47.

176   **to preserve the ancient right of the paterfamilias:** Guillermo Suárez Blázquez, "La *patria potestad* en el derecho romano y en el derecho altomedieval visigodo," *Revista de estudios histórico-jurídicos* 36 (2014): 159–87.

176   **a woman carrying a "formed fetus":** Marianne Elsakkers, "Gothic Bible, Vetus Latina and Visigothic Law: Evidence for a Septuagint-Based Gothic Version of Exodus," *Sacris Erudiri: A Journal of Late Antique and Medieval Christianity* 44 (2005): 37–76, with the quotation at p. 72.

178   **denied Christian priests the privilege:** E. Thompson, *The Goths in Spain* (Oxford: Clarendon Press, 1969), 29.

179   **Theoderic:** Sophie Patoura, "Le rôle historique des Balkans dans le processus de la chute de l'Empire romain d'Occident: Le cas des chefs goths Alaric et Théodoric," *Byzantinoslavica* 60 (1999): 367–73.

179   **"A youth of tall stature":** EV 10.46.

179   **"to enjoy the advantages of the Roman Empire":** J 57 for the details.

179   **a Gothic golden age:** David Gwynn, *The Goths* (London: Reaktion Books, 2018), with bibliography.

179   **united their kingdoms:** EV 12–14 for this detail and other quotations from the paragraph.

180   **"won the good-will of the neighboring nations":** EV 12 for this detail and other quotations, including *"duas gentes in uno."*

180   **civilitas returned:** Wolfram 1988, 296.

180   **"Everyone could carry on his business":** EV 12, mentioning "gates, they were never shut."

181   **Qusayr 'Amra, Jordan:** Garth Fowden, *Qusayr 'Amra: Art and the Umayyad Elite in Late Antique Syria* (Berkeley: University of California Press, 2004), 197–226.

182   **Ibn Habib al-Ilbiri:** Daniel König, *Arabic-Islamic Views of the Latin West: Tracing the Emergence of Medieval Europe* (Oxford: Oxford University Press, 2015), 154, with reference to *al-Qut* at p. 156.

182   **"for a thousand years":** Ibn Kaldun, quoted at König 2015, 173; displacing *al-Rum,* the Romans, at p. 183.

183   **Hurushiyush:** König 2015, 134–49.

183   **a road map to their common future:** Christian Sahner, "From Augustine to Islam: Translation and History in the Arabic Orosius," *Speculum* 88 (2013): 931.

183   **Petrarch, Giorgio Vasari, Flavio Biondo:** Gwynn 2018, 90–94.

184   **"the Goths to the unknown edge of the globe":** Quoted at Gwynn 2018, 110. A list of Visigothic kings had already, for a century or more, been circulating in Spain and Portugal in a popular book, *Crónica del moro Rasis.* It had been translated from Latin into Arabic, then into Castilian and Portuguese, and may have inspired Quevedo to connect the glory of a Gothic past to the dream of a future in the Americas; see also König 2015, 164, 185–87.

184   **a virtuous race of brave, patriotic warriors:** Christopher Krebs, *A Most Dangerous Book: Tacitus's* Germania *from the Roman Empire to the Third Reich* (New York: W. W. Norton, 2011).

Chapter Eleven: Smoldering Ruins and a Lost Key

185   **"History aims":** Eunapius Fr. 62.2, my translation.

185   **"the immutable laws of the universe":** Claudian *G,* lines 54–60, translated by Platnauer.

185   **"A wound, though deep":** Jerome *Ez.: Preface to the Commentary on Book 1.*

185   **"nothing had happened":** Orosius 7.40, translated by Fear, slightly modified.

186   **"For when we return to a place after considerable absence":** Quintilian, in *Institutio Oratoria,* translated by H. Butler (Cambridge, MA: Harvard University Press, 1920–22), 11.2.17.

186   **intentionally left the wreckage in place:** Gloria Ferrari, "The Ancient Temple on the Acropolis at Athens," *American Journal of Archaeology* 106 (2002): 11–35.

186   **Seven addresses:** In addition to Sallust's house and Marcella's, the five other sites are: the Lateran (*Book of the Pontiffs* 1.233), Anicia Proba's house (Jerome *L* 130.7), the house of the Valerii family (*Life of Melania Junior* 14.3), Santa Maria in Trastevere (*Book of the Pontiffs* 1.205), and the Forum of Peace (Procopius *H* 1.12). From Riccardo Santangeli Valenzani, "Dall'evento al dato archeologico: Il sacco del 410 attraverso la documentazione archeologica," in *SoR,* 35–37.

186   **connection to the dead apostle:** In the third century, a church located outside Rome's walls, named St. Sebastian's, also claimed to have Saint Peter's body.

187   **Sallust's house:** L. Richardson Jr., *A New Topographical Dictionary of Ancient Rome* (Baltimore: Johns Hopkins University Press, 1992), 202.

187   **"half-burned":** Procopius *H* 3.2.

188   **"were insufficient for the increased population":** Oly. Fr. 25.

188   **its own version of a catastrophe:** Matthew Kneale, *Rome: A History in Seven Sackings* (New York: Simon & Schuster, 2018).

189   **No one really understood what they were looking at:** Paolo Liverani, "Alarico in Laterano e sull'Esquilino: Due casi e qualche riflessione," in *SoR*, 277–94.

189   **pioneers in the archaeology of Rome:** Marcella died in 1961, and her husband, Adolfo, was buried at her side in Rome's Campo Verano cemetery. The family's story has been recounted by Domenico Palombi in *Rodolfo Lanciani: L'archeologia a Roma tra Ottocentro e Novecento* (Rome: L'Erma di Bretschneider, 2006), and in Palombi's shorter piece "Lanciani, Rodolfo Amedeo," in *Dizionario biografico degli italiani* 63: 353–60 (Rome: Istituto della Enciclopedia Italiana, 2004).

190   **translated his discoveries into English:** "Signora Rodolfo Lanciani," *New York Times*, February 18, 1914.

190   **sent bulletins to the United States:** "Discoveries at Rome: Prof. Lanciani Describes His Explorations and Discoveries," *New York Times*, March 19, 1887 (unattributed); "Glimpses of Old Rome," *New York Times*, April 2, 1887 (unattributed); "Palaces of Noble Romans: Ground They Preferred—Some Recent Discoveries," December 29, 1889, *New York Times* (no byline but sourced as "Prof. Lanciani"); "Latest Finds in Rome: Rodolfo Lanciani Describes the Dredging of the Tiber," *New York Times*, June 26, 1892 (attributed to Lanciani); "The City of Rome," *New York Times*, January 20, 1900 (under Lanciani's name); "New Tales of Old Rome," *New York Times*, November 30, 1901 (under Lanciani's name).

190   **In his eighty-four years:** "Prof. Lanciani Dies: Famous Scientist," *New York Times*, May 23, 1929, although the paper mistakenly reported that he had been eighty-two.

192   **"felt more than ever the vast difference":** R. Lanciani, *Pagan and Christian Rome* (Boston: Houghton, Mifflin, 1892), 276. Lanciani excavated the tomb of the boy poet buried at the Salt Gate (1892, 280–82).

192   **"I have witnessed excavations":** R. Lanciani, *The Destruction of Ancient Rome: A Sketch of the History of the Monuments* (New York: Macmillan Company, 1899), 57–58, with the paragraph breaks inserted for clarity.

194   **"bigoted Christians":** Lanciani 1899, 70.

194   **"in the Gothic attack":** Recorded in the biography of Pope Celestine, discussed by Ralph Mathisen, "*Roma a Gothis Alarico duce capta est*: Ancient Accounts of the Sack of Rome in 410 CE," in *SoR*, 87–90.

194   **"it cannot clearly be documented":** Johannes Lipps, "Alarichs Goten auf dem Forum Romanum? Überlegungen zu Gestalt, Chronologie und Verständnis der spätantiken Platzanlage," in *SoR*, 116.

194   **Ennio Quirinio Visconti:** The discovery of the Esquiline Treasure, made

between June 1793 and March 1794, is described in *Lettera di Ennio Quirino Visconti intorno ad una antica supelletile d'argento scoperta in Roma nell'anno 1793*, 2nd ed. (Rome: Le Stampe del Salviucci, 1827).

195 **"We are not far . . . from the date of the sack":** Lanciani 1899, 64.

195 **One such quake ruptured the pipes:** Silvia Orlandi, "Le tracce del passaggio di Alarico nelle fonti epigrafiche," in *SoR*, 342.

195 ***"quasi nulla":*** R. Santangeli Valenzani in *SoR*, 38, comparing the thin evidence to the heavy impression Alaric's attack has made.

195 **Italgas:** P. Quaranta, R. Pardi, B. Ciarrochi, and A. Capodiferro, "Il 'giorno dopo' all'Aventino: Dati preliminari dai contesti di scavo," in *SoR*, 185–214, with the bronze padlock at p. 191.

197 **"It is obvious that the capture of so great a city":** Sozomen 9.10, with Mathisen 2013 in *SoR*, 96–102.

197 **"punishment for God's wrath":** Sozomen 9.6, my translation.

197 **"casual disregard and complete":** Sozomen 9.6, my translation.

Epilogue

199 **"To weep with them that weep does ease some deal":** From Shakespeare's *Titus Andronicus,* dramatizing the conflict between Romans and Goths through the life of a fictional Roman general (act 3, scene 1, lines 253–54).

199 **Gibbon called the burial Cosenza's "secret spot":** Gibbon 1970 (originally 1781), 173.

199 **"with many treasures":** J 30.

199 **including the Nazis, who went to Cosenza:** Kneale 2018, 29–30.

199 **Cosenza's enterprising mayor:** James Bone, "Romans in Arms over Museum to Visigoth King Alaric the Barbarian," *Times* (UK), July 5, 2013.

WORKS CITED AND FURTHER READING

An expanded list of sources consulted in writing this book, including resources in languages other than English, is available at www.religiousdirt.com, the author's website.

Balsdon, J. *Romans and Aliens*. Chapel Hill: University of North Carolina Press, 1979.

Boin, D. *A Social and Cultural History of Late Antiquity*. Malden, MA: Wiley, 2017.

Brown, P. *The World of Late Antiquity, AD 150–750*. New York: W. W. Norton, 1970.

Burns, T. *Barbarians Within the Gates of Rome: A Study of Roman Military Policy and the Barbarians, ca. 375–425 A.D.* Bloomington: Indiana University Press, 1994.

Cameron, A. *Circus Factions: Blues and Greens at Rome and Byzantium*. Oxford: Clarendon Press, 1976.

———. *Claudian: Poetry and Propaganda at the Court of Honorius*. Oxford: Clarendon Press, 1970.

Cameron, A., and J. Long with L. Sherry. *Barbarians and Politics at the Court of Arcadius*. Berkeley: University of California Press, 1993.

Christensen, A. *Cassiodorus, Jordanes, and the History of the Goths: Studies in a Migration Myth*. Translated by H. Flegal. Copenhagen: Museum Tusculanum Press, 2002.

Cooper, K. *The Fall of the Roman Household*. New York: Cambridge University Press, 2007.

Elton, H. *Frontiers of the Roman Empire*. Bloomington: Indiana University Press, 1996.

Gibbon, E. *The Decline and Fall of the Roman Empire*, vol. 2, *395 A.D.–1185 A.D.* Originally 1781. Reprint, New York: Modern Library, 1970.

Goffart, W. *The Narrators of Barbarian History (AD 550–800): Jordanes, Gregory of Tours, Bede, and Paul the Deacon*. Princeton, NJ: Princeton University Press, 1988.

Graham, M. *News and Frontier Consciousness in the Late Roman Empire*. Ann Arbor: University of Michigan Press, 2006.

Gwynn, D. *The Goths*. Lost Civilizations series. London: Reaktion Books, 2018.

Halsall, G. *Barbarian Migrations and the Roman West, 376–568*. New York: Cambridge University Press, 2007.

Heather, P. *Empires and Barbarians: The Fall of Rome and the Birth of Europe.* New York: Oxford University Press, 2010.

———. *The Fall of the Roman Empire: A New History of Rome and the Barbarians.* New York: Oxford University Press, 2006.

———. *Goths and Romans, 332–489.* Oxford: Oxford University Press, 1991.

Holum, K. *Theodosian Empresses.* Berkeley: University of California Press, 1982.

Humphries, M. "The Shapes and Shaping of the Late Antique World: Global and Local Perspectives." In *A Companion to Late Antiquity,* ed. P. Rousseau, 97–109. Malden, MA: Wiley, 2009.

Kaster, R. *Guardians of Language: The Grammarian and Society in Late Antiquity.* Berkeley: University of California Press, 1997.

Kennedy, R., C. Roy, and M. Goldman. *Race and Ethnicity in the Classical World: An Anthology of Primary Sources in Translation.* Indianapolis: Hackett Publishing, 2013.

Kneale, M. *Rome: A History in Seven Sackings.* New York: Simon & Schuster, 2018.

Kulikowski, M. *Rome's Gothic Wars: From the Third Century to Alaric.* Cambridge: Cambridge University Press, 2007.

Lanciani, R. *The Destruction of Ancient Rome: A Sketch of the History of the Monuments.* New York: Macmillan Company, 1899.

Lee, A. D. *War in Late Antiquity: A Social History.* Malden, MA: Blackwell, 2007.

Lenski, N. *Failure of Empire: Valens and the Roman State in the Fourth Century* A.D. Berkeley: University of California Press, 2003.

Liebeschuetz, J.H.W.G. *Barbarians and Bishops: Army, Church, and State in the Age of Arcadius and Chrysostom.* Oxford: Clarendon Press, 1991.

———. *Decline and Change in Late Antiquity: Religion, Barbarians, and Their Historiography.* Aldershot: Ashgate Variorum, 2006.

Mathisen, R. "*Peregrini, Barbari,* and *Cives Romani*: Concepts of Citizenship and the Legal Identity of Barbarians in the Later Roman Empire." *American Historical Review* 111 (2006): 1011–40.

Matthews, J. *Western Aristocracies and Imperial Court, AD 364–425.* Oxford: Clarendon Press, 1975.

McEvoy, M. *Child Emperor Rule in the Late Roman West, AD 367–455.* Oxford: Oxford University Press, 2013.

Merrills, A. *History and Geography in Late Antiquity.* Cambridge: Cambridge University Press, 2005.

Moorhead, S., and D. Stuttard. *AD 410: The Year That Shook Rome.* Los Angeles: J. Paul Getty Museum, 2010.

Oltean, I. *Dacia: Landscape, Colonization, and Romanization.* London: Routledge, 2007.

Schwarcz, A. "The Visigothic Settlement in Aquitania: Chronology and Archaeology." In *Society and Culture in Late Antique Gaul: Revisiting the Sources,* ed. R. Mathisen and D. Shanzer, 15–25. Aldershot: Ashgate, 2001.

Sivan, H. "'Alaricus Rex': Legitimizing a Gothic King." In *The Construction of Communities in the Early Middle Ages: Texts, Resources and Artefacts*, ed. R. Corradini, M. Diesenberger, and H. Reimitz, 109–21. Leiden: Brill, 2003.

———. *Galla Placidia: The Last Roman Empress*. Women in Antiquity series. Oxford: Oxford University Press, 2011.

Thompson, E. A. *The Visigoths in the Time of Ulfila*. 2nd ed., with an introduction by M. Kulikowski. New York: Bloomsbury Academic, 2008.

Van Nuffelen, P. *Orosius and the Rhetoric of History*. Oxford: Oxford University Press, 2011.

Wallace-Hadrill, J. M. "Gothia and Romania." In *The Long-Haired Kings*, ed. J. M. Wallace-Hadrill, 25–48. Toronto: University of Toronto Press, 1961.

Ward-Perkins, B. *The Fall of Rome and the End of Civilization*. Oxford: Oxford University Press, 2005.

Watts, E. *City and School in Late Antique Athens and Alexandria*. Berkeley: University of California Press, 2006.

Whittaker, C. *Frontiers of the Roman Empire: A Social and Economic Study*. Baltimore: Johns Hopkins University Press, 1994.

Williams, S., and G. Friell. *Theodosius: The Empire at Bay*. New Haven: Yale University Press, 1994.

Wolfram, H. *History of the Goths*. Translated by T. Dunlap. Rev. ed. Berkeley: University of California Press, 1988.

ILLUSTRATION CREDITS

17   Erich Lessing / Art Resource, NY. Art Resource No.: ART109610.

23   British Museum. Registration no: 1813,1211.1.

32   Image courtesy of Abby Rennemeyer.

45   The Picture Art Collection / Alamy Stock Photo MMRM2A.

81   Photograph by Magnus Hjalmarsson, 2012.

89   Scala / Art Resource, NY. Art Resource No.: ART86875.

101 Kunsthistorisches Museum, Vienna, Austria, inv. 524. Erich Lessing / Art Resource, NY. Art Resource No.: ART35135.

116 Album / Alamy Stock Photo. Alamy Image ID: PA6B5J.

177 Kunsthistorisches Museum, Antikensammlung VII B 23, Vienna.

190 Photo by P. P. Mackey, British School at Rome Library & Archive PPM 0904.

191 Image from the British School at Rome Library & Archive JHP [PHP] 0007.

200 Douglas Boin, 2016.

INDEX

Page numbers in *italics* refer to illustrations.
Page numbers after 208 refer to endnotes.